Reflections on
GOOSE POND

Stories of a Berkshire Mountain Lake

By David E. Cohen

Copyright © 2025 by David E. Cohen, 1st Edition

All rights reserved.

No portion of this book may be reproduced in any form without written permission from the publisher or author, except as permitted by U.S. copyright law. All photographs not otherwise attributed were created by the author.

Book and cover design by Amit Dey

Berkshire Mountain Books
P.O. Box 515
Lee, Massachusetts 01238

www.berkshiremountainbooks.com
david@berkshiremountainbooks.com

ISBN (hardcover): **979-8-9928483-0-4**

100% of net profits donated to **The Western Massachusetts Appalachian Trail Management Committee** in support of its volunteer activities all around Goose Pond

for Eli

TABLE OF CONTENTS

Introduction vii

Prologue xi

Chapter 1: Water and Mountains 1

Chapter 2: A Tour of Goose Pond 11

Chapter 3: Geological History 43

Chapter 4: The Ice Age 57

Chapter 5: The Mohican Indians 63

Chapter 6: The Shakers 71

Chapter 7: Paper Mills 79

Chapter 8: The Dam 95

Chapter 9: Lake May Power 105

Chapter 10: The Huckleberry Trolley Line 113

Chapter 11: The MacDarby Farm 119

Chapter 12: A Presidential Visit 133

Chapter 13: Pinepoint 139

Chapter 14: The Mohhekennuck Club 179

Chapter 15: Three Goose Pond Families 189

Chapter 16: Chanterwood 205

Chapter 17: A Dugout Canoe 237

Chapter 18: The Appalachian Trail 241

Chapter 19: Wildlife 253

Epilogue 281

Acknowledgements 283

Author Bio 289

Recommended Reading 291

Endnotes 293

Pinepoint cabin on the day it entered our lives

INTRODUCTION

We were enjoying a family dinner in our Teaneck, New Jersey home on a Friday evening in September of 1971 when the kitchen phone rang. The caller, a Lee realtor, informed my parents of a lakefront cabin on Goose Pond going on the market the following morning. She was certain that this property was exactly what my parents had been looking for and she was equally certain that it would be sold before noon.

Having rented the old Wagner cabin on Goose Pond for the prior two summers, my family had already become enchanted by this little mountaintop lake. So, the following morning we awoke before sunrise, ate a wordless breakfast in the dark, piled into our Buick station wagon and drove up to Lee. I recall how we followed the realtor's car onto Lakeside Drive and then turned onto a dirt driveway that became progressively narrower and shadier, and how each of us was growing increasingly excited, sensing that the moment was upon us when we might soon have our own home on this lake.

I recall seeing how the property jutted out into the lake, terminating in a dark, lichen-covered rock ledge, cool to the touch and dropping down steeply into the water, and how soft the beds of pine needles were under our feet, fallen from the countless surrounding pine trees. And then there was the seventy-year-old cabin, the first on the lake, with its cozy color-coded bedrooms — a blue room, a red room, and a green room — its fieldstone fireplace, its exposed posts and beams, the chachkas and old dishes all included, and the darkened, slightly spooky sleeping loft overlooking the living room. And, of course, Goose Pond was right there, quietly beckoning.

I don't think it took thirty minutes on the property for my parents to make their decision. This was the wonderful day that Pinepoint would become my family's beloved "lakehouse." Fifty years later it would become my own full-time home.

My parents on Pinepoint

As the ensuing course of my family's lives whirled madly around over the next fifty-plus years, Goose Pond was always right here, serene and unperturbed, like the lighthouse perched high on a stormy shore, a powerful, but calming beacon always there for us.

Over the years, Pinepoint certainly had its share of changes. A lot of the old pine trees fell while new ones sprouted. Low points were filled in, the dock was rebuilt and then relocated, and our veritable fleet of small boats constantly evolved. When we finally had to bid our sad farewell to the old cabin, we also said goodbye to the chipmunks, mice, spiders, and bats with whom we had always shared it -- like it or not. After our new house sprung up, we learned the joys of Goose Pond even when it was frozen over during the frigid winter months. But, despite all the visible changes, Pinepoint, and the Pond, never had truly changed – not where it mattered.

Goose Pond was just here, always here.

COVID led many of us to slow down and take measure of our lives. While our approaching permanent re-location to Goose Pond had not yet been formally written into our life plan, I became increasingly conscious of the quiet, but irresistible force that this lake had exerted on my life. It was during this life pause that the seed of a thought that I had entertained in the past, of someday writing a book about the pond, sprouted roots, grew larger, and gradually moved front and center. By the end of 2020, I had decided to write the book you have before you.

It would be easy to think of Goose Pond as an isolated place, cut off from the rest of the world, its inhabitants going about their business away from the forces at play in the surrounding world.

Introduction

And, at first glance, the stories that follow, focused as they are on events surrounding a small patch of water sitting high on a Massachusetts mountaintop, appear, on their surface at least, to back up this belief. But on closer examination, it becomes clear that the lake's stories were a barometer of much larger events taking place far beyond its shorelines. Viewed this way, we can see that much of our pond's history is a reflection of the powerful flow of American history.

For starters, the arrival of Europeans on the North American continent led to a dramatic transformation of local human society from that of the indigenous peoples to that of the Europeans. These profound changes were accompanied by the disenfranchisement and involuntary relocation of Goose Pond's Mohican Indians and the subsequent founding of the colonial towns of Lee and Tyringham. On the heels of the American Revolution came yet another, the Industrial Revolution, which stretched from the mid-nineteenth-century to the early twentieth century, and was the driving force behind the development of Lee's robust paper industry, the Lake May Power plant, the construction of Goose Pond's dam, and the digging of Sucker Brook.

The growth of American literacy was a consequence of the birth of public education which, along with an American passion for reading printed discourse, led to an insatiable appetite for paper, a commodity manufactured, quite substantially, using the water flowing out of Goose Pond. In the late nineteenth-century, a growing appreciation for nature, as reflected in the popularity of naturalist American writers like Henry David Thoreau and John Burroughs, contributed to the establishment of Goose Pond's early family cabins, the Mohhekennuck Club, the Morse Camp, and the Appalachian Trail.

The invention of the automobile transformed personal mobility and opportunities for leisure, contributing to the rapid decline of the Huckleberry Trolley Line and the increasing interest in wilderness resorts like Chanterwood. We can see that the remarkably broad arc of Goose Pond's history stretches across the many centuries of Mohican society, to colonial America, through the Industrial Revolution, and finally to a lake enjoyed mostly for recreation and leisure.

Although this is a book of history, it is not, strictly speaking, a history book. I wanted to tell the tales of Goose Pond. It was therefore impractical to present its stories in a strictly chronological manner. I have organized chapters according to their topics, but even these topics, and their timelines, will sometimes overlap between chapters. Unavoidably, there will be some content repeated here and there, but usually from different perspectives. Some topics will be mentioned only briefly the first time around, but in more detail later, or vice versa. That said, the book was nevertheless written with the intent that the chapters would best be read in their sequence.

This book will certainly have its share of errors and omissions. I invite you to inform me of what I got wrong, or didn't make clear, or should have included but didn't, or did include but shouldn't have. I hope you will email me with your comments, questions, and corrections. If enough of those come through, maybe there will be a second, improved edition someday.

The creation of this volume has arisen from, and further deepened, my abiding love for Goose Pond. I hope that reading it will deepen yours too.

David

reflectionsongoosepond@gmail.com

Sunrise on Pinepoint

PROLOGUE

AS MY KAYAK glides out of Sucker Brook and enters Upper Goose Pond, the air seems to me unusually transparent today, the world appears – well, crystalline.

It's a morning in late October, early morning, the sun is still low, but the sky is already a luminous azure. Something about the sun in autumn; it's extra bright, and I am thankful for my wrap-around sunglasses and trusty Cape May baseball cap, the solar glare otherwise blinding. Without a whisper of wind, the water's surface is like a mirror, no, exactly a mirror, and the thickly forested hills, with their leaves wildly ablaze, are more than just reflected below, they are duplicated.

I hear a small splash behind me and, turning, I see concentric, circular, widening ripples in the water from a fish grabbing an insect struggling on the pond's surface. Looking skyward, I see one of our resident bald eagles soaring overhead. I lift my hand to shield my eyes from the sun. Wait! There are two of them today, both circling, circling, four sharp eyes searching for a careless fish.

The autumnal sun delivers a light caress of warmth on my face, a hint of coming relief from the air's morning chill. Taking a break from paddling, I reach for the insulated cup filled with strong black coffee, which has been sitting on the floor of my kayak. The dark, still-steaming liquid goes down smoothly. As I enjoy its chocolatey aroma and earthy, faintly volcanic taste, it warms me even a bit more, this time from within. The caffeine is certainly welcome, my brain still sleepy despite the glare all around me. I feel as though wide awake and sleeping simultaneously.

The log cabins along the shore (the Stilwell camp) are empty, deep in shadow, and closed for the season. But the hiker cabin is still open. I can't see it, but I hear the murmuring voices of some late-season Appalachian Trail hikers, a man and a woman, emerging from the cabin, an occasional laugh, and the faint smell of a breakfast frying over a campfire wafts my way. Eggs and bacon would surely be a welcome addition to my coffee and my stomach rumbles a little. Other than these signs of unseen hikers, the only other indication of human life – anywhere in the world! - is the faint continuous hum of traffic on the Mass Pike, which lies just over the hill, stretching from Stockbridge to Boston. Where have I heard that line before? I hear a big truck engine climbing a steep incline, its trailer heavily laden with its freight.

Mine is the only boat on Upper Goose and I see no one. Yet, at the outer edges of my solitude, I sense company. I wonder if it's a ghostly, but welcoming presence of some long-gone Mohhekennuck Club campers, those joyful Upper Goose nature lovers from years past, whose massive fieldstone fireplace still stands just ahead on the left, the sole remaining remnant after the big fire. Maybe those jubilant Mohhekennuckers of old never truly left and their joy now becomes my own.

The gentle splashes of my paddle seem cacophonous in the surrounding quiet. With each stroke, I feel droplets of cold, clear water sliding down my bare forearms. My shoeless feet are also wet, and a bit cold, from climbing into the kayak earlier, but my body is otherwise warm and dry from the layers of clothing I am wearing, including a well-worn hooded sweatshirt, soft with use.

Light from the rapidly rising sun is now reaching the fall foliage which is at its peak on the encircling mountains. The radiant oranges, yellows, and reds glow as if forged from fire itself. Yet there are also some treetops showing green -- the pines, of course, of which there are many. The vibrant colors in the trees' watery reflections call out to me, each shade competing for my attention, each more brilliant than the next and certainly no duller than its identical twin above the waterline.

The silence, the sounds, the chill, the warmth, the blinding brilliance, and the shadow, the sleepiness alongside vivid awakening, the wetness, the dryness, the blues and oranges, the solitude, but with invisible people nearby (maybe some ghosts too), the world around me and then its precise duplication below. The competing dualities are soothing, mutually enhancing, otherworldly, and even dreamlike. Or could it be that this — *this*, here and now — is Reality and everything *else* (out there) is the Dream?

Welcome, my friends, to Goose Pond.

A Sunrise on Goose Pond

CHAPTER 1

WATER AND MOUNTAINS

*O*NE COULD QUITE arguably take the position that any written history of a lake, or a pond for that matter, should properly start with the story of its water. After all, its water is what makes a lake a lake, or a pond a pond. So, if it's with the water that we start, any such story might logically begin fourteen billion years ago, when there was a pretty dramatic, cosmic actually, event known universally as the Big Bang, which, by way of creating all the space, time, matter, and energy comprising our universe, marks the true beginning of the story of Goose Pond's water (and, yes, of Everything Else too.) It wasn't until the 300,000th year of all existence that the infant cosmos had cooled sufficiently to permit some of its swarming superheated subatomic particles to coalesce into hydrogen atoms, themselves (a billion years later) going on to combine with oxygen atoms, and thereby creating the very same molecules of water (H_2O) which, thirteen billion years later, now fill Goose Pond.

One might understandably have assumed that, when the Earth itself was initially formed, some four billion years ago, it would have had its water on it right from the start. But early planet Earth, scorching hot and lacking any protective atmosphere, had, in its formative days, no water on it whatsoever. Earth scientists believe that the water that fills Goose Pond, indeed the water that fills our oceans and our water glasses, very likely arrived on Earth by hitching rides as ice frozen on the surfaces of countless asteroids and comets colliding with our slowly cooling planet. (If we were to think about how many asteroids it would have taken to bring enough ice to fill our lakes and seas, we might appropriately be quite thankful that this asteroid shower ended well before we showed up.)[1]

Digressing now to a far more earthly level, those familiar with Goose Pond know that it consists of two crescent-shaped ponds, a larger one many call "Lower" Goose Pond and a smaller one to its northeast named Upper Goose Pond, each connected to the other by a narrow, winding channel (officially named Sucker Brook), which is navigable, with a little care, during much of the year.

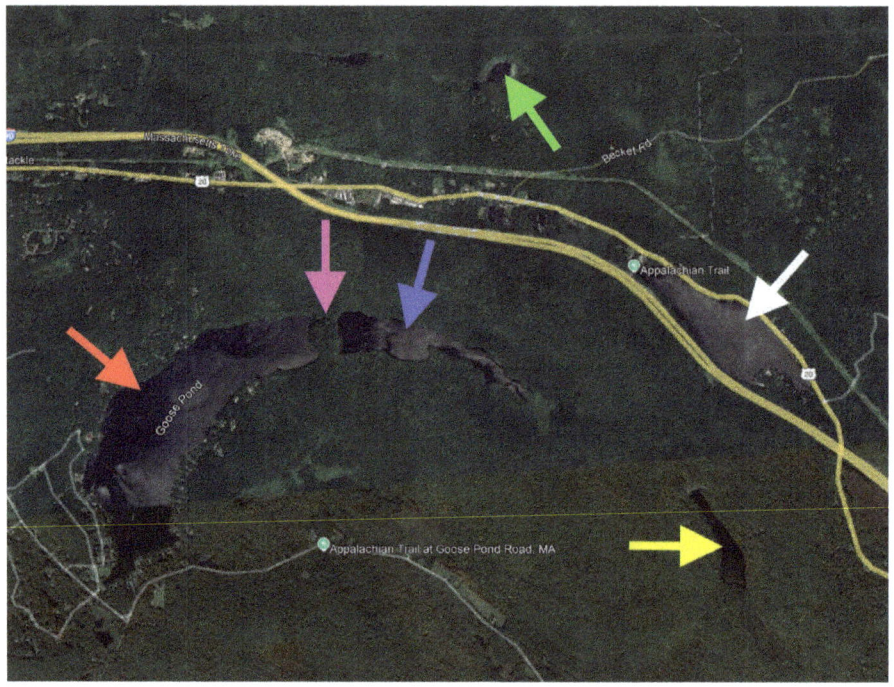

Figure 1.1 Satellite map of the Goose Pond watershed. "Lower" Goose Pond (red arrow), Upper Goose Pond (blue arrow), Upper Upper Goose Pond (yellow arrow), Greenwater Pond (white arrow), Basin / Mud Pond (green arrow) and Sucker Brook (pink arrow) all drain into the same stream whose water eventually joins the Housatonic River. The Mass Pike (I-90) and Route 20 are the two roads that traverse from left to right north of Goose Pond. Modified, courtesy of Google Earth.

Whether these paired ponds should technically be considered as a single, but subdivided, lake or rather as two distinct, but conjoined, lakes will depend on who you ask and has been a question at the center of some debate about applicable boating regulations on these waters. But, if you were to ask me, I would argue that they should properly be considered as two topographically and historically separate and distinct lakes, which they were for many thousands of years, long before becoming connected as the consequence of a man-made dam and a hand-dug channel, both constructed as recently as 1839. Consider that, even after the Suez Canal was completed, we continue to designate the Mediterranean and Red Seas as distinct bodies of water. And certainly, there is no debate about the individual identities of Lakes Huron and Michigan whose connection is quite a bit wider (and older) than Sucker Brook.

Earlier, I put the word "Lower" in quotes because the larger, lower (i.e. more southerly) pond is officially just called Goose Pond, not Lower Goose Pond. Upper Goose is, however, always called Upper Goose (except in the nineteenth-century when it was, for a time, called Long Pond). To make things a bit more confusing, the term "Goose Pond" is often used loosely to describe *both* ponds together. And for a while, in the 1800s, Goose Pond was called Lake May for reasons that will become clear later. I will nevertheless sometimes use the term "Lower Goose Pond" whenever I am referring specifically to the larger, lower body, and in certain historical contexts, I will call it Lake May, but I will never call anything Long Pond.

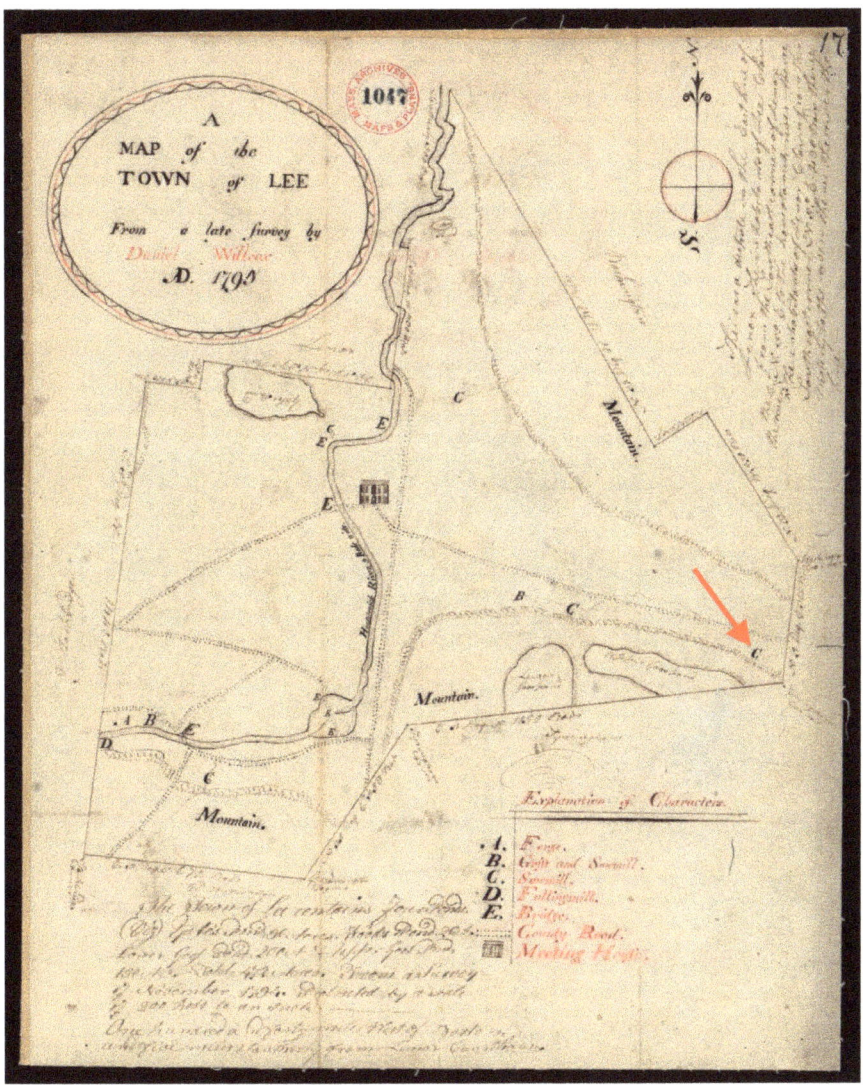

Figure 1.2 *Map of Lee from 1795. On close examination of this map, it can be seen that Lower and Upper Goose Pond had been given their names as early as 1795. Also, note that there is no connection drawn between Upper and Lower Goose Ponds. The far-right sawmill (red arrow) was likely the historically important "Griffin Bros" sawmill.*

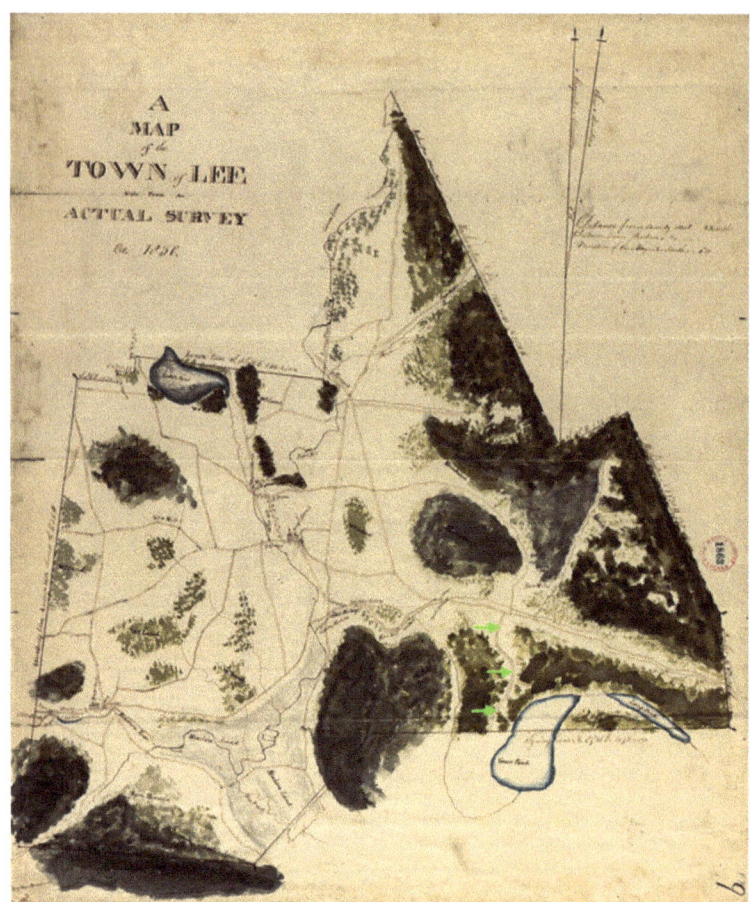

Figure 1.3 Survey of Lee from 1830. Notice Goose Pond in the lower right corner outlined in blue. Upper Goose is called "Long Pond" on this map. Curiously, a connection is drawn between the two ponds even though the dam had not raised the water high enough to fill any connection until 1839. Note that Chanter Road (green arrows) was then the only road to Goose Pond and that Forest Street access to Goose Pond, beside the Goose Pond stream, had not yet been constructed. Compare to Figure 1.5.

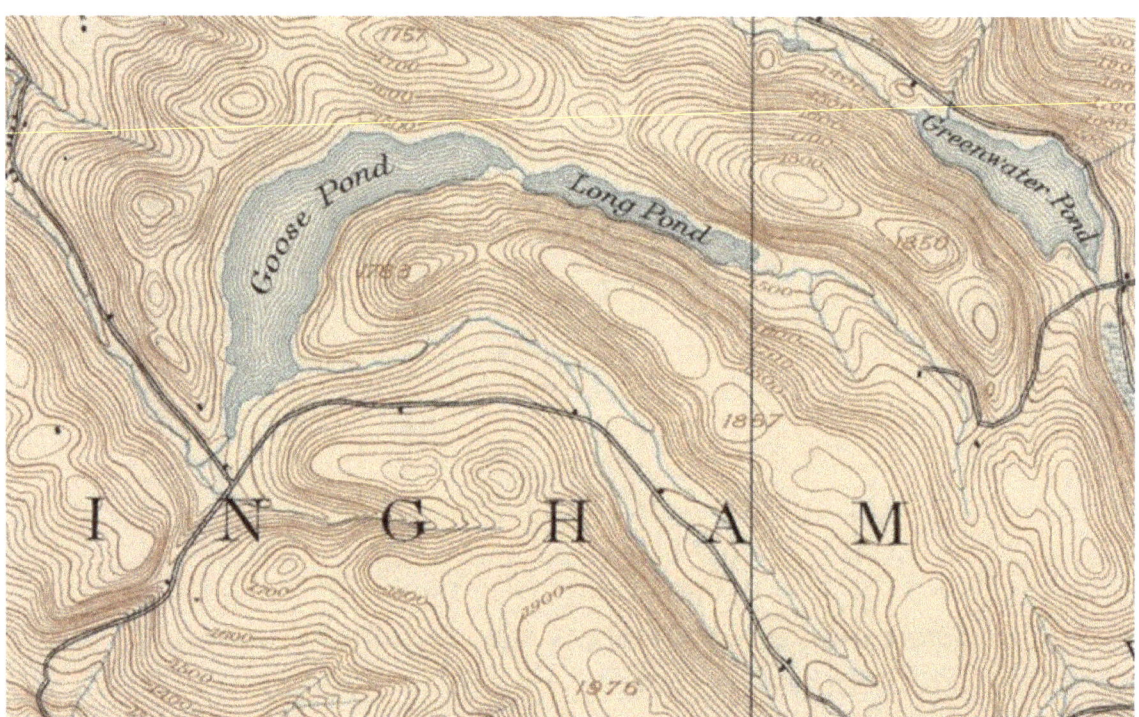

Figure 1.4 Map from 1886 showing Upper Goose Pond as "Long Pond". Courtesy of Joe Janis.

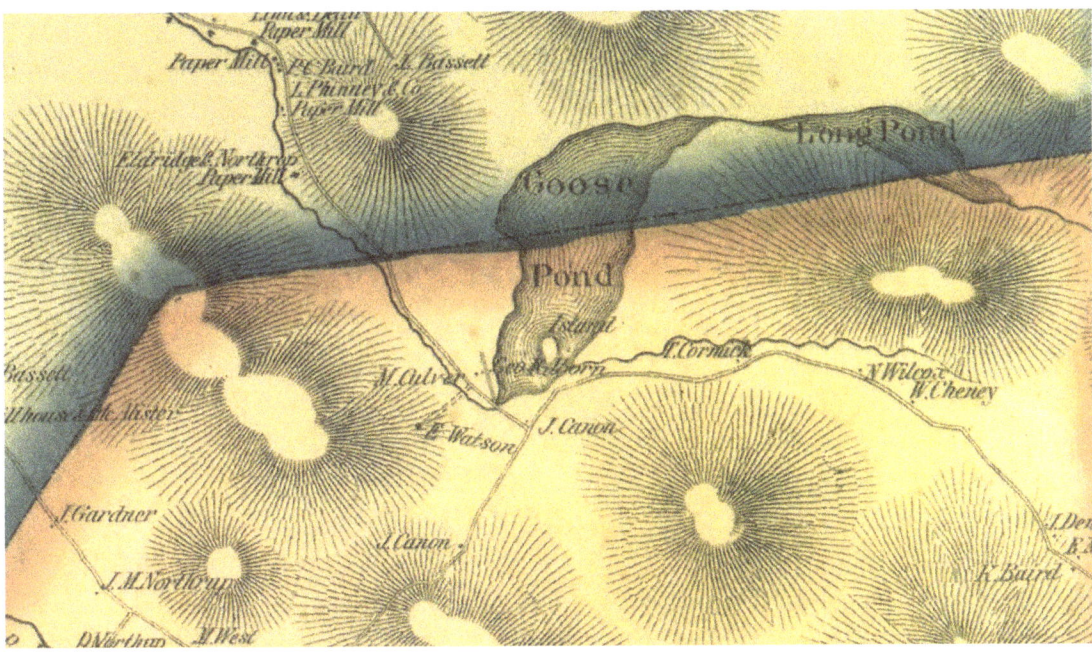

Figure 1.5 Map drawn by H.F. Walling in 1858 showing Upper Goose Pond as "Long Pond". When compared to Figure 1.3, this map now demonstrates that the Forest Street/Mountain Road/Goose Pond Road access to Goose Pond had been completed during the interval of 1830-1858. This road can be seen on this map as it starts near the dam and parallels the Goose Pond stream towards the top of the map. Courtesy of old-maps.com.

Figure 1.6 Survey map dated as recently as 1924 continues to show Upper Goose Pond's name as having the alternate name of Long Pond. Courtesy of Tim Puntin.

People commonly ask why Goose Pond is called a pond, and not a lake. I cannot opine any more meaningfully on this topic than RW Smith does in his entertaining little book, *Three Thumbnails,* to which curious readers are referred.[2] As to why someone back in the 1700s thought to name the pond "Goose" remains a mystery, although these birds have been consistently present in the lakes of Massachusetts for many centuries.

Lower Goose Pond's surface covers 263 acres (at its summer level), measures approximately one and a half miles long, and a half-mile wide, with a perimeter of four miles and a maximum depth of forty-eight feet. Upper Goose Pond covers sixty-one acres, measures approximately three-quarters of a mile long, three-eighths of a mile wide, and has a perimeter of two and half miles and a maximum depth of thirty-three feet. If you were to drain the two ponds dry (please don't) you would be the proud owner of 5,400 acre-feet (or 1.7 billion gallons) of water.

Two streams feed directly into Goose Pond, one of which is Cooper Brook, which drains into Lower Goose Pond at its western end, close to the dam. The other is Higley Brook, which originates from a dam on Upper *Upper* Goose Pond (in Becket) and empties into Upper Goose Pond at the swampy area at its far eastern end. Goose Pond gets additional water from springs that bubble up from deep subterranean aquifers, and from all the water that arrives by way of the thunderstorms that reliably disrupt our afternoon lakeside barbecues.

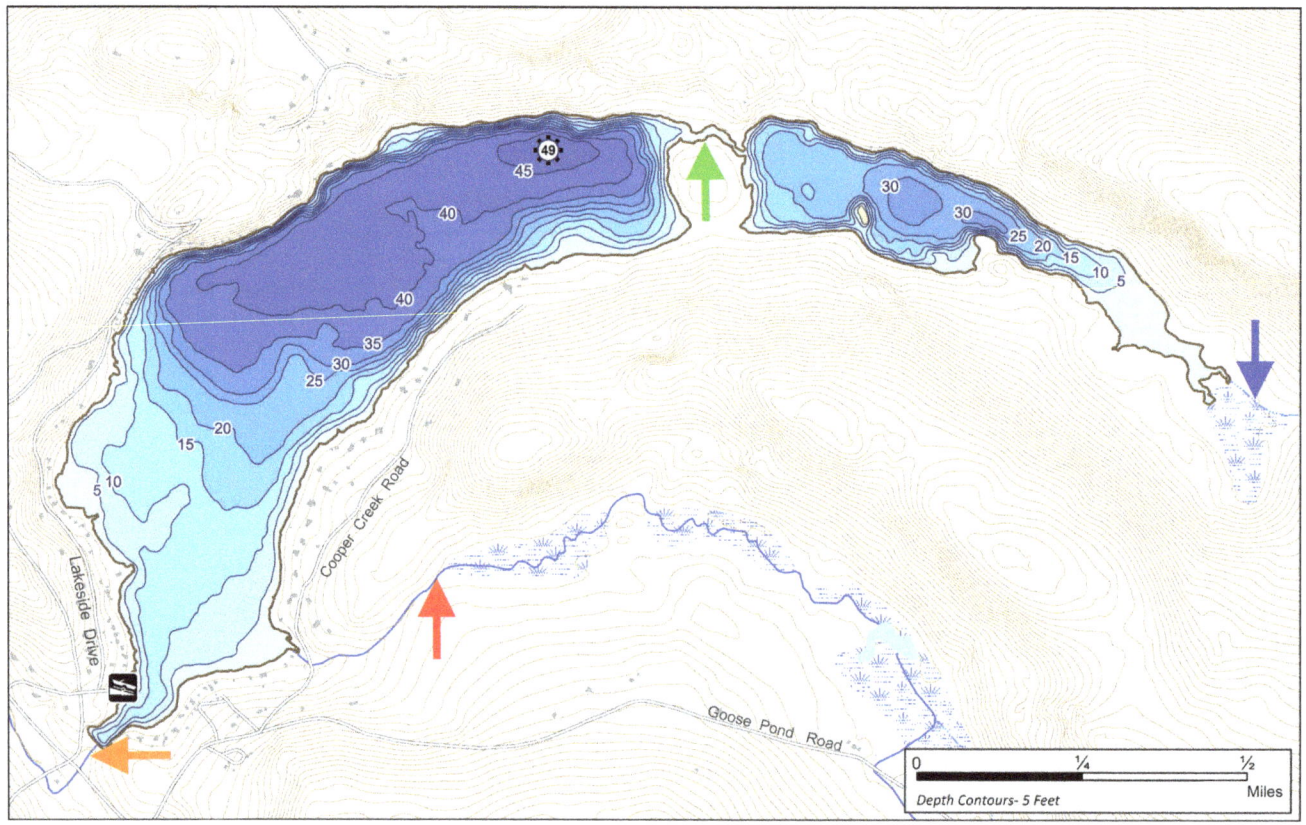

Figure 1.7 *Goose Pond depth map showing water inflow and outflow. Cooper Brook (red arrow), Higley Brook (blue arrow), Sucker Brook (green arrow), and the outflow via Goose Pond stream (orange arrow). Modified, courtesy of Commonwealth of Massachusetts Division of Fisheries and Wildlife.*

Figure 1.8 Upper Upper Goose Pond, c1990's. Courtesy of the Crewdson family.

Goose Pond's outflow is through the man-made dam located at its southwestern end, and emptying into the otherwise unnamed Goose Pond stream. Topographic maps hint that, in ages past, this stream might have drained to the south, along where George Canon Road currently runs down into the Tyringham valley. But now, evidently diverted by a long-ago geological or glacial event, the stream runs a northerly route alongside Goose Pond Road and Forest Street and eventually empties into the Housatonic River.

But before Goose Pond's water reaches the Housatonic, it is first joined by the water draining two other nearby lakes, one of which is Greenwater Pond, located to the east of Goose Pond and sandwiched tightly between Route 20 and the Mass Pike. This pond drains via the Greenwater Brook, which combines with the Goose Pond stream at the lower terminus of Forest Street where it intersects with Route 20. The third lake of this trio is Basin Pond (formerly called Mud Pond, and briefly named Lake Lee), which has its own draining stream that directly joins the Greenwater Brook upstream from its connection to the Goose Pond stream. (See Figure 1.1) The conjoined waters flowing from these three lakes finally enter the Housatonic River bound for the Long Island Sound and then to the Atlantic Ocean.

Goose Pond's water has, in years past, been sought after for more than just waterwheels and recreation. In 1931, the Mountain Mill and Lake May Power Company offered to sell Goose Pond's water to the City of Pittsfield for drinking, promising a daily supply of 7,887,000 gallons.[3] While Pittsfield's citizens never did get the opportunity to drink Goose Pond's water, Lee's did. From 1962-1972 the town of Lee gained access to Goose Pond water as a backup to its drinking water supply. Westfield Paper Company's gifting of the water to the town of Lee prompted plenty of heated debate about who rightfully owned the water in the pond itself, an interesting question that appears never to have been definitively resolved.[4] There are still visible remnants of a two-foot diameter steel pipe buried in the ground representing some of the infrastructure installed during this period. The valve to draw Goose Pond's water into the town's drinking supply was turned on at least three times during droughts in those years, events not particularly popular among the lake's residents who were understandably distressed about dramatically receding shorelines.[5]

Figure 1.9 Remnants of the water pipe used when Goose Pond water was supplying the town of Lee with drinking water. This pipe section is visible near the intersection of Chanterwood Road and Forest Street.[6]

With its water surface at a summer elevation of 1477 feet above sea level, Goose Pond is situated on the northernmost summit of Long Mountain, which itself rises from the valley at the western edge of the Berkshire Mountain range. Long Mountain is, as its name suggests, quite long, and also narrow, running in a north-south orientation down towards Otis, and making up the eastern side of Tyringham valley opposite the foothills of Beartown Mountain. The neighboring towns of Lee and Tyringham (each at an elevation of 900 feet) lay settled in their respective valleys at the foot of Long Mountain. The most northern end of Long Mountain has also been called Pixley Mountain, named after a founding Lee citizen by the name of Reuben Pixley.[7] (see Figure 10.4)

As you travel up Forest Street from Lee to reach Goose Pond, you will be following the Goose Pond Stream, climbing up from the valley into the western margin of the Berkshire Mountain range. Forest Street, and its neighboring Goose Pond Stream, climbs, or drops (depending on your direction of travel), 500 feet in two miles, an incline that, in my younger days, permitted an excellent workout, and many years before that provided the power for some highly relevant industrial development like sawmills, paper mills and a hydroelectric power plant.

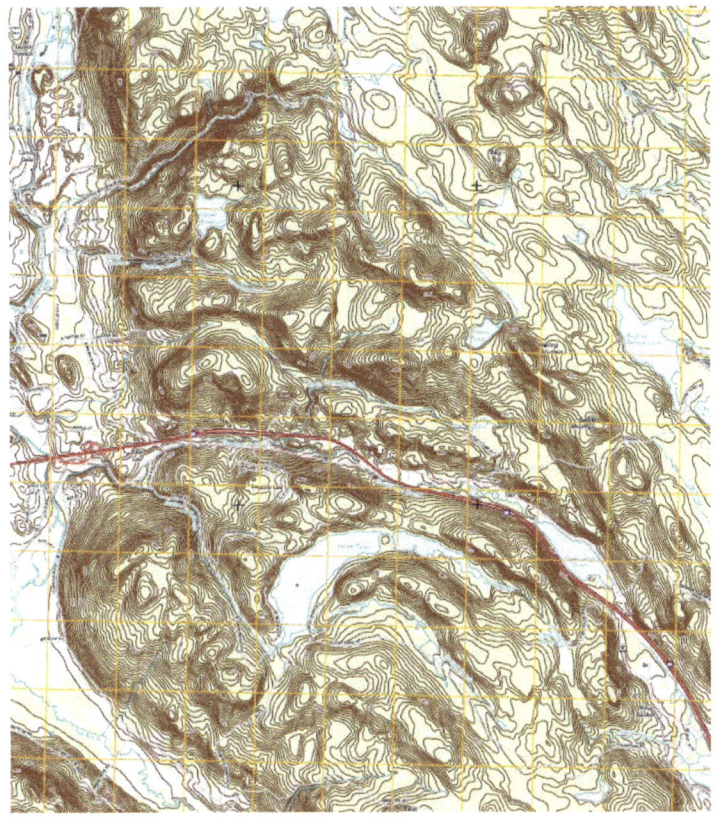

Figure 1.10 U.S. Geological Survey (USGS) map of Goose Pond environs. Long Mountain extends from the lower right corner up to the Mass Pike (in red). Goose Pond lies near the northern summit of Long Mountain. The Tyringham valley lies in the lower left corner. The western margin of the Berkshire Mountain range runs in a north-south direction on the left side of the map. The town of Lee lies in the valley to the west of the Berkshire Mountains. Courtesy of U.S. Geological Survey.

Figure 1.11 Topographical map showing the relationship between Goose Pond (blue arrow), the western edge of the Berkshire Mountains, Beartown State Forest, and the valleys holding Lee and Tyringham townships. Long Mountain is bordered to its west by Hop Brook in Tyringham, and to the east by the West Branch of the Farmington River. Courtesy World Topographic Maps.

Flowers in the swamp of Upper Goose Pond

CHAPTER 2

A TOUR OF GOOSE POND

*I*MAGINE YOURSELF PADDLING A KAYAK or canoe close to shore, starting your journey at Goose Pond's dam, and proceeding clockwise around the sister ponds' edges. During this tour, I will share some stories related to the sights along the way. Figure 2.1 provides a map of the main attractions we will visit.

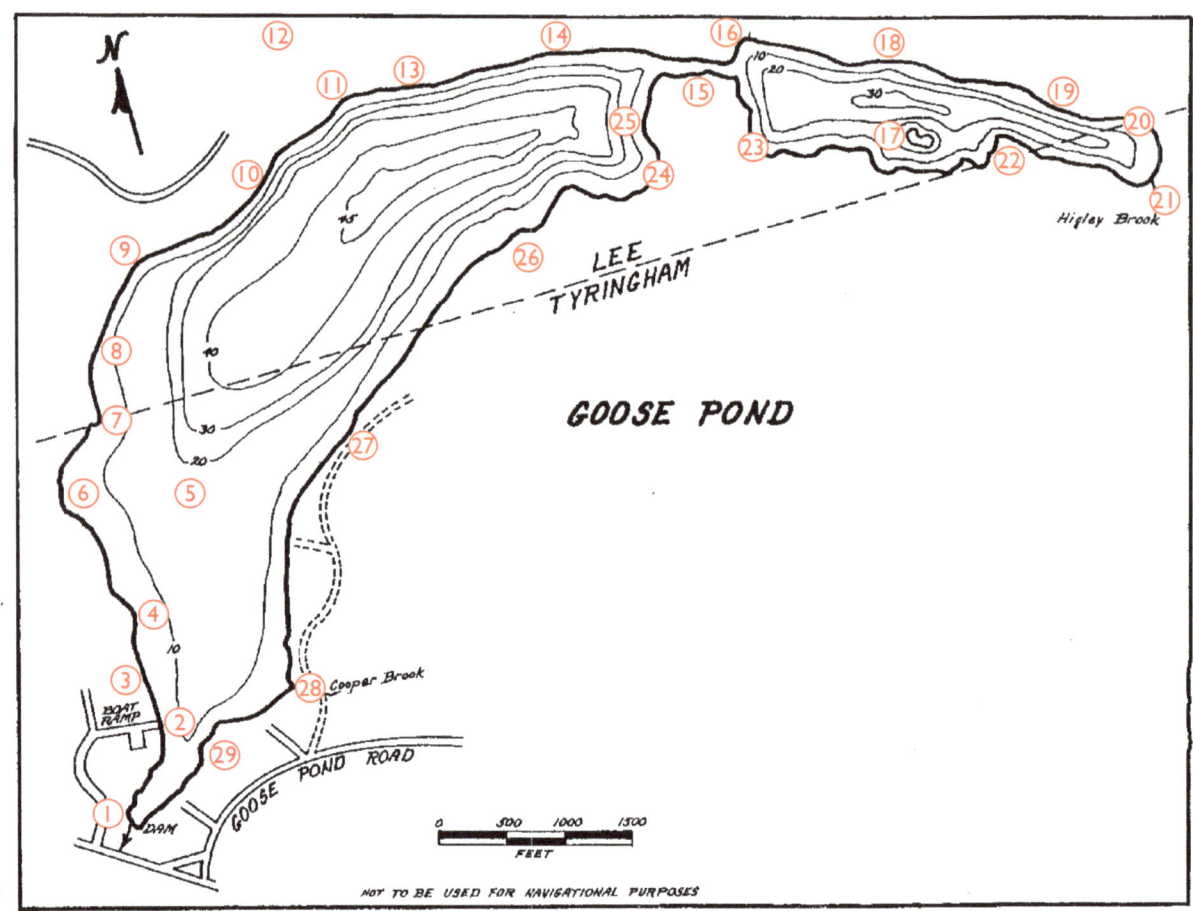

Figure 2.1 Goose Pond Tour Map. 1 Dam. 2 Boat Ramp. 3 Lakeside Drive community. 4 Pinepoint. 5 Stump Island. 6 Submerged Chanter Road. 7 Town Line. 8 Wagner cabin location. 9 Chanterwood section. 10 Bass Rock. 11 Berkshire Hills (aka Leisure Lee). 12 Ski Trail. 13 Stone Chair. 14 Trustees property. 15 Sucker Brook. 16 Hiker Cabin. 17 Island (Elwell's Rock). 18 Stilwell cabins. 19 Mohhekennuck Club. 20 Swamp. 21 Higley Brook. 22 Peninsula. 23 Upper Boynes Cove. 24 Lower Boynes Cove. 25 Goose Pond Yacht Club mooring. 26 Smith cabin location. 27 Cooper Creek Road community. 28 Cooper Brook. 29 Goose Pond Road community. Modified, courtesy of Commonwealth of Massachusetts Division of Fisheries and Wildlife.

Shortly after leaving the dam (see Figure 2.1, #1), our first sight is the boat ramp (see Figure 2.1 #2), a public access open 365 days a year and providing public boat launching, and parking for recreational boating, fishing, and ice fishing. This access, established in 1958 by the Berkshire County Commissioners, was constructed on land donated by the Goose Lake Development Corp. as well as on an easement across the property of Hooker Moore, himself descended from the MacDarby family.[8] The public access ramp is managed by the Department of Fish and Game, monitored by the Massachusetts Environmental Police, and maintained year-round by the Township of Tyringham. Recently added modern enhancements include paving of the ramp, designated trailer parking spaces, and a new dock.

Figure 2.2 *Aerial view of the Goose Pond dam. Courtesy of Wallace Prysock.*

Figure 2.3 *Public Boat Ramp.*

Proceeding north along the shoreline you will encounter the shorefront homes of my own Lakeside Drive neighborhood (see Figure 2.1 #3). Once comprising the 175-acre MacDarby farm, many of these lots were subsequently developed by the Goose Lake Development Corp. Lakeside Drive, an unpaved, private, dead-end street, ends at the Lee town line.

A few hundred yards from the dam, you will encounter a small peninsula jutting into the lake, dotted with pine trees, and sporting a ledge of dark, ancient bedrock dropping down into the lake. Historically dubbed "Pinepoint," this spot has a well-documented history of its own and holds a special place in my heart. (see Figure 2.1 #4) Just past Pinepoint is a small, private beach shared by many of the residents of the Lakeside Drive neighborhood. This beach was initially created by a Girl Scout troupe in the 1930s for use as a day camp.[9]

Figure 2.4 Original Cavarly cabin on Pinepoint, circa 1905. Other than the MacDarby farmhouse on Lower Goose and the nineteenth-century Griffin homestead on Upper Goose, the Cavarly cabin was the first cabin built on Goose Pond. Courtesy of Charles Mecklum.

Figure 2.5 *Pinepoint, as it is now, in autumn. The rock ledge on this point, called "Lee gneiss," is over one billion years old. The house is a bit younger. (gneiss is pronounced "nice").*

If you were to paddle (or swim) a few hundred feet off Pinepoint, you would encounter some shallow water, marked during the summer months with a buoy and providing swimmers the opportunity to stand in a few feet of water and inattentive boaters the risk of grinding up their motors' propellers (see Figure 2.1 #5). Before 1839, this area was a full-time island, and today, during the winter's six-foot drawdown, its rocks can still be seen rising above the ice, so calling this otherwise submerged area an island has some justification. Its name, Stump Island, reflects the continued presence of the two-hundred-year-old tree stumps still present under the surface.

Figure 2.6 *Stump Island on a misty morning. This photograph was taken after the annual six-foot drawdown that takes place each fall.*

Just past the Lakeside beach on your left, you will see a small shallow bay (see Figure 2.1 #6). Before the dam was raised in 1839, this bay was dry and crossed by a segment of Chanter Road (distinct from Chanterwood Road), which, in years past, was the major access road to Goose Pond, running up the mountain from Route 20, through the "Chanterwood" section, and connecting to Coopertown Road near the dam.

When the Pond's water level was raised by the enlarged dam, this submerged segment of Chanter Road was re-routed higher up the hill.[10] I suspect that some remnants of the submerged section of Chanter Road might still be visible to curious snorkelers in this bay. Many sections of what remains of Chanter Road can still be found in the woods of the Lakeside and Chanterwood neighborhoods, and its origination off Route 20 still boasts a street sign. Figure 1.3 shows Chanter Road as the only road to Goose Pond in 1830. Figure 1.5 reveals that, by 1858, Forest Street/Goose Pond Road had been completed all the way to Goose Pond. It seems likely that Forest Street/Goose Pond Road, initially called Mountain Road, was constructed in 1839 in order to facilitate the transportation of the workers and equipment required for the major expansion of the Goose Pond dam that was accomplished that year.

Figure 2.7 *Road sign for Chanter Road at its origin from Route 20, just west of Leisure Lee.*

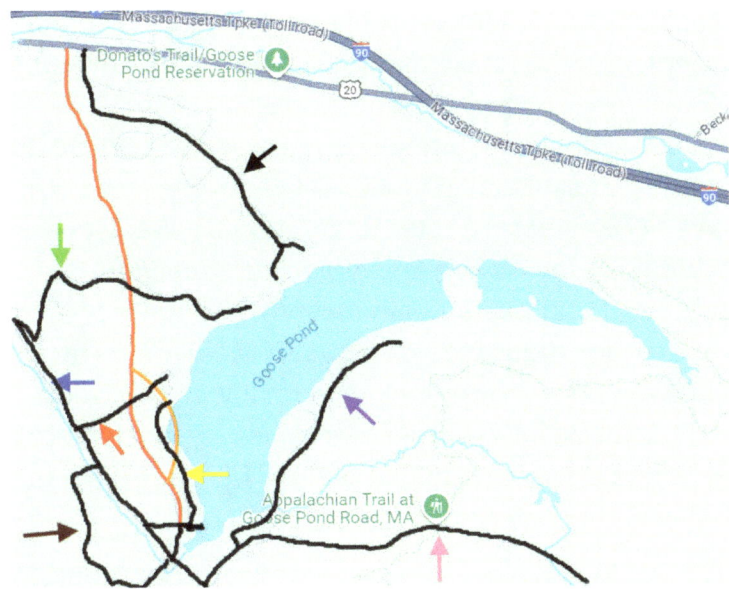

Figure 2.8 *Map of the approximate, original course of Chanter Road (solid red line) which was for many years the principal access to Lower Goose Pond. The orange line indicates the course of Chanter Road before becoming submerged following the 1839 enlargement of the dam. It was rerouted to higher ground once the dam raised the water level. The northern section of Chanter Road is still functional, but the road largely disappears as it approaches the Chanterwood area but its roadbed is still visible in the woods behind Lakeside Drive. Also shown are Chanterwood Road (green arrow), Forest Street/Goose Pond Road (blue arrow), what I call the "Wagner Road" (red arrow), McDarby Road/Stonebridge Ways (orange arrow), Goose Pond Road (pink arrow), Cooper Creek Road (purple arrow), Leisure Lee Road (black arrow), and Lakeside Drive (yellow arrow). Modified, courtesy of Google Maps.*

Up to this point, we have been paddling in the town of Tyringham, but now we are crossing the town line into Lee (see Figure 2.1 #7) The Tyringham-Lee town line slices East-West through Lower Goose and then again through the far end of Upper Goose. During our tour of the shoreline, we will be crossing this line four times. Goose Pond has not however always been located in Lee and Tyringham. This is because Lee has not always been Lee, nor Tyringham Tyringham.

In 1757, Robert Watson, of Sheffield, claimed to have purchased a large parcel of land from the Mohican Indians and proceeded to rename this land as Watsontown. Shortly thereafter, it was discovered that Watson had not actually paid the Indians, who were still demanding payment. Watson somehow ended up in jail for an unrelated offense. When some local men finally

Figure 2.9 *Hand-drawn map of Goose Pond from RW Smith's* Three Thumbnails *in 1978. Notice the short section of submerged Chanter Road. Many of the "sights" on our tour are designated in this drawing. Courtesy of Flint Smith.*

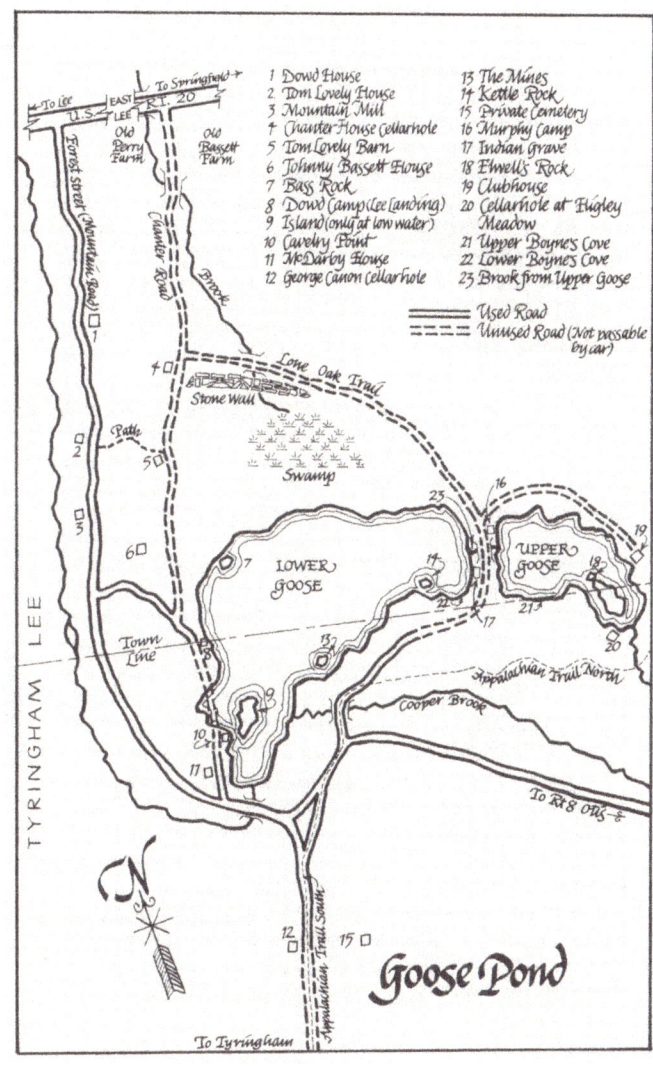

paid the Indians for this land, the deed was signed over to them by Benjamin Kokhkewenaunant, John Pophnehauauwah, and Robert Nunghauwot, and the land's name changed again, this time from Watsontown to Grennock (as in Lee's "Greenock Country Club").[11]

On June 29, 1763, without any apparent explanation, Grennock's name was changed to Hartwood. It was from the adjacent territories of Hartwood, Hoplands, Glassworks, and Williams Grant that Lee was eventually carved in 1777 and named after Revolutionary War General Charles Lee, who was featured (none too favorably) in the hit Broadway musical *Hamilton*.

Hence, it has only been since 1777 that Goose Pond has actually been in the town of Lee. Before then, Goose Pond's northern shores existed for thousands of years in Mohican territory, then briefly — and fraudulently — in Watsontown, then in Grennock, and finally in Hartwood.

Before Tyringham became Tyringham in 1762, the pond's southern stretches lay in a territory originally known as Brewer Mills (named after John Brewer who built a sawmill here in 1739), and subsequently as Housatonic Township No. 1.[12]

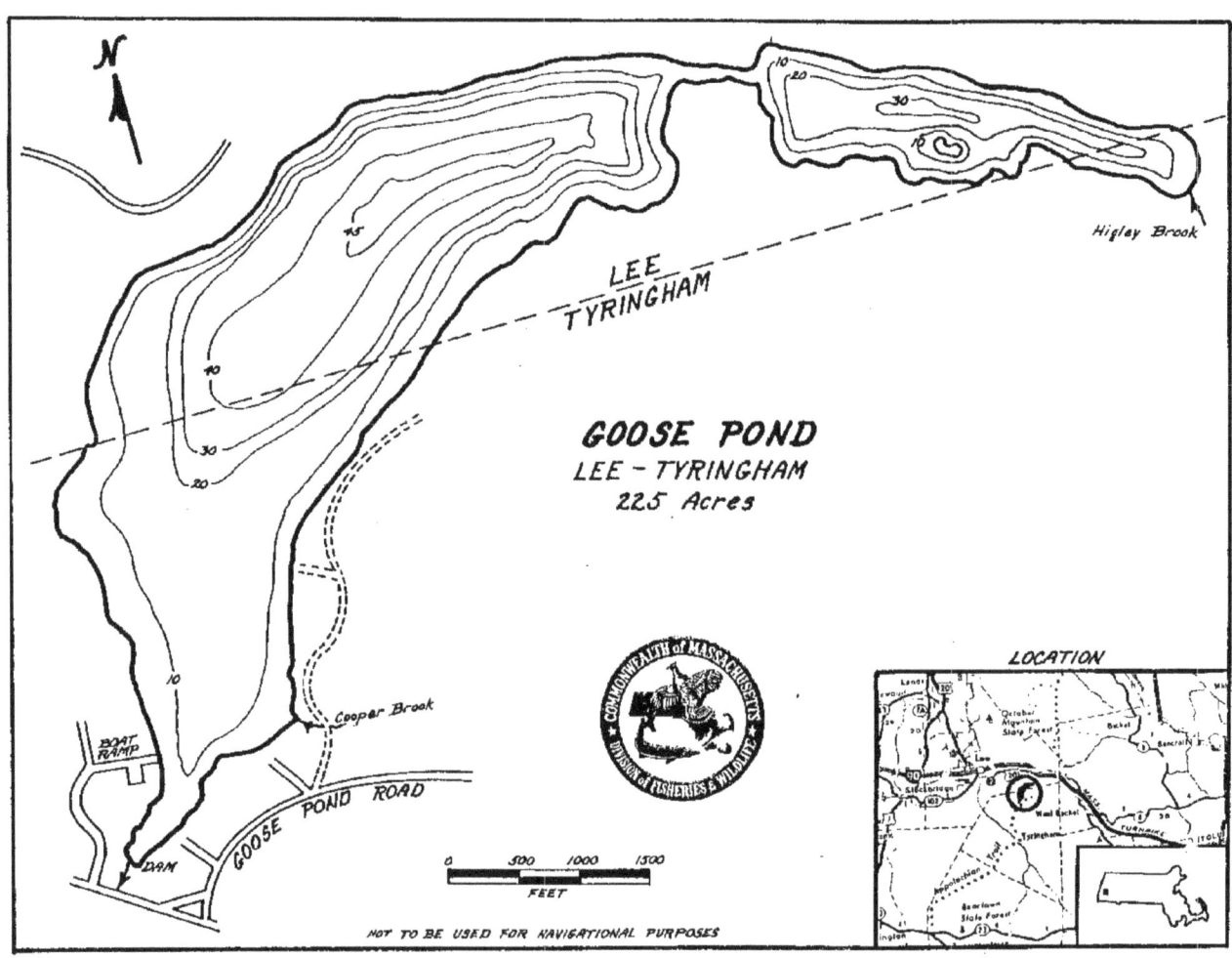

Figure 2.10 *Map of Goose Pond showing the Lee/Tyringham town line. Courtesy Commonwealth of Massachusetts Division of Fisheries and Wildlife.*

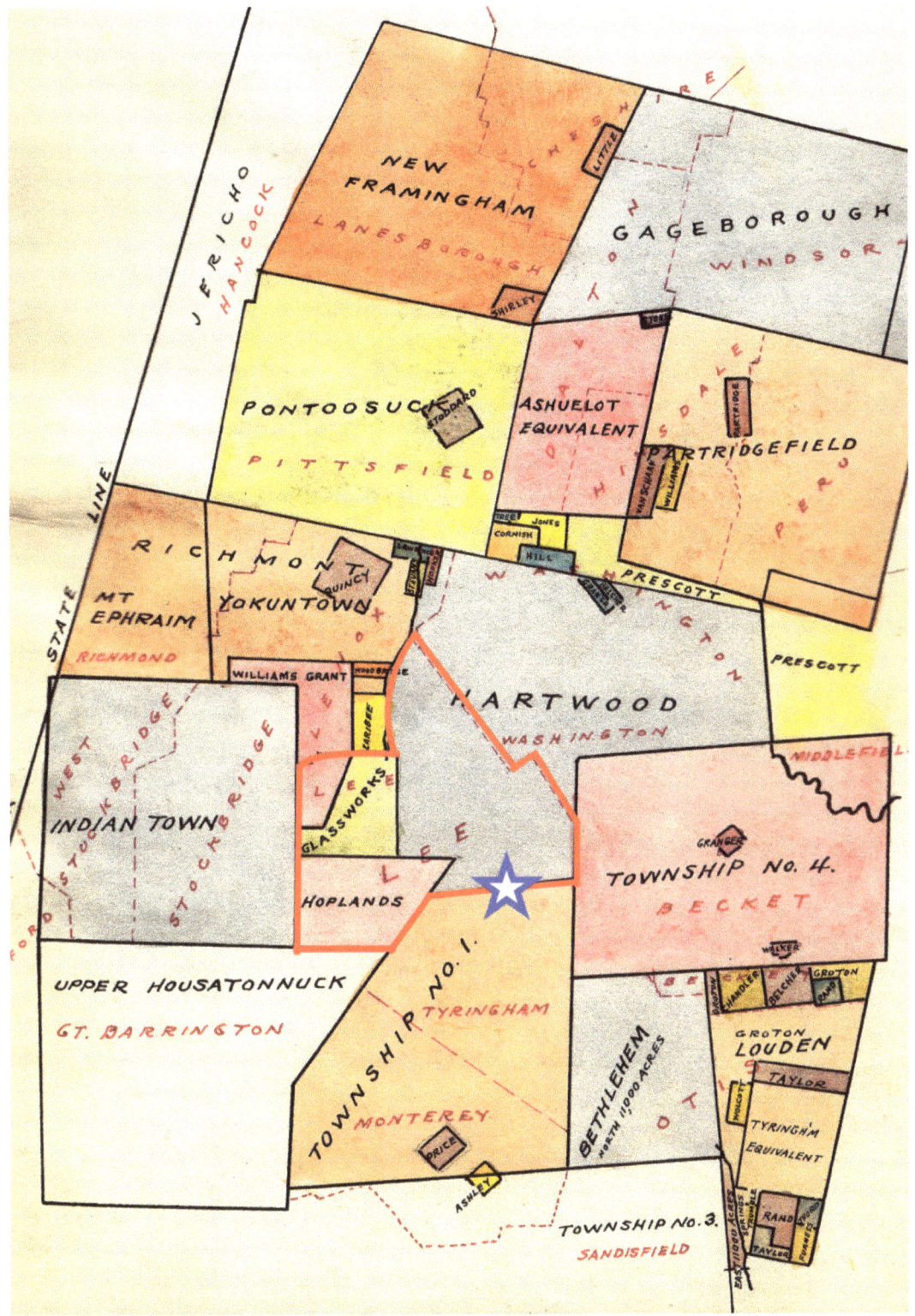

Figure 2.11 *This pre-Revolution map shows how the town of Lee (outlined in red) had been carved, in 1777, out of the previously British territories of Hartwood, Hoplands, Glassworks, and Williams Grant. Hoplands had itself been derived previously from Upper Housatonnuck (aka Great Barrington.) Tyringham's name in 1777 was still Housatonic Township No. 1. The location of Goose Pond has been designated with a blue star. Modified, from LenoxHistory.org.*

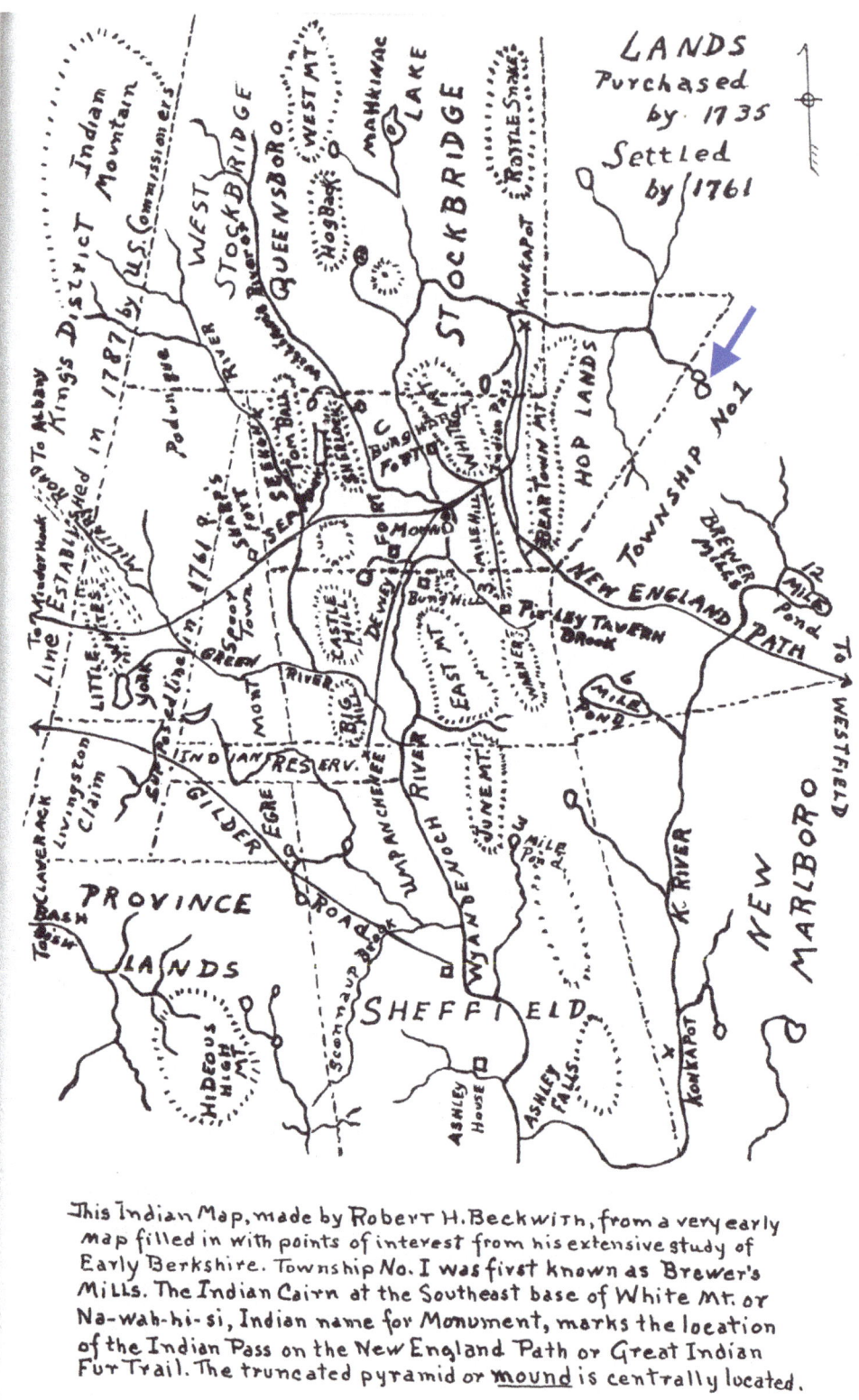

Figure 2.12 This "Indian Map," drawn by Robert H. Beckwith in 1761, shows Goose Pond (blue arrow) near the border between Township No. 1 (aka Tyringham/Monterey) and Hop Lands (later Lee). Note the designation of Brewer Mills. It seems likely that Tyringham's Hop Brook got its name from Hop Lands. This is the earliest map showing Goose Pond I was able to find. From A Hinterland Settlement, by Eloise Myers.

Since we are now on the topic of geography, I thought I might digress with a curious and little-known conflict between Massachusetts and New York. Goose Pond is now universally agreed to be situated within the Commonwealth of Massachusetts, but it was not always agreed that this was so. It's not that the Pond has ever been moved from one state to another, mind you, but rather that there was not always agreement on which colony had legitimate claim to the Berkshire Mountains.

It turns out that during the seventeenth century, the lands comprising the Berkshire Mountain range were claimed by, not one, but two colonies: one British and the other (initially) Dutch, resulting in a disagreement that lasted for over 200 years. Massachusetts claimed these lands based upon its 1628 Charter for the Massachusetts Bay Company, which extended Massachusetts' claims as far west as the Pacific Ocean. But New York also claimed the Berkshires, along with the lands as far east as the Connecticut River, a claim based upon the Dutch explorations of Captain Henry Hudson, and subsequently codified by the Dutch charter of the New Netherlands in 1614. Although England took possession of New Netherlands in 1664, renaming it New York, the boundary between Massachusetts and New York remained an area of contentious disagreement, leading even to some armed conflict and loss of life. None other than John Adams himself lent his impresario to this debate with his "Examination of the Claim of New York, May 1774."[13] A settlement of these contested claims was (more or less) tentatively reached in 1773, but the American Revolution delayed the "drawing of the line" until 1787 when this was completed by three Congressional Commissioners. Interstate squabbles nevertheless continued until 1897, when the physical lines were finally marked on the ground and the border definitively established. This landed Goose Pond, once and for all (we can hope), within the Commonwealth of Massachusetts. New York appears to have ultimately accepted its losses rather magnanimously.

Having now just paddled across the town line into Lee (yes, it's in Massachusetts), in front of the large new home currently being built on this shoreline there used to be a small log cabin – known by old-timers as the Wagner cabin. (See Figure 2.1, #8) This cabin was built by Anna Wagner circa 1922, during a time when many of the Pond's other early cabins were also being built. No longer standing, this cabin has held a special place in my own heart, as it was here that my family first discovered Goose Pond when we rented it for the two summers of 1970-1971.

Figure 2.13 Wagner cabin in 1970.

Before the Wagner cabin was built, this spot, or one nearby, had been called "Lee Landing", owned then by Wolcott Dowd.[14] For twenty-five cents, Dowd would rent out his rowboat at Lee Landing to local kids for the day, but only if they were willing to carry the oars and anchor lines up from his house on Forest Street, known then as Mountain Road. The cost of renting Dowd's boat was half that of the rowboats that could then be rented at the Hooker Moore boat livery near the dam. For his less affordable daily rental fee of fifty cents Hooker would however provide you a rowboat with its oars and anchor lines already on board.

After passing the old Wagner camp, we encounter the so-called Chanterwood section. (See Figure 2.1, #9) Here you will see a series of seasonal waterfront cottages. This is the most rustic of the Lower Pond's developed neighborhoods. Lacking direct road access, most of these charming cabins require their inhabitants to hike through the woods to get down to their camps. However, unlike what we'll find when we get to Upper Goose, these Chanterwood cabins do at least have the convenience of electricity.

Figure 2.14 *Sign on one of the older Chanterwood section cabins. Courtesy of Edward Habermehl.*

Chanterwood's name is derived from an eighteenth-century Quaker farmer named William Chanter, known locally as "Friend William", who owned the 180-acre Snow Farm in this area around 1770.[15] Chanter's farmland was known for its crystal-clear spring water, which prompted its subsequent purchase by a local paper mill in the 1860s.[16] The cellar hole remains of William Chanter's homestead is still visible in the woods, along with a very impressive stone dam up the hill which presumably was also a Chanter project, flooding a large swampy area, its purpose unclear. (See Figure 2.9)

Figure 2.15 *Cellar hole of the homestead of "Friend William" Chanter, located in the Chanterwood section. The aerial photograph in Figure 11.3 might illustrate the extent of the Snow Farm. The GPS coordinates of this cellar hole are N 42.29212 W 73.21009. This cellar hole corresponds to site #4 in Figure 2.9.*

Figure 2.16 *Stone dam located near the old Chanter cellarhole in the woods behind the Chanterwood section. It is likely that this dam was built by Quaker William Chanter, most likely for flooding of the swamp rather than for generating waterpower. Its GPS coordinates are N 42.29241 W 73.20538.*

From the 1920s to the 1980s, a commercial lakeside inn existed in the Chanterwood section. Starting as the "Morse Camp," and subsequently renamed "Chanterwood," this was a landmark on the Pond for many years, sporting a large dock, its canoes with a large letter "C" painted on their bows, a large lodge, rustic guest cabins, and classical music that could be heard piped from its outdoor speakers.

Continuing past the Chanterwood section, you will encounter a very large shorefront rock dropping into deep water. (See Figure 2.1, #10) Many have called this "Bass Rock," presumably for all the bass caught while fishing here. If even only half of all the old fishing stories are true, which of course isn't at all likely, I wouldn't expect there to be many bass to be caught here any longer. Remnants of an old rope swing can be seen dangling from the overhanging tree. I don't recall being the one who broke it, but it was a long time ago.

Figure 2.17 *Bass Rock is located on the north shore of Lower Goose between the Chanterwood Section and Leisure Lee.*

Figure 2.18 A vintage Goose Pond cabin, one of my old favorites, that used to stand just east of Bass Rock.

Beyond Bass Rock is a large beach area belonging to a private community known as Berkshire Hills, formerly Leisure Lee, established in 1967 and now containing more than eighty homes in a wooded environment (See Figure 2.1, #11). During 1968 to 1976, Leisure Lee operated its own rope tow and ski trail just up the hill from the Pond.[17] (See Figure 2.1, #12) The ski trail was 1000 feet in length and had a vertical drop of 150 feet. The rope tow was powered by an old truck whose chassis was mounted on blocks, and one of its rear wheels was used to pull the rope. A skier from those days shared online that the tow was unreliable and that holding onto the rope to the top was supremely challenging. The truck chassis and the remains of the rope tow mechanisms, and overgrown remnants of the ski trail itself can still be seen in the woods. There was also a "ski lodge" which has since been torn down.

Figure 2.19 Elements of the rope tow for the Leisure Lee Ski Trail. Note the truck chassis on blocks that powered the rope tow, using a rear wheel to pull the rope. The GPS coordinates of the truck chasis: N 42.29235 W 73.20216.

Figure 2.20 The remains of the Leisure Lee ski trail.

Figure 2.21 Hand-drawn map designating the private "Ski Area." Courtesy of Joe Janis.

Figure 2.22 Satellite photograph (2003) showing the location of the old ski trail (red arrows). The trail is labeled by Google Earth as follows: "Leisure Lee Ski Hill Tow Chalet (Former)" Modified, courtesy Google Earth.

We now approach what is arguably the most natural and beautiful shoreline of Lower Goose. This steeply sloped section of shoreline, studded with massive boulders dramatically deposited by the Wisconsin glacier, and shaded by overhanging trees, is part of a beautiful, undeveloped, protected 112-acre property generously donated by Henry Smith in 1986 to The Trustees of Reservations, a Massachusetts-based land conservancy, also known simply as The Trustees. (See Figure 2.1, #14) This "Goose Pond Reservation," with 2000 feet of natural shorefront, is largely inaccessible except for Donato's Trail, a 2.2-mile loop, which opened in 2019 and is accessible from Route 20. It is a lovely trail but don't expect much of a view of Goose Pond.

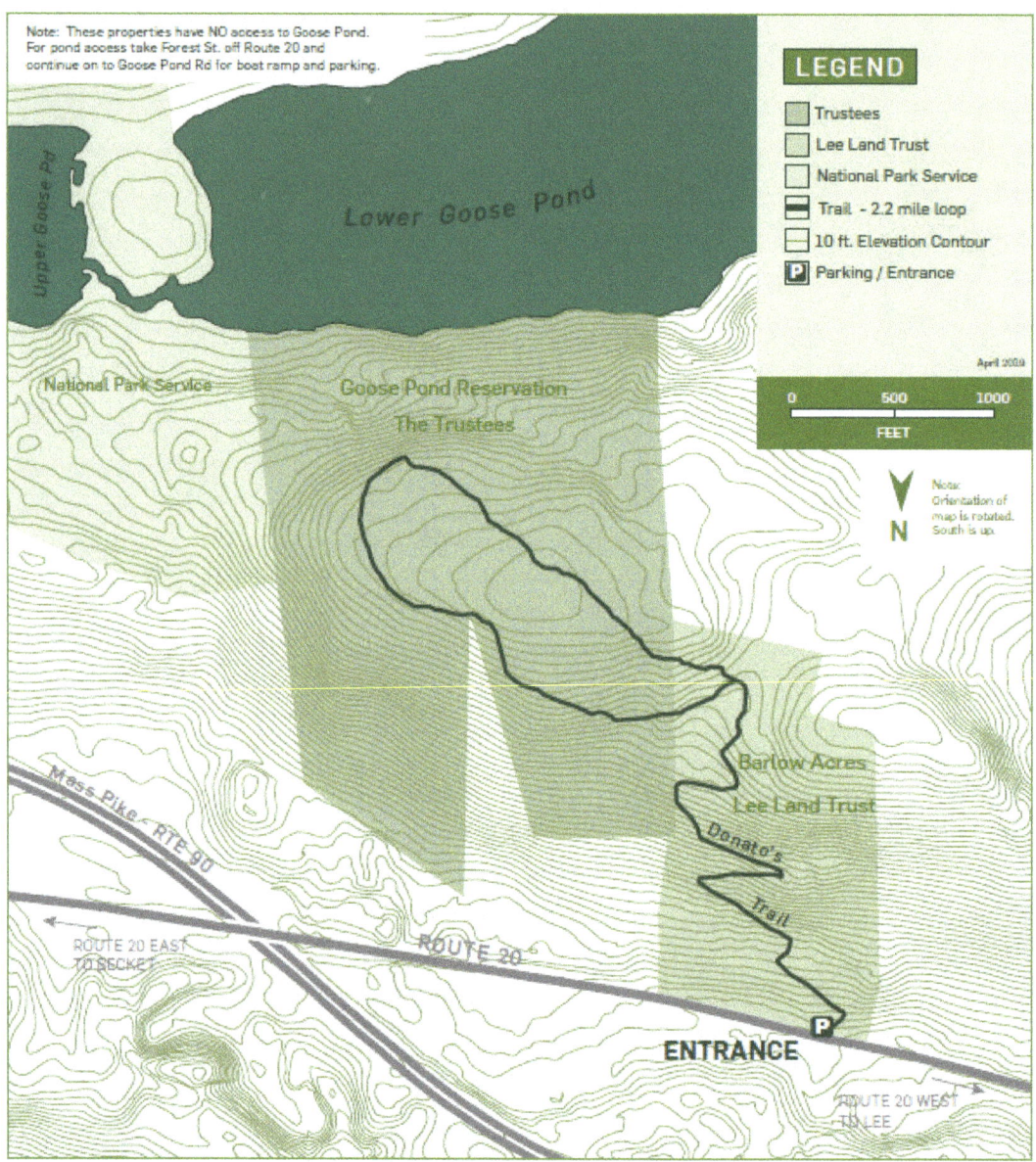

Figure 2.23 *Map of the Trustees Goose Pond Reservation and the Lee Land Trust. Note the location of Donato's Trail which is accessed from Route 20. Donato's Trail was opened in 2019 as a cooperative project by the Lee Land Trust and The Trustees. The trail is named after Donato Cedrone who bequeathed the so-called "Barlow Acres" to the Lee Land Trust upon his demise in 2000.[18] Courtesy of The Trustees.*

Figure 2.24 *Shoreline of the Goose Pond Reservation. There are dramatic glacial rock deposits along this shoreline and up the hill from the water.*

On the shoreline just past the Leisure Lee beach, and visible from the water, is a steep deposit of large boulders piled high 10,000 years ago by the glaciers of the last ice age. In this mass of boulders is what appears, for all the world, to be a large stone chair. Frequently referenced in local lore, it has been variously named as the "The Throne"[19] or "Couch Rock". (See Figure 2.1, #13) While popularly rumored to be an ancient man-made stone structure, geologists think this is more likely a creation of Mother Nature. If you find yourself exploring this section of shoreline one day, beach your boat here, scramble up the rocks, sit yourself on The Throne, and be a monarch for a day.

Figure 2.25 *"The Throne" is located just up the hill from the shoreline, east of the Leisure Lee beach. This throne was mentioned in RW Smith's Three Thumbnails. The location of the throne was recently re-established by Joe Janis.*

Figure 2.26 *This hand-drawn map was passed down to my family along with the Pinepoint house. Note the "Couch Rock" designated on the northern shoreline, presumably referencing what RW Smith called the "The Throne". Note the designation "Cavarly's": this became the property of Madge Cavarly's son Perry Cavarly. Madge's daughter, Margueritte, held the Pinepoint property. This map was drawn by Charles "Terry" Dietrich (Margueritte's husband) in the 1950's. Courtesy of Charles Mecklum.*

We have now reached the channel, officially named Sucker Brook – a wondrous, winding 500-foot-long passage snaking through the woods and taking us into the wilds of Upper Goose Pond. Although there is a slight current flowing (from Upper to Lower Goose), it is not truly a brook, and why it's called "Sucker" is a mystery. Few people refer to it as Sucker Brook anymore, most just calling it "The Channel." Before the original dam was expanded and this connection dug in 1839, Upper and Lower Goose were separated by dry land. (See Figure 8.3) In the absence of the dam, Sucker Brook (only a few feet deep) would even today be dry and the two ponds left without any watery connection.[20]

Figure 2.27 Sucker Brook seen from over Upper Goose Pond. It connects Lower Goose Pond (top) and Upper Goose Pond (bottom). Courtesy of Wallace Prysock.

Having now paddled through Sucker Brook, we are entering the mystical realm of Upper Goose Pond, the largest undeveloped lake in Massachusetts. I think most would agree that this is the crown jewel of Goose Pond. We will later learn how the entire shoreline around Upper Goose came to be owned by the National Park Service. Except for a few rustic cabins, this shimmering sliver of water is completely undeveloped and in its primordial state. It is wild, federally protected and accessible only by foot or boat.

Figure 2.28 Sucker Brook in winter. The channel's water does not freeze over during winter, likely a consequence of its slight current.

Figure 2.29 *Drone photograph of Upper Goose Pond, looking west. Lower Goose Pond can be seen towards the top of the photograph. Note the island in Upper Goose. Courtesy of Wallace Prysock.*

Figure 2.30 *Drone photograph of Upper Goose Pond, looking west. Note the island in the distance. Lower Goose is not visible in this photograph. Courtesy of Wallace Prysock.*

Upper Goose has its own idyllic little island which is a peaceful spot to beach your canoe and enjoy a swim or a quiet lunch on Elwell's Rock. (See Figure 2.1, #17) It seems a bit sad that no one has bothered to give this little island an actual name. On the highest point of this island stands a concrete rectangular pedestal about three feet tall and ten inches wide, like our very own *2001: A Space Odyssey* monolith. Over the years, I have heard many theories about our monolith's origins, some stranger than others.

Figure 2.31 Concrete pedestal can be seen on Upper Goose Pond island. Elwell's Rock is on the right.

Here is the pedestal's actual story. In 1937, Bill Stilwell (then an enterprising student at Wesleyan University -- my alma mater) and his father Winfred (himself also a Wesleyan alumnus), who were the owners of the rustic camp on Upper Goose's north shore, decided to build a telescope, even going to the trouble of grinding their own mirrors and lenses. In the course of this project, they became aware that the view of the night sky from inside their camp was limited by all the surrounding trees. They proceeded to build the concrete pedestal on the island, upon which the telescope could be mounted.[21] Back then the large trees we see now on the island were not there, and the Stilwell logbook records viewings of Jupiter and the Moon from this island. Sadly, the telescope has been lost to history, but the pedestal reminds us to look upwards at night.

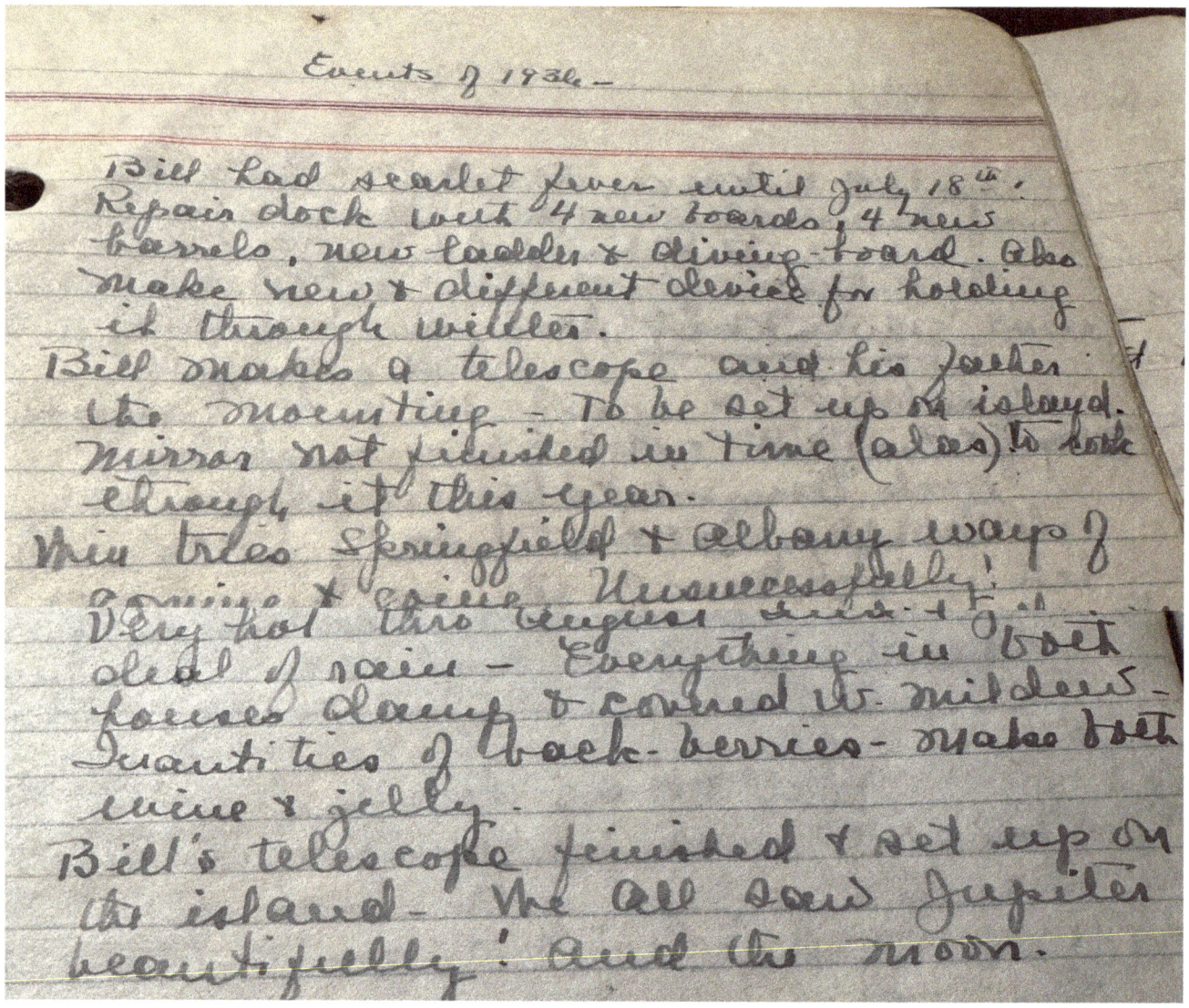

Figure 2.32 Entries in the Stilwell family's cabin log. The top 1936 entry describes the construction of the telescope and the island's concrete pedestal. The bottom 1937 entry describes the completion of the telescope and the viewing of Jupiter and the Moon. Courtesy of David Stilwell.

Figure 2.33 Drone photograph of Upper Goose Pond looking east. Courtesy of Wallace Prysock.

Figure 2.34 Drone photograph of the island in Upper Goose Pond. Note the "zen rocks" piled in the water on the right. "Elwell's Rock" is on the left side of the island. Courtesy of Wallace Prysock.

Here is as good a time as any to learn about a unique Upper Goose island tradition. The water just south of the island is very shallow and its bottom rocky. There is a tradition of wading in this shallow water, which gets quite warm during the summer, and using the endless collection of submerged stones to create dazzling displays of majestic towers, castles, piles big and small, daring balancing acts, and ingenious rock sculptures. This is a great way to spend a sunny summer afternoon, but, from personal experience, I strongly recommend sturdy water shoes. All summer long these stone sculptures come and go, grow and shrink, rise and fall. Wintertime pretty much knocks them all down, leaving a blank canvas for the next season's creations.

It is my own kids' firm conviction that they started this rock-building tradition. My kids had learned an activity called "zen rock building" at the Nature Place Day Camp in New York. This activity required calm concentration, steely nerves, and imagination as they would quietly balance small stones, one on top of the other, as high as possible. I think this exercise may have been a tool used by their camp counselors to make the campers stay quiet and give the counselors a break. In the 1990s, we used to take our kids each summer for a picnic on this island and, after finishing their peanut butter and jelly sandwiches, they would apply their impressive zen rock-building skills using the endless rocks in the shallow water near the island. They claim that this was the start of this tradition. In my more recent conversations with the Stilwell family, owners of the small rustic compound across from the island, they related that these stone sculptures near the island started to mysteriously appear in the 1990s. So, my kids might be right. We all leave our little marks on the world.

Figure 2.35 *"Zen Rocks" at the Upper Goose Pond island. A much larger example can be seen at the top of Chapter 3.*

Continuing our tour, on your left you will pass the hiker cabin (and its dock) for hikers of the Appalachian Trail, as well as the historic Stilwell log cabins. (See Figure 2.1, #16, #18) A little way past the Stilwell cabins, nestled under the trees, are the remains of the legendary Mohhekennuck Club. (See Figure 2.1, #19) You will learn much about these cabins in subsequent chapters.

Now the pond starts narrowing and at its far end becomes increasingly shallow. We will now have re-entered Tyringham and the marsh at the far eastern end of Upper Goose. (See Figure 2.1, #20) I love this spot for its natural beauty and isolation—perfect for meditation and bird watching. Until a few years ago, there was an active beaver lodge here and a well-maintained beaver dam. The beaver are gone now, although I did see one here in 2023, maybe scouting out the location for another lodge. At the bitter end of this marsh sometimes you can hear the bubbling inflow from Higley Brook bringing us water from Upper *Upper* Goose located in Becket. (See Figure 2.1, #21)

Figure 2.36 Swamp at the far eastern end of Upper Goose Pond.

Figure 2.37 *Eastern end of Upper Goose Pond (the drone is looking west). The branching arms of the swamp are seen at the bottom of the photograph. This was taken in October when much of the swamp's typically rich vegetation had browned. Courtesy of Wallace Prysock.*

The origin of Higley Brook's name can likely be traced to the presence of a prominent Becket, Massachusetts family descended from a John Higley, himself born in Frimley, England in 1649. He emigrated to the British colonies at a young age, ultimately settling in Connecticut. An extensive Higley clan descended, many of whom subsequently settled in Becket. Among the Becket Higleys was Joseph Higley (1715-1790), who, along with his son, Micah Higley (b. 1743), purchased several Becket properties in 1773. Micah and his wife Olive Adams settled into Becket "Lot No. 48" shortly after their marriage in 1774 where they had two sons, Micah Jr. (b. 1776) and Benjamin (b. 1777). Micah's sister, Sarah, and her husband James Rudd, having married only two months earlier, fatefully moved next door.

Leaving his two infant sons at home with Olive on the snowy morning of December 19, 1778, Micah Higley went out hunting for deer, wearing a deer-skin cap. Also (independently) heading out for some deer hunting that day was his brother-in-law, James Rudd. Seeing movement behind a fallen tree, and unaware of Micah's presence in the woods, James mistook Micah's moving deer-skin hat for a moving deer, took aim and fired his gun, only to discover that he had just shot his brother-in-law Micah Higley, killing him instantly. Fortunately, Sarah was spared witnessing the tragedy of her husband killing her brother, herself having passed away the year before, at the age of twenty-four, and married for less than a year. Micah's two sons and their own families ultimately relocated to Ohio in 1811. I have not discovered exactly where these Higley homesteads in Becket were located, nor exactly where Micah met his tragic fate, but it seems entirely possible that the family homes were located alongside Higley Brook. I wonder if it was in Micah Higley's memory that the brook received its enduring name.[22]

Figure 2.38 *Higley Brook, seen from where it is bridged by the Appalachian Trail. This brook brings water from Upper Upper Goose Pond in Becket into the far eastern end of Upper Goose Pond.*

Figure 2.39 *Cellar hole near Higley Brook near the crossing of the Appalachian Trail. This cellar hole corresponds to the location #20 in RW Smith's hand-drawn map from* Three Thumbnails *(Figure 2.9). This cellar hole might have been a Shaker home or perhaps a Higley cabin. Thanks to Jim Pelletier for finding this on a LIDAR map and for taking me here.*

We are now paddling westward along Upper Goose's south shore back towards the Channel. On your left will be a peninsula which is a popular spot to beach a small boat and enjoy a picnic and a swim. (See Figure 2.1, #22) Just before reaching the channel, there is grassy Upper Boyne's Cove. (See Figure 2.1, #23) As you emerge from the channel, back into Lower Goose you will learn the truth of an enduring Goose Pond truism – that paddling Lower Goose reliably puts you into a headwind *in both directions* every time. I don't know how Mother Nature manages this feat, but trust me, this is a quite dependable, and widely acknowledged phenomenon.

You are now paddling westward (upwind of course) along Lower Goose's southern shoreline. Just to your left, shortly after leaving Sucker Brook, you will enter Lower Boyne's Cove, where you might spot the Goose Pond Yacht Club mooring. (See Figure 2.1, #24, 25) We will then pass by Kettle Rock and a spot called The Mines, neither of which I have been able to successfully identify.[23] I have heard rumors of an old iron mine on Lower Goose, but I have not come across any corroborating historical references of any iron mining, nor any geological evidence of iron's presence here. We will soon explore the pivotal stories surrounding the Annie Foote Smith cabin which used to stand here. (See Figure 2.1, #26) We are now paddling past the varied waterfront homes of the Cooper Creek neighborhood (See Figure 2.1, #27).

Figure 2.40 Cooper Brook entering Lower Goose Pond.

As you approach the western end of Lower Goose you will see the mouth of Cooper Brook. (See Figure 2.1, #28) It was always curious to me that the stream is called Cooper *Brook* but the accompanying road is called Cooper *Creek* Road. The road's original name was in fact Cooper Brook Road. However, a vociferous debate arose amongst some of the road's residents, some of whom preferred the sound of "Cooper Creek Road." The debate, ending with a gasoline-fueled sign-burning and the sale of a home or two, ultimately settled on what we have now, which is Cooper Creek Road.[24] It is interesting that we also have a "Coopertown Road" near the dam. The origin of the names for Cooper Brook, Cooper Creek Road, and Coopertown Road is not known.

Having now passed Cooper Brook, we are paddling by the lovely Goose Pond Road neighborhood. (See Figure 2.1, #29) And just past these homes, we come full circle back to the dam. We've just completed a (virtual) six-and-a-half-mile paddle. Take a breather.

Figure 2.41 *Double rainbow over homes in the Goose Pond Road section (2024).*

"Zen Rocks" at Sucker Brook

CHAPTER 3

GEOLOGICAL HISTORY

*T*HIS IS A COMPLICATED STORY about rocks and time. It involves lots of different rocks, extremely slow-motion action, powerful tectonic continental collisions, crushing pressure, melting heat, deep oceans — coming and going — soaring mountain ranges (also coming and going), erosion, and eons and eons of time. This may not be a chapter for everyone, but for those who might be curious about why Goose Pond exists where it does, and why it has the crescent shape that it has, this would be their chapter.

It has been said that much of the geological history of the Earth can be understood as various sequences of three basic processes: dramatic mountain-building events, less dramatic, and far more gradual, erosion of these mountains, and then the slow deposition of sediments under ancient oceans. Goose Pond's formation involved all three of these processes. During the last billion years, the area now occupied by Goose Pond has experienced not one, but two, dramatic mountain-building events, each followed by a prolonged period of erosion. In between these two mountain-building events, the Goose Pond environs had become submerged under a deep ocean and subjected to a prolonged period of deposition of underwater sediments. To fully understand Goose Pond's origins, we must unravel these long-ago geological processes.

The term "continental drift" sounds like a description of a lazy and gentle phenomenon, but the amount of energy required to move continents and ocean floors around on the Earth's surface is incomprehensible, certainly belying any sort of passive process. Recent computer simulations have suggested that this energy may have been delivered to Earth by way of its collision, over four billion years ago, with a large planetary object, named Theia, in an event that also spawned the Moon. Scientists postulate that this cataclysmic collision injected continent-sized molten "blobs" of superheated liquified rock 1200 miles below the Earth's surface, which continue to slowly float around and are thought to be providing the enormous power required for our planet's ongoing tectonic movement.[25][26]

Figure 3.1 *Theia colliding with Earth, 4 billion years ago. Courtesy of Wikipedia.*

One billion years ago, a very big rock -- bedrock actually -- the size of a continent, twenty miles thick, and seemingly immovable, was, nevertheless, on the move. It was on a collision course with yet another solid rock just as big, just as hard, just as deep, and also -- just as improbably -- on the move. One rock, (named Laurentia) in due course was destined to become the North American continent, and the other (Amazonia) that of South America. It was out of this continental collision, one billion years ago, that the very backbone, and shape, of Goose Pond was born.

During this geological period, the Proterozoic Eon of the Precambrian Era, we would find Earth utterly unrecognizable, its surface barren of plants, the only existing life microscopic and floating around in the oceans, the atmosphere paper-thin, consisting mostly of toxic methane, and with only the smallest traces of oxygen. Laurentia had a shape vaguely resembling today's

North American continent but flipped ninety degrees clockwise on its side, and our future eastern seaboard facing south and situated south of the equator. The section of Laurentia destined to later become the Berkshires was on the Laurentian coast — central and eastern Massachusetts would not be "sutured" onto the continent until much later (courtesy of a future territorial gift from the African continent.) Amazonia, also flipped on its side, was approaching from the south, slowly shrinking the ocean separating the two continents. As a consequence of this collision, the supercontinent Rodinia was being formed.

Meanwhile, twenty miles below the surface, this continental collision was generating unimaginable pressure in the underlying bedrock, heating it to the point of softening it (like putty), compressing it, deforming it, and transforming it to even denser, "metamorphic" rocks. During this process, the granite bedrock situated near Goose Pond's future home was being transformed into a much denser and harder rock, known to geologists today as "Tyringham gneiss." Adjacent to this gneiss were also deposits of softer, sedimentary rock, initially formed under even earlier oceans from the remains of ancient marine life, which, when subjected to this enormous pressure, were themselves metamorphosed into "Precambrian" marble. There was also quartzite rock, formed out of the compressed silicate sands (sandstone), which had also settled under ancient oceans. It was the contrast between the extreme hardness of the Tyringham gneiss and the relative softness of the nearby marble and quartzite that created the fundamental conditions necessary for the future formation of Goose Pond.

The collision between Laurentia and Amazonia resulted in an enormous mountain-building event known as the Grenville orogeny. The great Grenville Mountains, which may have reached altitudes of 20,000 feet, stretched from what later became Newfoundland to what we now call Texas. The deep core of the Grenville Mountains (near Goose Pond's future home that is) was comprised of a mixture of dense Tyringham gneiss alongside the much older and softer Precambrian marble and quartzites.

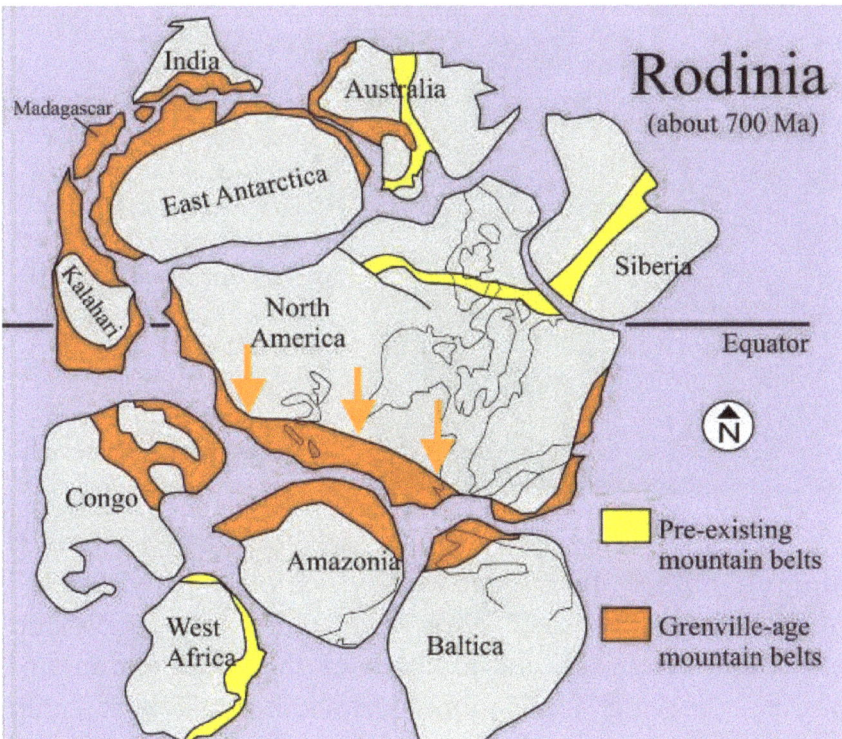

Figure 3.2 The Grenville orogeny and the formation of supercontinent Rodinia. The continent, mistakenly labeled in this figure as "North America", was then actually a proto-continent called Laurentia. The orange arrows on Laurentia's southern coast designate the Grenville mountains which formed on the coast of Laurentia. What we consider today to be central and eastern "Massachusetts" had not yet been added to the continent. Notice that our continent is flipped on its side and below the Equator. Amazonia later became South America. Baltica was destined to later become Europe. Modified, courtesy of Jim Lehane, Geology P.A.G.E.

Figure 3.3 Tyringham gneiss on the shore of Lower Goose Pond, demonstrating the characteristic compressed light and dark-colored layers of quartz, feldspar, and hornblende minerals. The gneiss was formed by the compression of granite during the Grenville orogeny. The curvaceous deformation of these layers developed during the subsequent Taconic orogeny. The Grenville rocks, such as Tyringham gneiss are 1.1 billion years old and are the oldest visible rocks in Massachusetts.

Figure 3.4 Lee gneiss on the shoreline at Pinepoint. The less abundant Lee gneiss is darker-colored than Tyringham gneiss due to its content of magnesium and iron. The undistorted, linear nature of the layers in this particular example indicates that this particular rock was spared any subsequent deformation during the Taconic orogeny.

On March 3, 1879, the U.S. Congress passed the *Organic Act,* which established the U.S. Geological Survey (USGS), whose mission was "the classification of the public lands and examination of the geological structure, mineral resources, and products of the national domain." The USGS further describes its mission as serving "the Nation by providing reliable scientific information to describe and understand the Earth; minimize loss of life and property from natural disasters; manage water, biological, energy, and mineral resources; and enhance and protect our quality of life."

To fulfill its mission, the USGS sent geologists out into the field, armed with hiking boots, compasses, and rock hammers, to seek out outcroppings of ancient bedrock, carefully measure their angles and inclination, and then piece their findings together into extrapolated geological maps of the bedrock lying far below their feet.

On a brisk November day in 2021, Nick Ratcliffe, a USGS geologist, who in the 1980s had previously been tasked with generating the definitive bedrock map around Goose Pond, and Steve Mabee, the Massachusetts State Geologist and geologist at the University of Massachusetts, took me on a day-long geology tour around Goose Pond. During our little educational expedition, Nick shared stories of his earlier days wandering around towns, cities, and private homes sporting his standard rock hammer complete with its three-foot handle. Not surprisingly, he had had numerous opportunities over those years to explain his activities (and his rock hammer) to local law enforcement. While successfully avoiding any encounters of our own with the local authorities during our little walkabout (despite the accompaniment of Nick's omnipresent three-foot hammer), Nick and Steve shared with me a remarkable geological story.

Figure 3.5 Nick Ratcliffe, USGS Retired (left) and Steve Mabee, Massachusetts State Geologist (right) during our geology tour, November 2021.

Figure 3.6 *Nick Ratcliffe (left) and Steve Mabee (right) looking for the geological "unconformity" on George Canon Road. An unconformity is where rocks derived from very different time periods touch each other, like a baby sitting on her great-grandmother's lap.*

During his earlier bedrock mapping, Nick had discovered that the mineral layers of the Tyringham gneiss located on Goose Pond's northern shore were tilted upward towards the lake's south side, while the gneiss on the lake's southern shore was tilted upward towards the north side. During the formation of the Grenville mountains, the Tyringham gneiss, then many miles under the surface and subjected to intense pressure and heat, had buckled into an angled shape like a peaked roof (a formation known as an "anticline"). The axis where the two angled formations would have met, like the ridge of a roof, could be geometrically extrapolated from this mapping. While this roof-like axis had been situated miles below the surface *when it initially formed* a billion years ago, today, as a combined result of the erosion of the Grenville mountains and the uplifting of the rock by the subsequent birth of the Berkshire mountains, this extrapolated axis is now projected *above the existing lake's surface*.

But here is the truly extraordinary find -- a line drawn along the extrapolated axis of this billion-year-old fold in the Tyringham gneiss *exactly* overlies a centerline drawn through the center of Goose Pond's crescent shape as it exists today!

Far from being a coincidence, this finding demonstrates that Goose Pond's geologic origins can be traced directly to events that took place twenty miles below the surface during the Proterozoic Eon, one billion years ago. (At the time of the Grenville orogeny, this fold's axis was straight, not curved like Goose Pond's axis is today – the arc in this axis, giving the lake its crescent shape, would come later.)

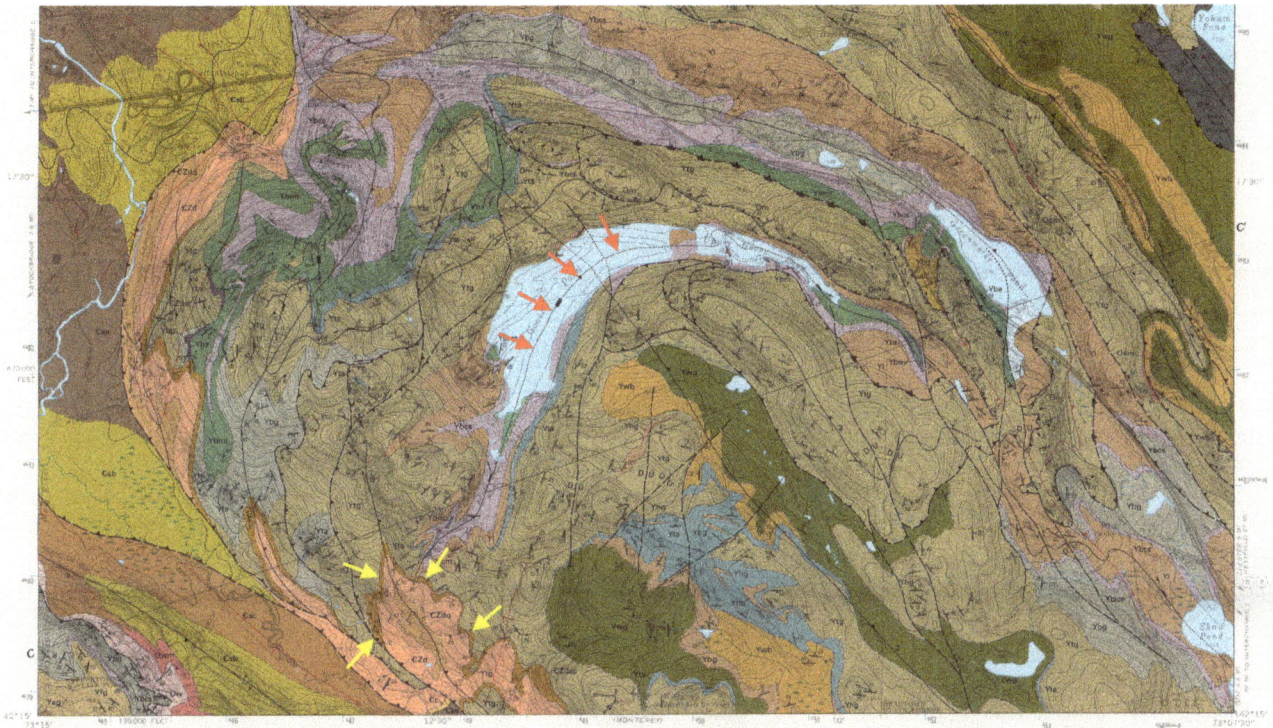

Figure 3.7 *Bedrock mapping of the Goose Pond environs. Ytg=Tyringham gneiss. Yl=Lee gneiss. The centerline (red arrows) drawn through the center of Goose Pond represents the extrapolated linear axis of the Grenville fold in the underlying Tyringham gneiss. It is not coincidental that this bedrock fold axis precisely corresponds to the Pond's topographical centerline — the fold created the lake's shape. The unconformity (yellow arrows) shows the billion-year-old Tyringham gneiss in direct contact with the 500 million-year-old quartzite "Dalton Formation" which formed under the ocean and laid on top a half-billion years after the Grenville orogeny. This particular unconformity, which can be identified on George Canon Road, has provided geologists with the necessary clues to determine the age of the older rock around Goose Pond. Between these two geologic events, there is a 500-million-year gap in the area's known geological history. Ratcliffe N.M.,1985, The Bedrock Geologic Map of the East Lee Quadrangle, Berkshire County, Massachusetts; US Geological Survey, Map GQ-1573.*[27]

The soaring Grenville mountains, subjected to the slow, but relentless, erosive forces of water and weather over hundreds of millions of years, were slowly converted into sand that washed into the ocean. Remarkably, this erosion of the Grenville mountains still continues today, evidence of which can still be seen in the Tyringham and Lee gneiss along Goose Pond's shoreline.

Figure 3.8 *Tyringham gneiss on Lower Goose demonstrating cracks resulting from the ongoing freeze-thaw weathering of the rock. This rock is an example of how the gradual degradation ("weathering") of the billion-year-old Grenville Mountains continues even today.*

Figure 3.9 *The grooves in this Lee gneiss on Pinepoint represent the modern-day continuation of the rain-induced erosion of the billion-year-old Grenville Mountains.*

As the Grenville mountains eroded into sand, the supercontinent Rodinia began to break up. The proto-North American continent, Laurentia, restored its independence but remained flipped on its side, our "New England Coast" still facing south and lying below the equator. As Rodinia broke up, the coast of Laurentia, later to host the Berkshire Mountains and Goose Pond, became submerged under the Iapetus Sea. Over millions of years, thick deposits of sediments derived from marine life settled on the Iapetus seabed. The layered sediment formed limestone which later became compressed by intense pressure and, in the area of Goose Pond's future home, was finally transformed into the famous Stockbridge Marble -- mined to create monuments as well as portions of the U.S. Capital Building. Today Stockbridge marble is still being mined in Lee, primarily for the production of lime for agriculture and for marking athletic fields. Also deposited under this ocean were sandstone sediments, later transformed into quartzites.

Figure 3.10 *Stockbridge Marble depositions at the Lee Marble Quarry. This marble is formed by the compression of limestone derived from millions of years of underwater marine sediments that were deposited and compressed after the Grenville orogeny. The subsequent erosion of this soft, exposed marble led to the formation of the valleys holding Lee, Tyringham, and surrounding towns.*

We have arrived at the emergence of the Berkshire Mountains. Fast forward to the Paleozoic Era, just 500 million years ago, and another grand tectonic collision was in the making. Across the Iapetus from the southern shores of Laurentia lurked the continent Baltica, which many years later would host Parisian cafes, London bridges, and the European Union. As Laurentia and Baltica approached one another, between these two continents lay an arc of volcanic islands called the "Taconic Islands."

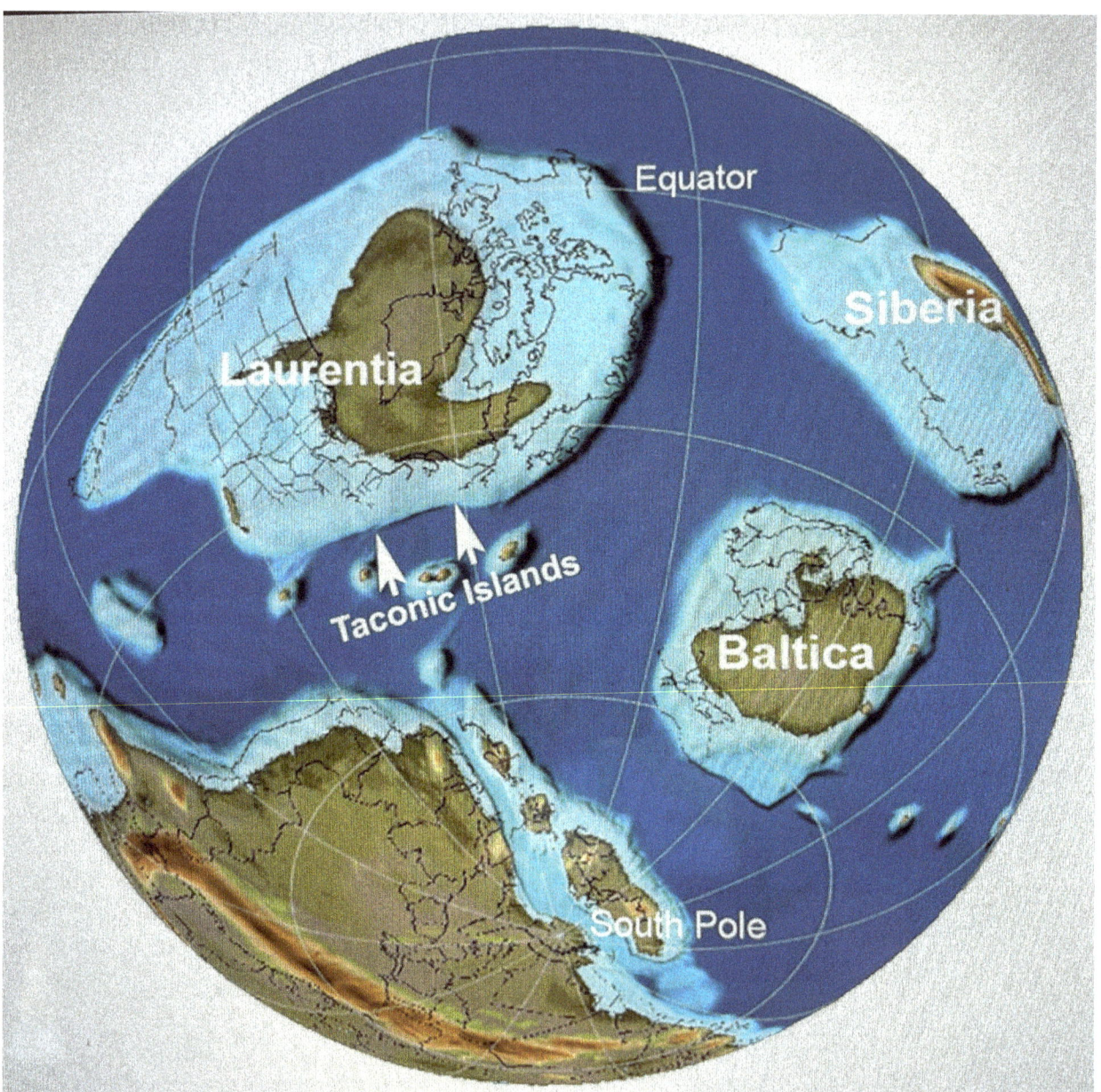

Figure 3.11 *The Taconic Orogeny, the birth of the Berkshire Mountains, resulted from the collision of the volcanic Taconic Islands with Laurentia, the Proto-North American continent, 500 million years ago. The collision caused the ancient Grenville rock to be thrust up and over the submerged Stockbridge marble, thereby forming the Berkshire Mountains. Reproduced with permission from Paleontological Research Institution, Ithaca, New York, from Geologic History of the Northeastern United States.*[28]

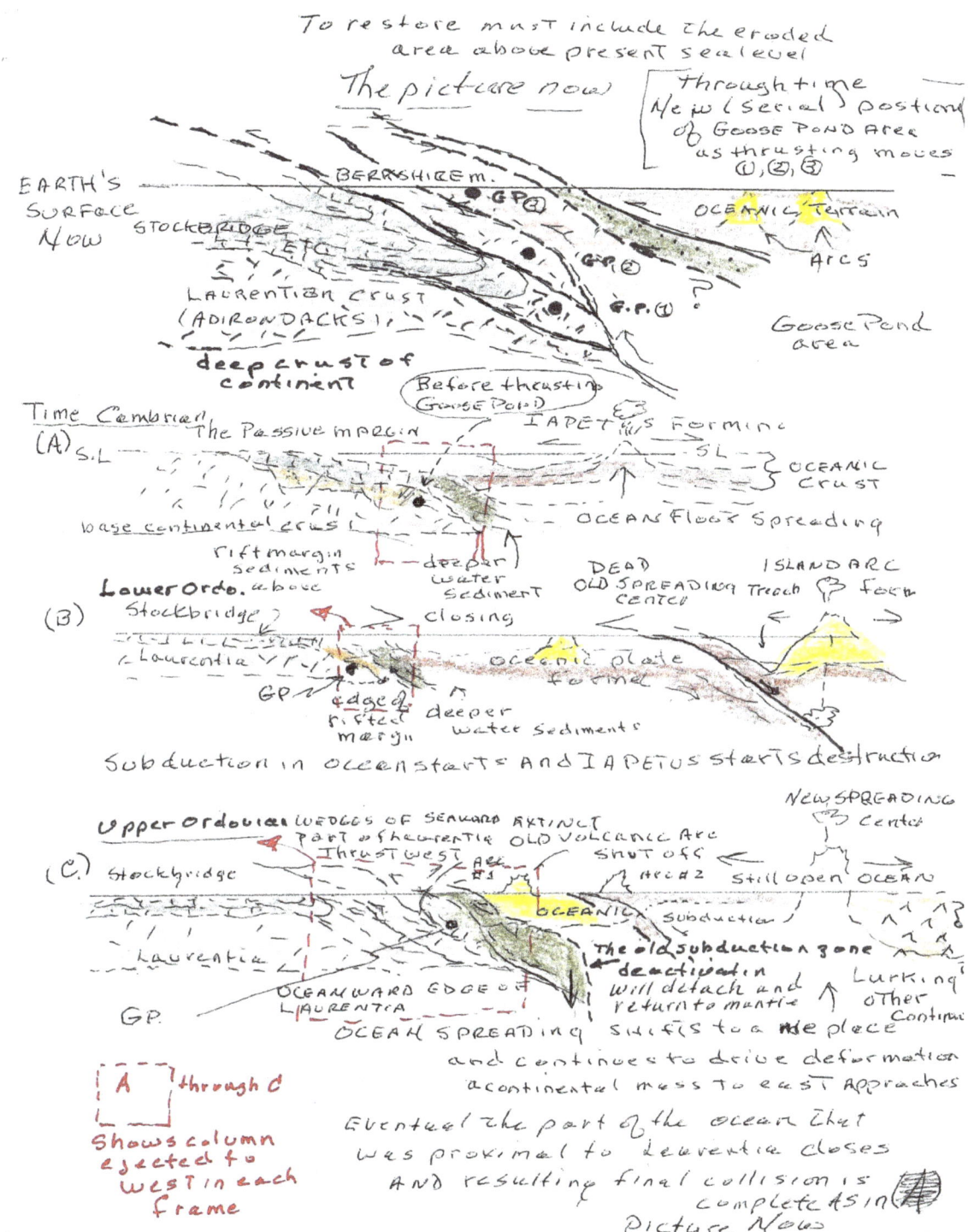

Figure 3.12 *Nick Ratcliffe's illustration of the Taconic Orogeny. Nick's description: "This sketch figure is a time/ space reconstruction of the geologic history of this part of the Berkshire massif during the collision of the ancient continent of Laurentia(west) with an island arc complex to the east that buried part of Massachusetts with stacked thrust slices. Following this Taconic compression, uplift occurred and rocks that were deeply buried were brought to the surface. So you might say the Earth's crust at Goose Pond and western New England has been up and down many times in the last 550 millions years." (Note: in this sketch, Goose Pond is designated with "GP") Courtesy of Nicholas Ratcliffe, retired geologist with the U.S. Geological Survey.*

When the Taconic Islands collided with Laurentia, a second mountain-building event occurred, this one called the Taconic Orogeny -- the birth of the Taconic and Berkshire Mountains. As with the Grenville event before, enormous pressures built up in the bedrock below, heating, softening, and deforming the ancient Tyringham gneiss and other, softer rocks below. This eventually led to the bedrock thrusting through surface faults up over the Stockbridge Marble, pushing back the Iapetus Sea and creating the Berkshire Mountain range.

Recall that a great fold in the bedrock had already occurred during the Grenville orogeny. During the Taconic orogeny, this fold became further deformed and tilted over, like a canoe on its side, resulting in a geologic formation known as an "inverted syncline." The outside of this sideways "canoe" was the hardened Tyringham gneiss, while the inside of the "canoe" was the softer Stockbridge marble and quartzites. Now this tilted fold had been thrust upwards toward the surface of the Earth.

Figure 3.13 *Massive ledge of Tyringham gneiss found in the Chanterwood section, showing extensive deformations and faults created by the subsequent Taconic orogeny. Joe Janis is standing in front, for scale. The GPS coordinates: N 42.28861 W 73.20146.*

The Earth was not yet done molding our pond. It was millions of years later, in yet another, more recent, geologic event, that Goose Pond's underlying bedrock fold became further deformed into a curved arc, and this is what gives Goose Pond its crescent shape.

Like the Grenvilles before, the towering Berkshire Mountains were subjected to the erosive forces of water, weather, and chemical breakdown. This resulted in the rounder, gentler hills we see today. The nearby valleys, now holding Lee, Tyringham, and nearby towns, were carved out because of the easier erosion of the softer Stockbridge Marble, then still exposed in the valleys.

In one of the final steps of Goose Pond's geologic origins, the actions of erosion on our sideways-flipped, bent rock "canoe" preferentially eroded the softer marble and quartzites located inside their surrounding casing of hardened Tyringham gneiss and thereby carved out a valley that followed the course of the flipped-over and bent Grenville fold. A crescent-shaped valley was thereby created, later to be filled, perhaps aided by glacial actions, with water and called Goose Pond.

Figure 3.14 *Fireplace in the old Cavarly/Pinepoint cabin built in 1902. All of the fireplaces and chimneys in the original Goose Pond cabins used local rocks like this. In this fireplace, there are samples of Tyringham gneiss (lighter color) and Lee gneiss (darker color) formed during the Grenville Orogeny. The photograph on the upper left side of the mantle is of my mom.*

Figure 3.15 *Collection of rocks on the concrete pedestal near the boat ramp. Courtesy of Zach Cohen.*

Should you find yourself standing on the pond's shore one day, take in the idyllic scene before you and contemplate how where you are standing had been submerged under an ancient ocean several times, other times buried under miles of rock, sometimes elevated to awesome alpine heights, and then buried under a mile of ice. It was once south of the Equator, once near South America, and another time near Europe, later joined with Africa. It was once a south-facing coast, later an eastern coast, and only later came to be inland. It was twice the inner core of towering mountains. It was once tropical, once frozen, and now temperate. And it wasn't always North America, and only recently became modern Massachusetts. Bob Dylan said it all, "for the times, they are a-changin'…"

A Tree on Lower Goose Pond

CHAPTER 4

THE ICE AGE

*A*S THE EARTH ENTERED its Pleistocene Epoch, some two million years ago, a long series of ice ages descended on much of the planet. The most recent of these ice ages, the Wisconsin Glaciation, started 75,000 years ago and, until 14,000 years ago, covered the area of Goose Pond with ice up to two miles thick. This caused not only profound topographical changes but also, quite predictably, major pre-historic human migrations throughout the Northern Hemisphere. The great Wisconsin glacier, covering much of North America, moved slowly, but inexorably, in a south-easterly direction, its extraordinary weight and ponderous movement leaving its mark on the contours of Goose Pond's future lakebed, as well as on its surrounding topography.

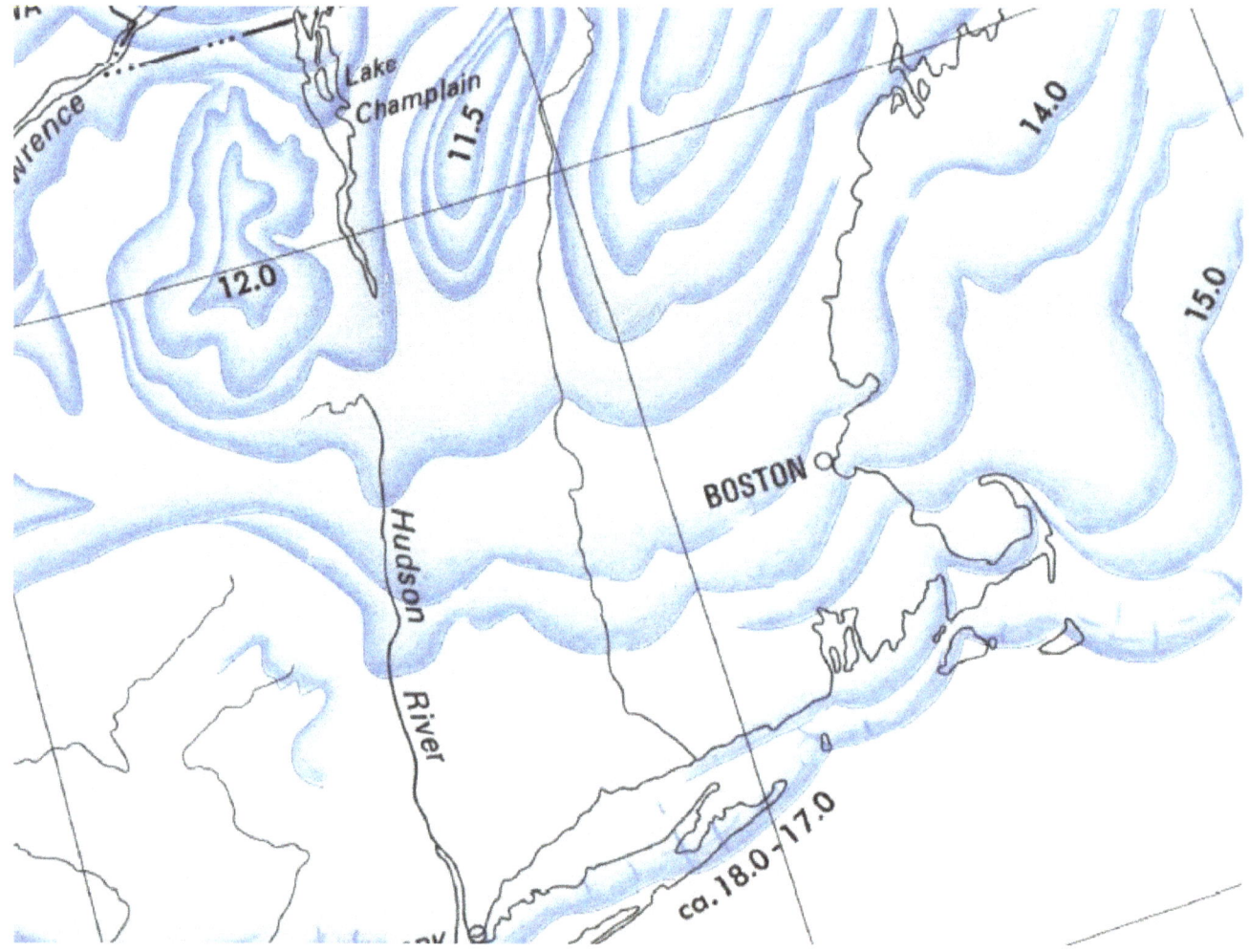

Figure 4.1 *Map indicating the timeline (in thousands of years before the current era) of the recession of the Wisconsin glacier's leading edge in Massachusetts. In the vicinity of Goose Pond, the glacier receded about 14,000 years ago. While the glacier's movement was in a southeasterly direction, its leading edge receded (i.e. melted) in a northerly direction. Cape Cod was formed by the Laurentide Ice Sheet which preceeded the Wisconsin glacier by thousands of years. Courtesy of the Geological Survey of Canada.*

When a glacier grinds up the incline of a hill, it smooths and flattens the uphill side as it climbs, dragging along with it rocks and boulders of all sizes, sometimes for distances of several miles. When the glacier then slides over the hill's crest the ice releases these boulders down the hill, while freeze-thaw cycles on the ground generate meltwater beneath it; meltwater filled with sand and acting like liquid sandpaper, further carving out the downhill side, making the rock-strewn decline even steeper. Geologists call this characteristic glacial shaping of the uphill and downhill sides of a mountain "Roche moutonnées", a rather strange term coined in 1786 by Horace Bénédict de Saussure, a Genevan alpine explorer, who likened these glacially modified, asymmetric hills to the shape of fashionable wigs worn at that time by French gentry — wigs which were smoothed by mutton fat (hence the name "moutonnées").

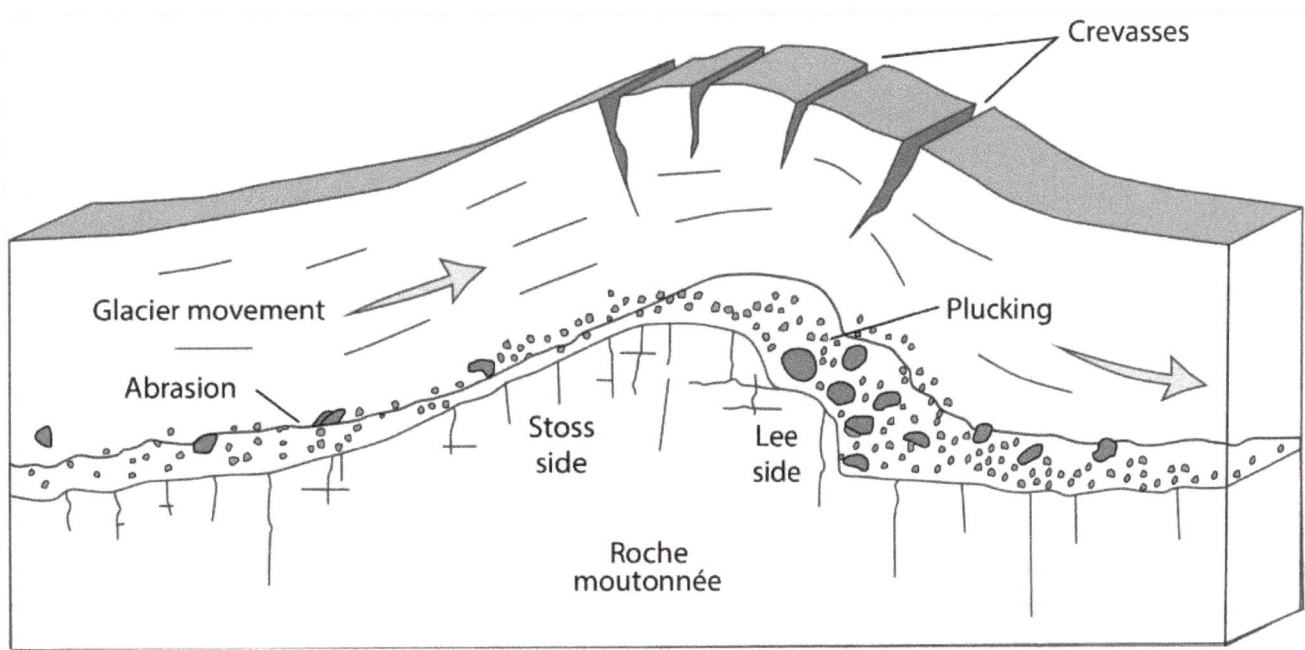

Figure 4.2 *Illustration of the Roche Moutonnées effect of glacial movement over a hill. The glacier moved in a southeasterly direction over Goose Pond. The pond's northern, steeper shoreline dropping into Goose Pond is the "Lee side" of the glacial effect. The southern, less steep shoreline is the "Stoss side" of the glacial effect. Courtesy of Ministère des Ressources naturelles et des Forêts, Quebec, Canada.*

Figure 4.3 *An eighteenth-century French wig, similar to the mutton-fat-smoothed style that inspired Horace Bénédict de Saussure when he was choosing a name for the topographical impact of glaciers on hills. Notice the gradual incline up the back of the head (the "Stoss side") and the steep decline over the forehead (the "Lee side") and compare to Figure 4.2.[29] Courtesy of Lightinthebox.com.*

As we look at Goose Pond's shoreline topography and depth map, their resemblance to the fat-smoothed wigs of eighteenth-century French gentry are quite evident, a consequence of how the Wisconsin glacier ground its way up over the lake's northwestern hills, descended into the area of its future lakebed, and then ascended back up the hills on its southern shore. What we see is that the northern shoreline is distinctly steeper than the southern one and that the lakebed of the northern part of the Pond is deeper, and steeper than the lakebed of its southern sections, all in keeping with the impact of glacial action on inclines and declines of the land underneath. We can also see how the northern shoreline (more so than on the southern shore) is peppered with huge masses of rock piles on the hills and shore, called "glacial erratics," which are the boulders carried by the glacier and dropped on the downhill side of the hills to the Pond's north. Conversely, the southern lakebed is shallower and less rock-strewn, and the rising hills to the south are less steep. It is entirely possible, maybe even likely, that the Goose Pond valley ultimately became a water-filled lake as a consequence of these shaping actions and the great melting during the glacial retreat that followed.

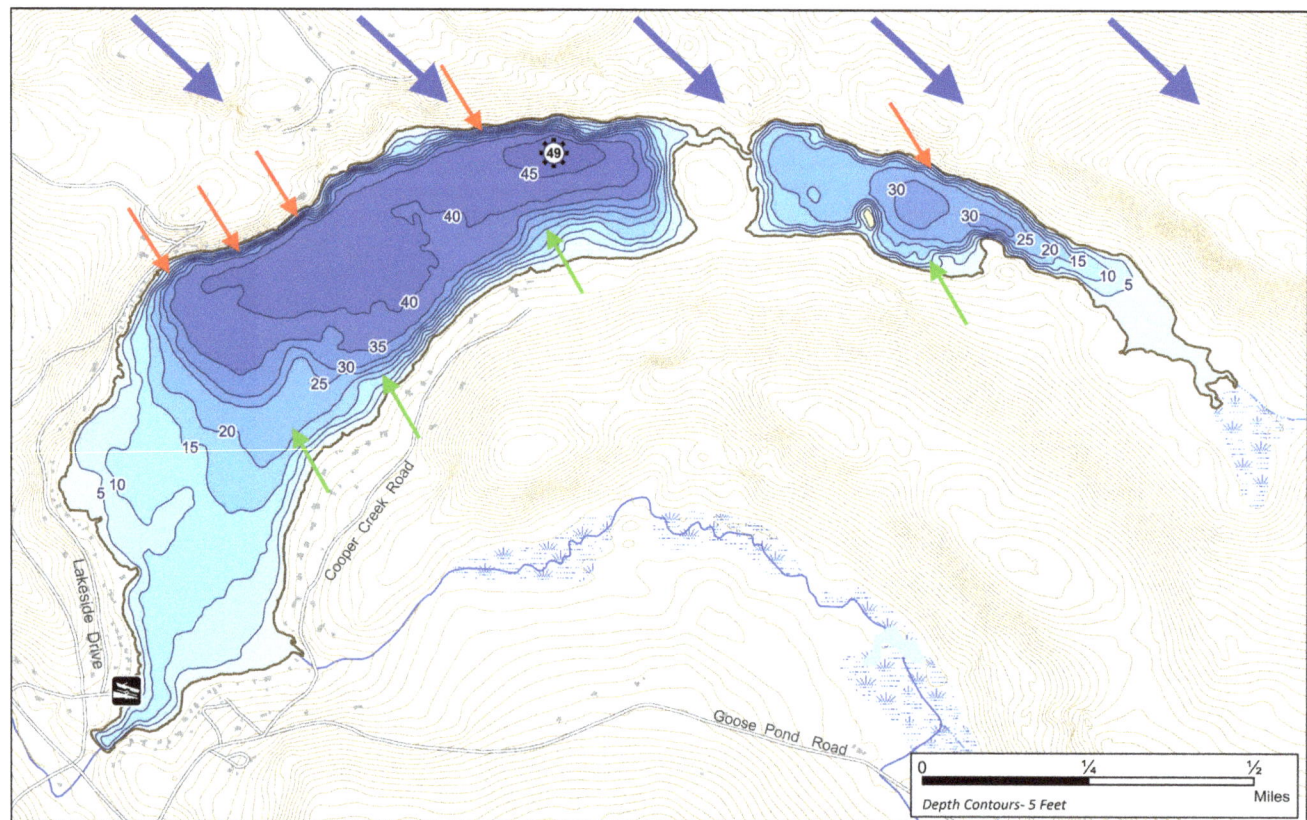

Figure 4.4 *Glacial impact on Goose Pond's lakebed depth map. Blue arrows indicate the direction of glacial movement. The steeper lakebed decline ("Lee side" red arrows) on the north shore and the more gradual incline ("Stoss side" green arrows) on the south shore are consequences of the glacier's movement in the south-eastern direction and the Roches Moutonnées phenomenon. Modified, courtesy of Commonwealth of Massachusetts Division of Fisheries and Wildlife.*

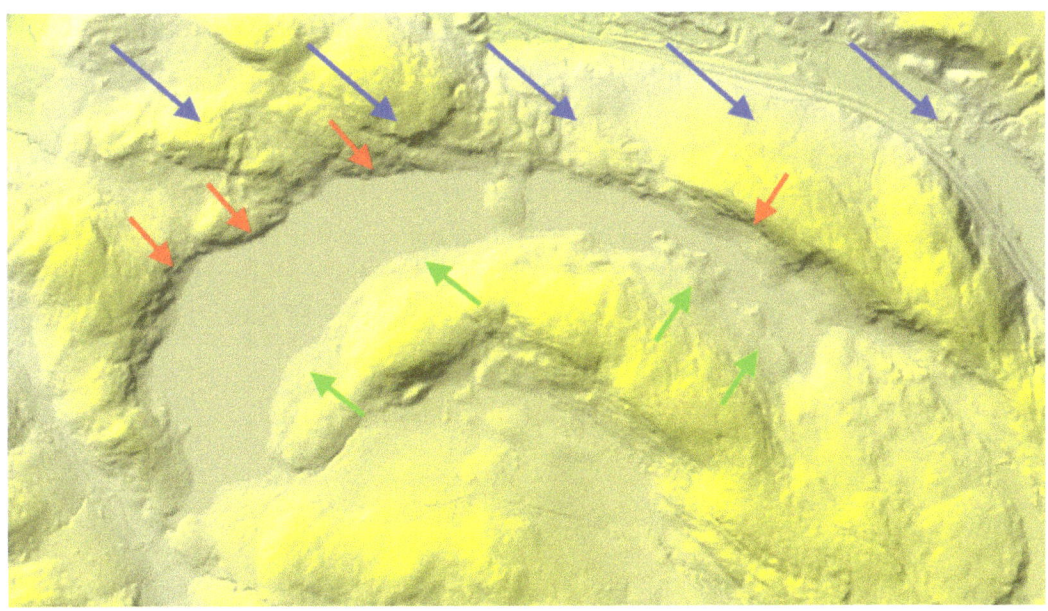

Figure 4.5 *USGS LiDAR map showing the impact of glacial action on the shoreline topography around the lake. Blue arrows indicate the direction of glacial movement. The shoreline on the north shore (Lee side) shows much steeper declines (red arrows) down towards the lake and the southern shore (Stoss side) shows a more gradual incline (green arrows) from the lakeshore, both of which are a result of Roche Moutonnées effect of glacial action which moved in a southeasterly direction. Modified, courtesy of U.S. Geological Survey.*

Figure 4.6 *An example of the extensive deposits of rocks, known as "glacial erratics," on Goose Pond's northern shoreline, dropped by the glacier as it descended the steep slope into the future lakebed.*

Goose Pond's creation story is indeed one for the ages — an epic drama, starting with the formation of its water molecules right on the heels of the Big Bang, followed by the Earth's birth ten billion years later and the subsequent delivery of its water by way of a seemingly endless deluge of icy asteroids plummeting from space. This was followed by the formation of Goose Pond's embryonic, curved spine, which was sculpted from superheated, subterranean rock by a series of powerful continental collisions, mountain ranges coming — and then going — and let's not forget the interminable ocean floods; only then to be further shaped, and perhaps filled, by an Ice Age glacier as recently as 14,000 years ago, and (finally) finished by Modern Man, just in the last 200 years, with the building of its dam and the digging of its channel.

Winter on Pinepoint

CHAPTER 5

THE MOHICAN INDIANS

THERE IS A WIDELY CIRCULATED LEGEND of an Indian grave on Goose Pond's shore. Those familiar with this legend commonly refer to a pair of local newspaper articles, the first in 1917 and the second in 1940:[30]

The history of Elwell Rock at upper Goose is not well known to the present generation I presume Ellwell, and an Indian, after fishing from the rock when Elwell by some mishap fell into the pond. Not being able to get out alone the Indian tried to rescue his companion, with the result that both were drowned. As the news became known a rescuing party went to the spot, among them tradition says, was Kendal Baird, then of West Becket, who being an expert swimmer and diver, tried by diving in the dark water to find the drowned men, but in vain. The bodies were not found until the grasses floated them to the surface

The graves were marked with four rough stones about four or five inches high, and have often been seen by the writer in a clump of bushes and large pines that grew there at that time. No doubt they could be found at this time by careful search

Figure 5.1 Excerpt from the July 13, 1917, front-page story in The Berkshire Gleaner *entitled "Stories of Goose Ponds", written by Edward A. Morley. The reference to "Elwell Rock" refers to the large rock on the northern side of the Upper Goose Pond island. The location of the gravesite has been redacted.*

INDIAN BONES FOUND

Said to Be Those of Man Drowned In 1865.

A mystery waa quickly solved Wednesday by Chief-of Police Frank, T Coughlin after four boys had disturbed the bones of the dead. The boys, John Turner, 14, William PinkaU, 13, Wallace Olds, 17, and Vernon Baker, 15, were digging worms at the of Lower Goose pond when the Shovel of one struck a skull. The boys, after taking the skull and ribs attached to a part of the backbone from the earth, brought them to one of their homes. Chief Coughlin, accompanied by State Patrolman Edward Haughey, investigated and the bones were taken to Chief Coughlin's office.

Dr George S. Wickham was called and stated the bones were many years old. The skull is believed to be that of Chief Mohhekenuck, who was was drowned in Upper Goose pond about 75 years ago. Chief Coughlin took the bones and returned them to the grave.

In the issue of the Berkshire Gleaner dated July 13, 1917, can be found a story related by Edward A. Morley which is in part as follows: It seems that a man by the name of Ellwell and the Indian were fishing from a rock on Upper Goose pond. (The rock being known today as Ellwell rock) when Ellwell by some mishap fell Into the pond.

The Indian tried to rescue his companion with result that both were drowned. As the news became known a party went to the spot, among them Ifendall Baird, who being an expert swimmer and diver, failed to find the bodies. The bodies were not found until later when they came to the surface They were buried between the

Figure 5.2 Excerpt from a front-page story in The Berkshire Gleaner, *August 23, 1940. The redacted word describes the gravesite's location.*

In 1978, RW Smith wrote yet another version of this story in *Three Thumbnails* (bracketed content added for clarity):

> *"Across from the Clubhouse [Mohhekennuck Club] and somewhat below it, the bulge of land (really an island) causing the Channel ends at a great rock. Here the pond abruptly widens into Upper Boynes Cove. The big rock is called Elwell's Rock and the water is very deep straight down from it. Many years ago, a man named Elwell drowned there while trying to rescue an Indian who had slipped off the rock and who also drowned. Elwell*

may have come from Otis but now nothing seems to be known about him. Presumably, his body was taken to wherever he came from and buried there. But if the Indian had a home nobody at the time knew where it was or what his name was, either. So they buried him on the [omitted] And a couple of gray shore rocks for markers [omitted]. Years ago, before TV and supervised play were hardly thought of, growing boys two or three together used to roam around in good weather in the woods and pastures and along the shores of ponds. When they saw anything that looked interesting or different, they would investigate it. About every 25-30 years, a couple of boys, while roaming around Goose Pond, would find this grave, probe into it, turn up a bone and then go all out to gather all they could find. Bearing their gruesome burden, they would hotfoot it to the police chief in Lee with a breathless 'Jeez, look what we found at Goose Pond! Sumbody musta got murdered!' It would end up, of course, with the bones being taken back and reburied, but not before the news media had got a picture of the bones tastefully arranged with respect to the skull on a white background. The boys would get their names in the paper with a short story about it. And that would be that. I don't believe the Indian has been dug up and had his picture taken since the late 1920's. Perhaps TV and supervised play do have an unsuspected benefit after all."[31]

These three narratives, each slightly different from the other two, provide us with several competing versions of the Elwell story. The 1917 version stated that Elwell fell in, that the "Indian" jumped in to save him, that both drowned, and that both were buried side-by-side near Goose Pond. But the 1978 version says that the *Indian* fell in, that Elwell tried to save *him*, and that they both drowned but that only the Indian was buried by the pond. I have found only one published story of the bones being dug up and that was in 1940, while Smith says they were dug up frequently but not since the 1920s.

In 1970, a relentlessly curious Lanesboro history buff by the name of Edward Knurrow looked deeply into this story. In his pursuit of his research, Knurrow interviewed yet another interested party by the name of Frank Gardner, a 78-year-old roomer at the Morgan House in downtown Lee. The interview took place on Saturday, November 28, 1970, Gardner perhaps visiting his family in Lee for Thanksgiving. Gardner shared with Knurrow how he (Gardner) had previously sought information about the swimmer/diver Kendal Baird (named in the 1917 article) and discovered that there had indeed been a local man by that name born in 1803. Gardner's logic was that an expert swimmer/diver would likely be about thirty years old at the time of such a dive, so Gardner estimated that the drowning event likely took place around 1835. Gardner had furthermore searched vital records up to 1850 for a Mr. Elwell in Lee, Tyringham, Otis, and Becket and came up emptyhanded. But he reported to have found some other evidence of an Elwell family on Webster Road, in Otis or Becket, who lost a family member to a Goose Pond drowning (but the handwriting on this last bit was not entirely decipherable).[32]

In light of these additional findings, we might be led to believe that the drowning -- and burial -- events likely took place around 1835 (not 1865), and that Elwell may have hailed from Otis or Becket.

But apparently unbeknownst to the Morgan House's Frank Gardner, or to *The Berkshire Gleaner* writers of 1917 and 1940, a little-known Stockbridge newspaper called *The Berkshire Star*, had long before published the first (or final!) word on this mysterious saga way back in 1822!

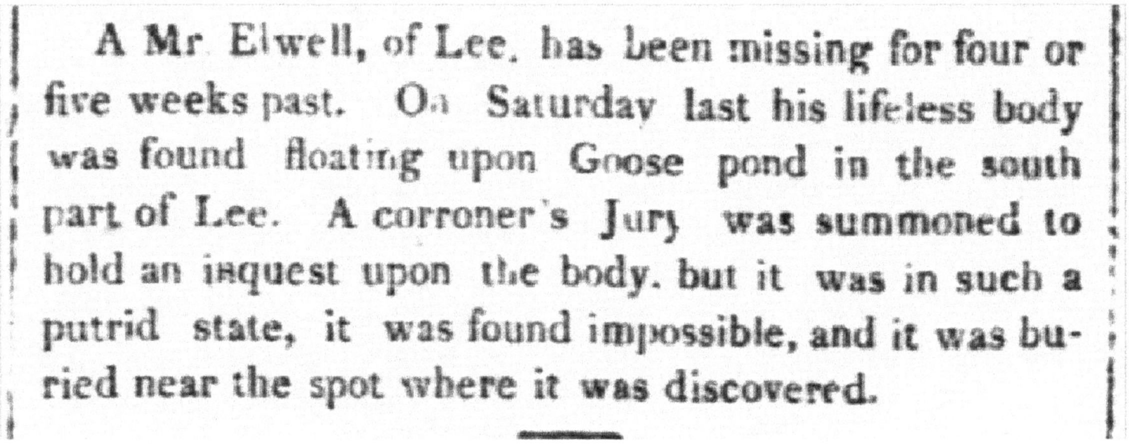

> A Mr. Elwell, of Lee, has been missing for four or five weeks past. On Saturday last his lifeless body was found floating upon Goose pond in the south part of Lee. A corroner's Jury was summoned to hold an inquest upon the body, but it was in such a putrid state, it was found impossible, and it was buried near the spot where it was discovered.

Figure 5.3 The Berkshire Star, *August 22, 1822.*[33]

This last is the oldest telling of this story that we have, and a contemporaneous one at that, dating the discovery of poor Elwell's body definitively to Saturday, August 17, 1822, and describing the death of only one man: Elwell (from Lee, not Otis or Becket.) Either poor Elwell wasn't given a first name by his mom and dad or, far more likely, the newspaper didn't see the point of sharing it.

And, quite remarkably: there was no mention of an Indian.

Where did the supposed role of an Indian in these events come from? Did someone insert the drowning of an Indian into the original 1822 story to embellish it after the fact, or did the *The Berkshire Star* reporter consider a drowned Indian unworthy of mentioning?

We should also consider that by 1822 there were very few, if any, Indians left in Berkshire County, most (or all) of them having already been relocated to their Wisconsin reservation. We can nevertheless be quite certain that the owner of any buried Indian skull would have been unlikely to have carried the alleged name of "Chief Mohhekennuck" -- an obvious usurpation of the local tribe's name.

And there's this: why would diver Kendal Baird have been needed if, in 1822, Elwell's body was found already floating? And if Baird had in fact been sent on his dive sometime prior to the discovery of Elwell's floating body, why would Elwell have been considered missing for four or five weeks? Even if there was then a nineteen-year-old kid named Kendal Baird from West Becket, we will never know if he was in fact an ace diver, nor if he actually dove for any bodies in Upper Goose.

Since poor Elwell was considered missing for four to five weeks in 1822, we can quite reasonably assume that there were no witnesses to his drowning. And if there were, in fact, two unwitnessed drownings, how would we ever know that one fell in and that the other jumped in for a rescue? And how would we know which one did the falling and which one tried the rescuing?

How would we even know if poor Elwell's demise even had anything to do with the rock that was subsequently named after him? Or that they were actually fishing?

Then there's the question of Elwell's Rock itself. The stories indicate, without any evidence -- or witnesses mind you -- that the drowned person(s) in this story fell into the water from this rock. But in 1822, the dam as we know it had not yet been built. Hence, the water level in 1822 would have been at least thirteen feet lower than it is today and the area adjacent to Elwell's Rock would have been dry land and hardly posing any serious risk of drowning. It would certainly seem unlikely that Elwell, with or without an Indian friend, would have been fishing from a rock that was surrounded only by land. But at least now we can explain how two alleged non-swimmers would have even reached Elwell's Rock in the first place without a boat - the "island" was then a dry peninsula.

That a marked shoreside grave from 1822 exists on Goose Pond holding the remains of poor Mr. Elwell is clear. But how he came to drown and whether the remains of an Indian lie beside him or not will remain one of Goose Pond's most closely held secrets.

Any Indian who might (or might not) in fact be buried on Goose Pond's shores would surely have belonged to the local Mohican Indian tribe -- a tribe whose name had been derived from that of the mighty river that runs to Goose Pond's west. Today we know this particular river by another name, coined in honor of a famous English explorer, Henry Hudson, who claimed to have "discovered" it in 1609 while sailing his ship *Half Moon* for the Dutch East India Company. His "discovery" led the Dutch to claim for themselves the territory of New Netherlands (later renamed New York) and its mighty "Hudson River."

But this powerful river had already been given a name long before Henry sailed his boat upon it claiming its discovery. The river had been called "Mahicannituck" by the people who had lived there for three thousand years - these were "The People of the Waters That Are Never Still" which they pronounced "Muh-he-con-ne-ok" (later shortened to Mohicans). By the time of Henry's great discovery, there were 25,000 Mohicans settled along both shores of this great river, their villages extending as far south as Manhattan Island and as far north as Lake Champlain. I think that the Hudson River is long overdue for the resurrection of its original name. After all, we managed to name the entire Commonwealth of Massachusetts after its indigenous people in the East known as the Massachusett...

The life led by the Mohicans is eloquently described in a passage taken from *A Brief History of the Mohican Nation – Stockbridge Munsee Band*, written in 2004 by a Native American, Dorothy Davids:

"The Mohican' lives were rooted in the woodlands in which they lived. These were covered with red spruce, elm, pine, oak, birch, and maple trees. Black bear, deer, moose, beaver otter, bobcat, mink, wild turkey, and pheasant thrived in the woods. The sparkling rivers teemed with herring, shad, trout, and other fish. Oyster beds were found beneath the river's overhanging banks for some distance up the Mahicannituck. Berries, cherries, and nuts were abundant. It was a rich life.

Mohican women generally were in charge of the home, children, and gardens, while men traveled greater distances to hunt, fish, or serve as warriors. After the hunts and harvests, meat, vegetables and berries were dried. These along with smoked fish were stored in pits dug deep in the ground and lined with grass or bark.

During the cold winter months, utensils and containers were carved, hunting, trapping, and fishing gear were repaired, baskets and pottery were created, and clothing was fashioned and decorated with colorfully dyed porcupine quills, shells, and other gifts from nature.

Winter was also the time of teaching. Storytellers told the children how life came to be, how the earth was created, why the leaves turn red, and so on. Historians also related the story of the people: how they learned to sing, the story of their drums and rattles, what the stars could teach them. Children learned the ways of the Mohicans..."

Figure 5.4 *Map indicating the location (in yellow) of the Mohican Indians. Courtesy of Spinningspark at Wikipedia.*

Figure 5.5 *The "Many Trails" symbol of the Mohican Indians, designed by Edwin Martin, a Mohican Indian, symbolizing endurance, strength, and hope.*

The Mohican Indians

During his July 4, 1854 speech in Reidsville, New York, a prominent Mohican named John Wannuaucon Quinney said, 'Wise men foretold the coming of a strange race, from the sunrise, as numerous as the leaves upon the trees, who would eventually crowd them from their fair possessions.'

This "strange race" had indeed come. On April 25, 1724, the English paid the Indians 460 pounds, three barrels of cider, and thirty quarts of rum for what is today Berkshire County.[34]

The Mohicans suffered from all the well-known injustices that Native Americans faced across the land. There were conflicts with European immigrants over land, missionaries, and fur trade as well as suffering from the myriad novelties the Europeans brought with them such as smallpox, measles, diphtheria, and scarlet fever. Unsurprisingly, the Mohicans' rights were never well represented in colonial courts. Their challenges were further compounded by the Beaver Wars with the Mohawk tribe throughout the 1600s. Ultimately, in the early 1700s, the Mohicans were pushed east of the Hudson River, many settling in the Housatonic River Valley – which includes the land around Goose Pond and in Stockbridge (previously Wnahktukuk). The Mohicans came to be called "Stockbridge Indians." By 1749, there were only 218 members of the Mohicans, and by 1774 their land was reduced to just 1200 acres.

The Mohicans had fought alongside the colonists in the American Revolution, including in the Battle of Bunker Hill, and were duly repaid for their brave service, first with the gift of a whole ox and a barrel of whiskey, this authorized by none other than General George Washington, and then with their involuntary relocation in the early 1800s to a reservation in Bowler, Wisconsin where they were joined by the Munsee. They now identify variously as the "Stockbridge-Munsee Community" or as "Mohican Nation" or as "Stockbridge-Munsee Band of Mohicans." There are now approximately 1500 tribal members, about 1/3 of them living on the Wisconsin reservation.

The town of Lee was founded in 1777 on land that had been purchased from the Mohican Indians in 1757. The numerous arrowheads collected from Goose Pond's shores demonstrate that the Mohicans were indisputably present right here on Goose Pond, probably for hundreds, or even thousands of years, peacefully and joyously enjoying the lake's plentiful fish, verdant forests, and cool waters, long before any of us showed up. It was in the Mohicans' honor, years later in 1909, that the members of the Mohhekennuck Club on Upper Goose Pond would name their club. Surely, no history of Goose Pond would be complete without telling the stories of the Mohicans.

Figure 5.6 *Arrowhead found on Stump Island by Madge Cavarly's son Perry when he was fourteen years old, in 1944. Young Perry treasured this find. Perry's own son, Perry III, had his honeymoon with his bride Adrienne on Pinepoint. Courtesy of Adrienne Cavarly.*

Figure 5.7 *Arrowheads found by Edward Walton on Goose Pond's shores, primarily in Sucker Brook. Courtesy of Bruce Walton.*

Double Rainbow on Lower Goose Pond

CHAPTER 6

THE SHAKERS

THE "UNITED SOCIETY of Believers in Christ's Second Appearing", later known as the "Shaking Quakers" and ultimately simply as the "Shakers", was an English Protestant sect founded in 1747 as an offshoot of the Quakers. The Shakers believed that knowledge of Christ was available directly to individuals, without churches, priests, or the *Bible*. Their lives were based on communal living, simplicity, pacifism, justice, celibacy, gender equality, spirited dancing, and a profound belief that a more perfect society could be achieved on Earth. They were called Shakers because of their dramatic shaking during their intensely spiritual worship.

One of the early founders of the English Shakers, Ann Lee, emigrated from Manchester, England to America in 1774 after having experienced a spiritual epiphany. Upon her arrival in America, she founded the first American Shaker community near Albany, New York. Her ideas soon spread and by the mid-nineteenth century, there were several thousand Shakers in America, many of them in Tyringham, Massachusetts until 1960.

Deed research and an 1886 manuscript both demonstrate a Shaker presence specifically around Goose Pond, although precise information about its nature has remained elusive. Artifacts showing the Shakers' presence in wider Tyringham still exist near Jerusalem Road, where the remains of a Shaker barn foundation, a cemetery, and the stone foundation of a ritual Fountain Stone can be found.[35] The Shaker community in Tyringham, at its peak, had several hundred members and included a furniture factory, claimed to be the sect's first.[36] By 1874, the settlement had dwindled in size with many members departing to join other Shaker communities. Shaker communities continued to shrink after laws were passed that prohibited them from taking in orphaned children.

half a mile in length. The two had no visible natural connection but a small opening was made to augment the supply from the lower pond. Formerly the power was used only for driving a saw mill at the mouth of the pond and the water could not be drawn more than a few inches. The land in the vicinity was largely owned by the Shakers. This was purchased, cut into lots and resold with the condition that they could be flooded but that the water should be drawn by May 10th each year sufficiently not to interfere with the usual crop of hay. Since the dam was raised the water can be drawn about 13 feet.

Figure 6.1 *Edward S. Rogers writing of Goose Pond. He refers to a Shaker presence around Goose Pond in this passage in his 1886 treatise entitled* The East Lee Disaster, Apr 20th, '86.

Figure 6.2 *Deed research around Upper Goose Pond reveals the existence of two Shaker properties belonging to James and Susan Masters, and Oliver, Thomas, and Daniel Hulet near Higley Brook. These were likely wood lots but at least one cellar hole has been identified nearby which might have been a Shaker home. Courtesy of Douglas Winiarski.*

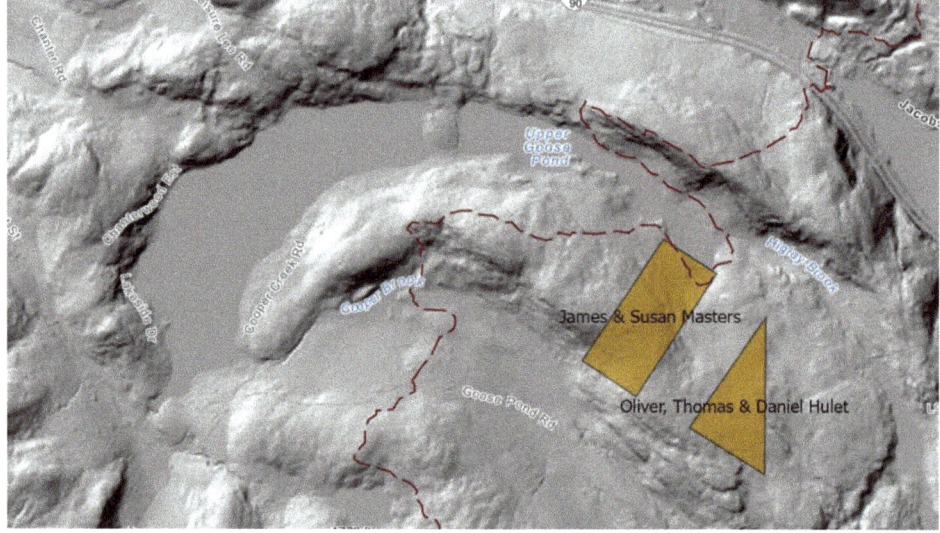

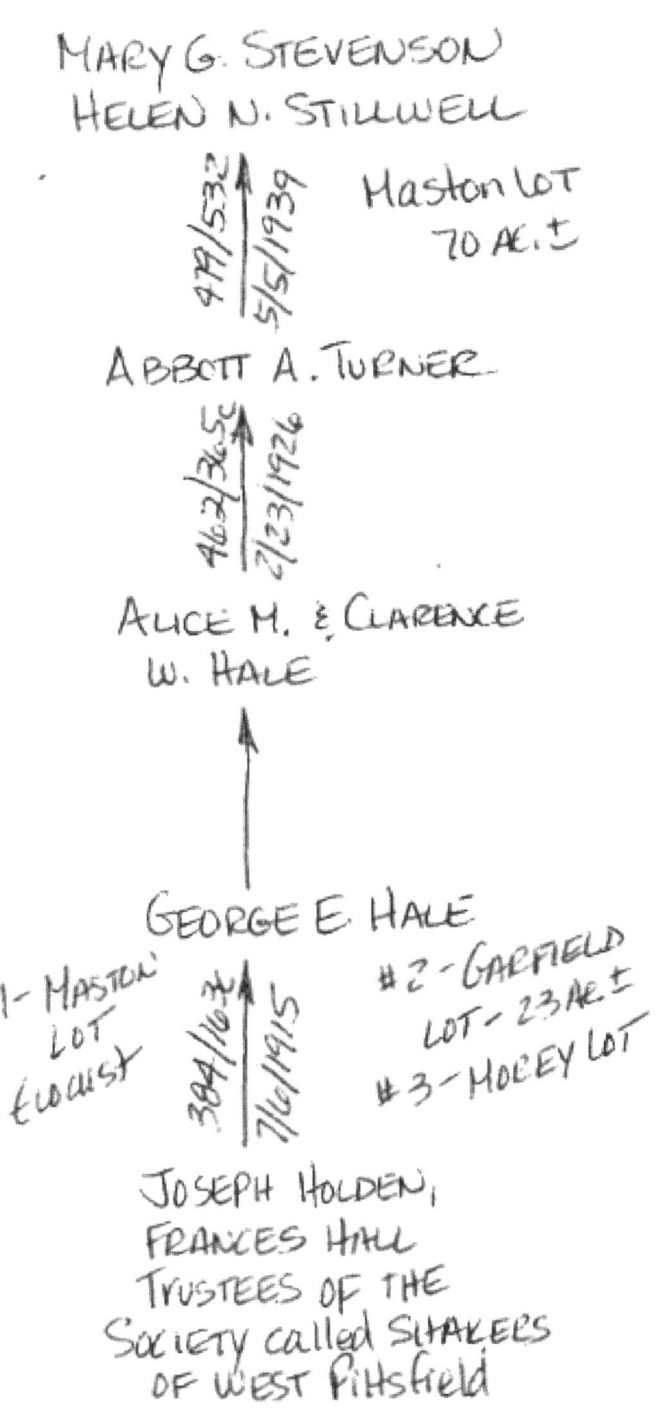

Figure 6.3 *Deed research, performed by the Stilwell family, discovered 1915 ownership of their seventy-acre Maston/Shaker Lot on Upper Goose Pond by the Shakers of West Pittsfield. Courtesy of David Stilwell.*

Figure 6.4 *Map of Tyringham (1739-1840). Seen here are Goose Pond (yellow arrow) and the Shaker's Mt. Horeb Holy Land (red arrow). Modified, courtesy of the Tyringham Historical Commission.*

Figure 6.5 *Stone foundation of a Shaker barn, currently located at a designated Appalachian Trail campsite in Tyringham.*

Figure 6.6 Gravestone in a Shaker Cemetery, just north of Jerusalem Road in Tyringham. There are nearly one hundred such gravestones in this cemetery.[37]

Figure 6.7 *Foundation of the "Fountain Stone" located in Tyringham, in the "Mt. Horeb Holy Land" site, just south of Jerusalem Road and adjacent to the Appalachian Trail. This site, when it was free of trees, would have had a dramatic 360-degree view of the surrounding mountains. This foundation had supported a "Foundation Stone" inscribed with sacred texts (See Figure 6.8). Shakers would hold energetic worship around this stone believing that a fountain of spiritual water would be rising from it. This artifact was discovered in 2023 by Professor Doug Winiarski, Professor, Department of Religious Studies, University of Richmond.*

Figure 6.8 *Two remnants of the Fountain Stone. Located in the Tyringham library.*

Figure 6.9 Shaker village in Tyringham. From The Book of Berkshire: Describing and Illustrating its Hills and Homes and Telling Where They Are, What They Are, and Why They are Destined to Become Homes in America, for the Season of 1887, *by Clark W. Bryan.*

Moonrise over Upper Goose Pond

CHAPTER 7

PAPER MILLS

THE RELATIONSHIP BETWEEN Goose Pond and the paper-making industry was truly symbiotic. By nature of Goose Pond's unusual mountaintop location, with its large volume of water sitting 500 feet above the valley, the fast-running stream that drains it has provided the power for dozens of successful paper mills since the early nineteenth century. And then, in due course, it was these mill operators' ever-expanding thirst for waterpower that motivated them, in 1839, to enlarge the Pond's pre-existing dam, adding thirteen feet to the lake's depth, and to dig a channel between the two lakes, both actions profoundly altering Goose Pond in ways that will surely endure for many generations to come. We cannot tell the story of Goose Pond without also telling the story of papermaking in the Berkshires.

> *"It goes without saying, I suppose, that there is no other one fabric so essential to the world as paper. To strike it from the world's products would be to doom mankind to a return to barbaric ignorance. It is in co-partnership with the printing press, the inspiration to civilization, the messenger of Grace, Mercy and Peace, the preserver of governments, the voice of the people, the destruction of tyrannies, the soul of all progress."*[38]

Early nineteenth-century America was a time of great societal change. Literacy levels were expanding thanks to the proliferation of public schools. Concurrently, there was an explosive growth of popular American literature as well as a vociferous societal discourse in the arenas of politics, civics, religion, agriculture, philosophy, journalism, technology, science and industrialization. These combined developments generated a voracious American appetite for paper. Fulfillment of this insatiable demand was made possible by the Industrial Revolution which was rapidly mechanizing both power production and papermaking processes. Goose Pond, quietly perched on its mountaintop, was more than ready to do its part in fulfilling this national demand for paper.

It was in 1799, when Zenas Crane, twenty-two, arrived in the Berkshires by horseback. Despite his young age, he was already experienced in the Boston paper-making industry and was seeking to build his own paper mill. The combination of the power provided by the water of the Housatonic River, the ready availability of raw materials, a robust railroad system[39] that provided access to the hungry New York paper market, clean low-iron spring water for paper production, abundant sources of lime, plenty of rainfall, available machine shops to manufacture necessary machinery, local livestock to provide materials for paper "sizing" and cheap land made the Berkshires appealing to this ambitious young man. After purchasing fourteen acres of land in Dalton, along with water rights, all for $194, he opened the first paper mill in the Berkshire Mountains in 1800.

Before the invention of paper, the skins of 300 sheep would be required to print just a single copy of the *Bible*. The impact that the inventions of paper and the printing press had on human civilization is obvious and by 1840, the town of Lee, Massachusetts, with dozens of paper mills then in operation, had become the most productive paper-making town in all of America, thereby earning its nickname, Papertown, USA.[40]

When Zenas Crane opened his Dalton mill, the primary raw material for papermaking was cotton rags. The rag market in Boston had, by then, grown so intense that its mills were importing most of their rags from Europe and even some from exhumed Egyptian mummies.[41] But in the Berkshires, Crane had discovered a robust supply of local rags, which lasted for thirty years. Teams of workers, on so-called "rag routes," would scour the local towns and farms, purchasing and bartering for old rags. Later, when flax farming took off in the Berkshires, the linen so produced would further fulfill the ravenous appetite of the local paper industry for raw material. Nevertheless, by 1832, Lee's rapidly expanding paper mills, which consumed nine hundred tons of rags annually were, like in Boston, importing 75% of their rags from Europe. In 1867, when the process of manufacturing paper from wood pulp was established in practice (inspired by an astute observer of wasp nest-building), the abundant Berkshire forests stood ready to feed the beast (at least for a while).

In the days of rag paper, the first step for the collected rags would be processing in a mill's "rag room", where women would hand sort the rags according to fabric, color, and quality, remove the dust ("dusting"), open the seams, remove the buttons, and finally cut them into two-to-four-inch squares with knives mounted on posts. After a paper mill would burn down, local kids would descend upon the cooled ashes searching for the treasured piles of discarded buttons.[42]

Figure 7.1 The "Rag Room" at the Bay State Mill (Dalton, 1895). Courtesy of the Crane Museum of Papermaking.

These rag squares would then be transferred to the "beater room", which, early on, was the only mechanized step of paper production, and the reason these early mills needed power from waterwheels. In fact, in those days, it was the very act of requiring power that then made a mill a "mill", and a pond a "mill pond".

Inside the beater room, we would find a "Hollander beater," an oval wooden tub with a stone or metal plate at its bottom embedded with iron "knives." Over this plate rested a tree trunk cylinder, which was similarly embedded with blades and would be turned using the power from a waterwheel through the action of multiple gears and belts. Many of these knives were forged locally by a Lee blacksmith named Cornelius Barlow Water and rags would be mixed in the beater, and then subjected to these grinding blades for several days, creating a fiber pulp, all under the supervision of an "engineer", who would adjust the "engine's" configuration and the duration of beating according to the type of paper being produced. While these beaters would undergo some refinements over the years, they were not substantially changed for the next hundred years.[43]

Figure 7.2 The "Beater Room" at the Pioneer Mill in Dalton (1895) showing multiple Hollander Beaters. In the early years, the Hollander Beater was the only step requiring power. It was called an "engine" and the operator an "engineer." Courtesy of the Crane Museum of Papermaking.

The pulp would then be transferred to a "vat room," where a highly skilled "vatman" would mix the pulp with clean spring water, pour the mixture over frames holding fine wire mesh, and skillfully shake the frames to interweave the fibers to make wet sheets of paper. The "coucher" would then lay these wet sheets on felt pads where they would be subjected to screw presses to remove excess water. The pressed sheets would then be draped over rails in the "dry loft" to dry for several days. Once dried, they would be taken to the "sizing room" where they were dipped into vats of animal glue (easily obtained from abundant local livestock) which would prevent ink absorption. The paper would also be treated with lime which was easily obtained from the local limestone and marble quarries around Lee. The final steps would be accomplished in the finishing room where final pressing, quality checking, trimming, and wrapping took place.

Most Berkshire paper was shipped to New York City by rail or steamship, to be used in newspapers, business ledgers, writing paper, wrapping paper, book printing, or currency. Horace Greeley, the editor of the *Tribune*, leveraged a personal friendship with the owner of a Lee paper mill (Winthrop Laflin) to help him start his newspaper in 1841. Laflin agreed to provide Greeley with newsprint paper on three months' credit.[44][45] In the 1800s, the 277,000 subscribers of the *New York Herald* and the *New York Tribune* were reading newspapers largely made from Lee paper created using the water flowing from Goose Pond. In fact, in 1832, over half of all paper consumed in New York City was manufactured by Lee paper mills.[46]

These manual steps of producing paper became increasingly mechanized in the 1820s with the invention of John Ames' cylinder machine and in the 1840s with the introduction of the revolutionary Fourdrinier machine. The Fourdrinier machine combined the wire vat step with a series of felt rollers and drying steps and soon became capable of producing paper at a rate of 200 feet per minute at widths of up to 125 inches. These mechanical advances improved output and quality, but further increased the need for skilled mechanics, for substantial capital investment, and for expanded sources of power.

Figure 7.3 *The Fourdrinier machine was first introduced to Berkshire County by the May brothers in 1848. It was much more expensive than Ames' cylinder machine but produced superior paper. The Paper-Making Machine by Clappertown, 1856.*

Figure 7.4 *The Fourdrinier Machine at the Bay State Mill (Dalton, 1892). Courtesy of the Crane Museum of Papermaking.*

Herman Melville wrote about the Fourdrinier machine in his 1855 book *The Paradise of Bachelors and the Tartarus of Maids*:

> "Something of awe now stole over me, as I gazed upon this inflexible iron animal. Always, more or less, machinery of this ponderous, elaborate sort strikes, in some moods, strange dread into the human heart, as some living, panting Behemoth might. But what made the thing I saw so specially terrible to me was the metallic necessity, the unbudging fatality which governed it."

In 1806, not far behind Zenas Crane, Samuel Church opened the second paper mill in the Berkshires, his in South Lee, on the site of the Onyx papermill that still operates today. Soon after, in 1808, Samuel's brother, Luman Church, built the Eagle Mill in North Lee, which was in operation until 2008 and is now being converted into residential housing. In 1819, Luman built the Forest Mill, which was located just below the confluence of the Goose Pond and Greenwater Pond streams, where the abandoned Tayford Company building stands today.

Two brothers, hailing from Putney, Vermont, named Edward (E.S.) May and Sylvester (S.S.) May, both the grandsons of the famous American artist Sybil Huntington May, soon arrived on the East Lee papermaking scene and were destined to make changes to Goose Pond, which are visible still to this day. Edward, born in 1809, started his business life as a wool manufacturer in Walpole, New Hampshire. Sylvester, younger by four years, arrived in Lee in 1834 as an apprentice at Lee's Columbia Mill, owned then by Winthrop Laflin.[47] Sylvester has been described as a private man, but his brother Edward was a Massachusetts state representative (in 1854, and 1874) and a Lee selectman from 1846 to 1848.[48]

The first paper mill on the Goose Pond Stream proper was built in 1837 by Sylvester May and his partner Jared Ingersoll. After burning down in 1839, the mill was rebuilt in 1840, and Ingersoll's interest was purchased by Sylvester's brother Edward May. The two May brothers built a large house, known as "Maywood," with two identical wings for each of their families, which still stands today at the bottom of Forest Street. In 1848, the May brothers introduced Berkshire County's first

Figure 7.5 *Sylvester "S.S." May. It was because of the influential two brothers, Sylvester and Edward May, that Goose Pond was, for a time, renamed Lake May. Courtesy of Lee Library Historical Collection.*

Fourdrinier machine in one of their Goose Pond mills. In 1860, the May brothers purchased the 180-acre "Chanter Farm" in order to gain access to its excellent quality spring water.[49] The two May brothers lived and worked together on the Goose Pond stream for forty-six years until Sylvester's death in 1886. During most of those years, Goose Pond was commonly known as "Lake May."

Figure 7.6 "Maywood." *The residence built by Sylvester and Edward May which still stands at the bottom of Forest Street. There are two identical wings, one built for each brother. Built in 1845. These are modern photographs.*

Other mills followed, mostly upstream from the May's mill, such as the Thatcher and Washington mills in 1836 and an Ingersoll mill in 1837.[50] At that time, the small Goose Pond dam, which had been built seventy-five years earlier by a lone sawmill upstream, only raised Goose Pond's water level by eighteen inches. To provide for the increasing power demands of the multiplying mills, the May brothers joined forces with the other mill operators to expand the existing dam in 1839, thus increasing Goose Pond's water level by thirteen feet. It was during this project that the channel connecting Lower and Upper Goose Pond was dug, further increasing the volume of water available behind the dam.[51] Once the dam was modified, the May brothers purchased the old sawmill in 1845 and converted it into the "Middle Mill" which was located about one-third of a mile up from the base of the Goose Pond stream.[52]

Presumably as a consequence of the dam's expansion, many other mills soon proliferated on the Goose Pond stream such as the Upper Forest Mill, Mahaiwe Mill (1853), Congress Mill, National Mill, May & Rogers Mill, Couch & Clark Mill (1853), Linn & Dean's Mill (1855), Phinney & Co, Upper Mill, Northrup and Eldridge Mill, and the PC Baird Mill, most of which were located below the existing paper mill whose remains we see today. Each mill typically specialized in one or more specific paper products, such as fine writing paper, newsprint, currency, straw paper, wallpaper, glassine paper, "gun cotton", starch collars, or wrapping paper. By 1840, Lee mills were responsible for the manufacture of one-fourth of all paper manufactured in the United States.[53] By 1851 there were twenty-five paper mills in Lee with an annual revenue of $2 million.[54]

Benjamin Dean, one of the owners of the Linn & Dean Mill, was a particularly colorful character. *"He had a massive head, long, flowing gray hair and whiskers, and spent his leisure in writing 'poetry' as he called it, satirizing the Bar and Pulpit. He became a 'free thinker' and Spiritualist and was always ready for an argument. Someone said to him one day, 'You can find a rhyme for almost any word, but it would puzzle you to concoct a rhyme for Timbuctoo. Instantly Dean replied: 'The Missionary went to Timbuctoo, Where savages ate him and his hymn book too.'"*[55]

While Dean was busy free-thinking, satirizing, and creating rhymes, his partner Linn was busy getting himself summoned to the authorities in New York. Apparently at the request of their New York customer, Manahan & Miller, the Linn & Dean Mill had been producing bank note paper with a watermark "CSA". In 1862, Linn was summoned by the New York authorities, who accused him of collaborating with the Confederate States by printing Confederate currency. He pled ignorance of the paper's purpose, was acquitted, retired to New Jersey, and passed away in 1900. Manahan & Miller maintained that it had been acting patriotically, and with the approval of Washington, by trying to destabilize the Confederate currency by flooding the Confederacy with counterfeit currency. It appears that the authorities in Washington and New York were not communicating very effectively.[56]

A word here about power production is in order. When paper mills first rose the primary source of power was waterwheels turned by rivers and streams. As technology advanced power needs also grew, needs which were met by the introduction of hydraulic turbines (in the 1850s), and later by steam engines (in the 1880s) powered by the heat of burning wood or coal to create steam. Many photographs of Goose Pond mills in the 1880s showed large chimneys billowing black smoke indicating the use of fossil fuels for steam engines. Finally, in 1926 the Tayford Company and Lake May Power entered the scene, providing hydroelectric power to the local mills.[57]

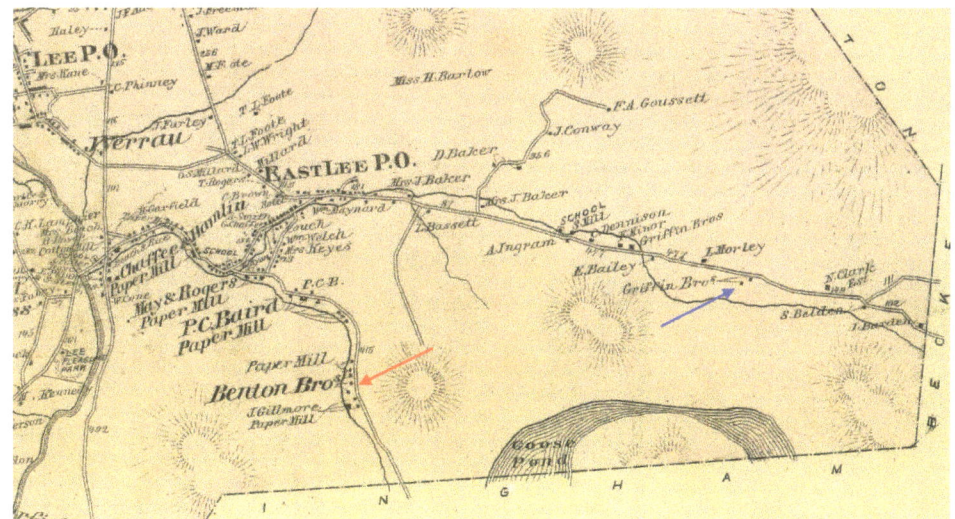

Figure 7.7 *Map of East Lee by F.W. Beers (1876) showing multiple paper mills on the Goose Pond stream. Notice the Benton Bros mill (red arrow) which was the predecessor of the abandoned mill whose remains still stand. Also, note the Griffin Bros sawmill (blue arrow) north of Lower Goose Pond. The Griffins were likely the first homesteaders on Upper Goose Pond. From the Atlas of Berkshire County 1876. Courtesy of old-maps.com.*

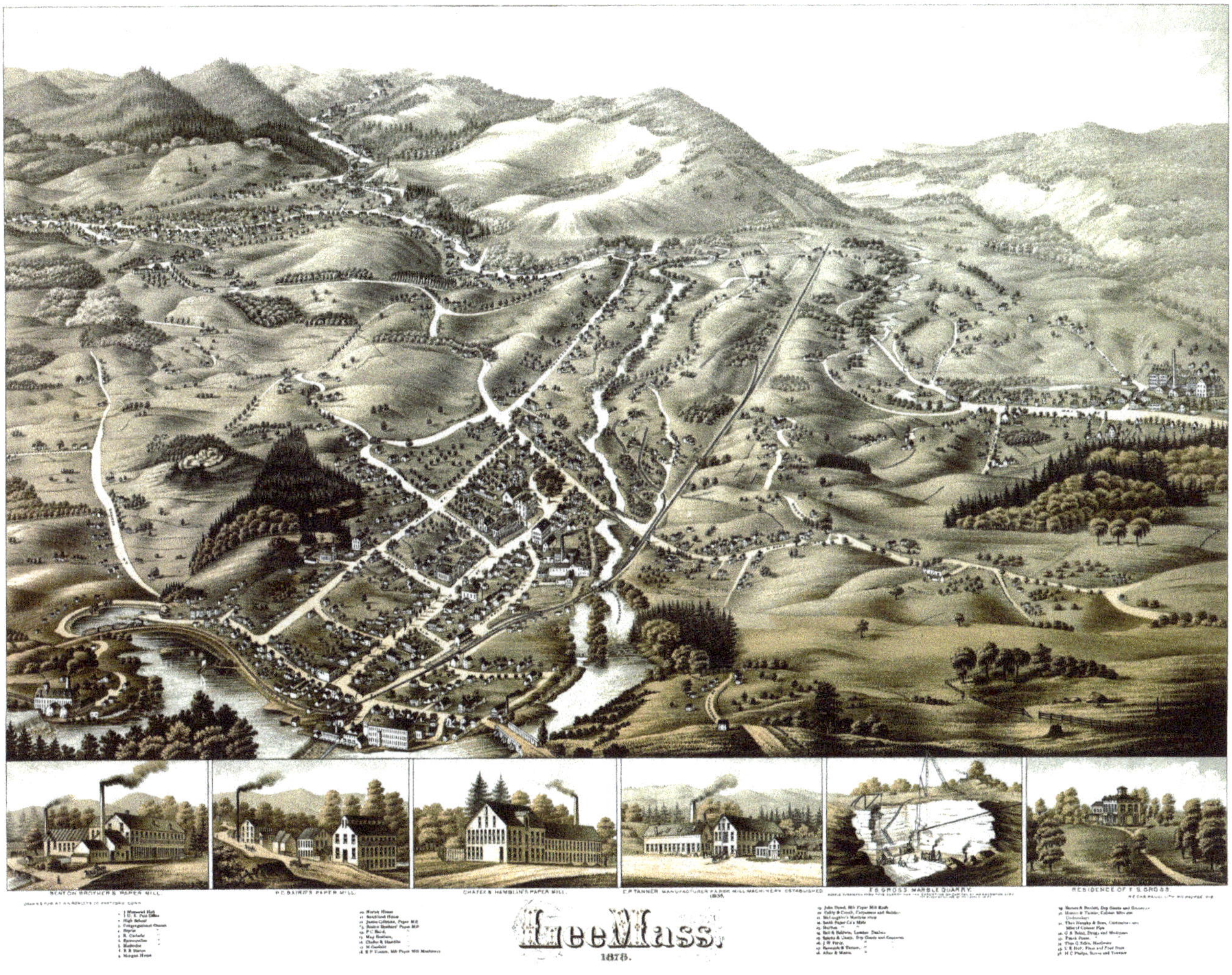

Figure 7.8 *Map of Lee, drawn by HH Rowling, 1878. Forest Street (aka Mountain Road) and its numerous mills can be seen heading up the mountains at the very top of the image. Note the extensive deforestation depicted behind the extensive series of mills at the top of the map, a consequence of the mills' ravenous appetite for wood.*

Figure 7.9 Baird Mill on Forest Street in 1870. Courtesy of Lee Library Historical Collection.

Figure 7.10 Mahaiwe Mill on Forest Street in 1880. Courtesy of Lee Library Historical Collection.

Figure 7.11 Baird Mill on Forest Street in 1860. Courtesy of Lee Library Historical Collection.

Figure 7.12 Baird Mill on Forest Street, 1876. Courtesy of Lee Library Historical Collection.

We have now reached the story behind the abandoned mill whose remains still stand today by the roadside. This particular mill had its start in 1854, when Caleb Benton and Harrison Garfield built their Mountain Mill, upstream from most of the other mills on the Goose Pond stream. Garfield and Benson were partners in the paper business for twenty-six years. Garfield, a highly educated man who started out in the meat market, was also a bank president, owner of several greenhouses, a Lee Selectman, a Massachusetts state congressman, and president of the Lee Library Association. Benson entered the paper business at a young age.[58] Like many other paper mills during this period, their first mill burnt down in 1861 and was rebuilt. By the 1860s, mill builders began to modify their methods to produce buildings less susceptible to destruction by fire using a building method known as "slow-burning construction", which utilized thicker, slower-burning lumber and enclosed stairwells and elevator trapdoors.[59] When Caleb died in 1866, his two sons, J. Frank Benton and Charles C. Benton took the mill over, renaming it the Benton Brothers Mill, added an enormous thirty-foot water wheel, and produced 1000 pounds of fine writing paper every day.[60]

During the Civil War, the Benton brothers switched to producing "gun cotton" for Union canons, and after the Civil War, they added starched collars to its writing paper production. The Benton brothers sold the mill in 1905 to a group of Lee businessmen led by Louis T. Stephenson and known as the Mountain Mill Paper Company, with the mill's name, reverting back to Mountain Mill.[61] Multiple ownership changes followed, the mill repeatedly changing its name to Hemlock Mill, Greenwood Mill, and finally, Westfield River Paper, which purchased the mill and the dam in 1933 after the company sold its old accounts to Strathmore Paper Company of Woronoco.[62] The name Hemlock Mill was the result of all the hemlock lumber (often called "Berkshire mahogany") with which it had been constructed.[63] Complicated and fluid financial relationships ensued between this mill and Lake May Power Company and Simkin Industries. By 1942, the mill had two "beaters" and a 72-inch Fourdrinier machine (manufactured at Lee's Clark-Aiken Company,) and was producing 52" wide paper and running twenty-four hours/day. In the 1960s the owners invested $1 million on renewing the factory and its machines. Towards the end of its operations, the mill employed an average of forty-five workers and produced glassine papers used for food wrapping.[64] It ceased operations in 1994 and ultimately donated the dam to the newly formed Goose Pond Maintenance District on October 1, 1997.

Figure 7.13 Benton Brothers paper mill in 1876. This mill was the predecessor of the current mill whose remains still stand on Forest Street. The note taped to the corner is enlarged. Courtesy of Lee Library Historical Collection.

Figure 7.14 Mountain Mill 1880. Note the children in front — who also worked in the mill. Courtesy of Lee Library Historical Collection.

Figure 7.15 Mountain Mill (formerly the Benton Brothers Mill) on Forest Street in 1890. NOTE: Many of this book's historical photographs which are specified to be of a particular mill can look very different from year to year. These substantial variations in a mill's appearance can perhaps be explained by its intervening destruction by fire followed by its rebuilding, or by the shifting names of mills, or by the mislabeling of the archived photographs. The author has adhered to the designations as they exist in the archives. Courtesy of Lee Library Historical Collection.

Figure 7.16 Mountain Mill employees in a Lee parade in 1912. Photo on left taken by Ira Bissell. Photo on right taken by Ralph W. Smith. Courtesy of Lee Library Historical Collection.

Figure 7.17 Remains of the Benton & Garfield Mill, aka Benton Brothers Mill, aka Mountain Mill, aka Westfield River Mill as it appears now on Forest Street.

In 1844, Charles Fenerty, working in Canada, and Friedrich Gottlob Keller, in Germany, simultaneously reported the successful manufacture of paper from wood pulp. It was in 1867, that Lee's Columbia Mill was one of the first paper mills anywhere to produce commercially viable paper from wood.[65] While the rapid migration from rags to wood for paper production opened up new sources of raw materials, it also hastened the end of the Berkshire paper industry. Paper mills already were consuming copious amounts of lumber to build their mills, fuel their steam engines, and heat their factories, and now they also required lumber as raw material for actual paper production. Just as paper mills had previously outgrown their rag supply, they soon outgrew their dwindling supply of wood.

Excessive lumbering in the Berkshire forests was not the only cause of deforestation. A fungus known as *Cryphonectria parasitica* arrived in America in the early 1900s by way of imported shrubs from Japan. This fungus led to the "Chestnut Blight" beginning in 1910 and quickly destroyed four billion chestnut trees in the United States. Even today, this fungus prevents chestnut trees from reaching maturity. Scientific research is ongoing at the American Chestnut Foundation to create a genetically modified chestnut tree resistant to this fungus.

In response to the local deforestation, coal filled the fuel need for a while, delivered by rail lines through a local coal yard named Hull & Dresser. Nevertheless, most of Lee's paper mills ceased operations by 1885, ending the brief, but glorious story of Papertown, USA.

Stone foundations of these mills, along with many smaller stone dams, can still be seen standing astride the Goose Pond stream, and remain as silent testaments to Lee's legacy of papermaking prowess, back when it was responsible for 25% of all paper manufactured in the United States (and for thirteen feet of Goose Pond's current depth).

Figure 7.18 Foundations of old paper mills and dams on the Goose Pond stream.

Today, as we travel up Forest Street to Goose Pond, we pass by, on our right side, the green, decaying remains of the now abandoned 1858 Mountain Mill (aka Greenwood Mill, aka Hemlock Mill, aka Benton Brothers Mill, aka Mountain Mill 2.0, aka Lake May Power, aka Westfield River Mill). However decrepit and sad this lingering industrial remnant may appear, it should nevertheless serve as a powerful reminder of what had been the signature industry here in the Berkshire Mountains, especially in the town of Lee, and particularly right here on the Goose Pond stream, an industry that provided paper for citizens all over America, and also had profound, and enduring effects on the Goose Pond we know and love.

October Sunrise on Lower Goose

CHAPTER 8

THE DAM

*I*T WAS CHILLY AND DARK at 5:30 a.m. on April 20, 1886, a Tuesday, when the dam on Mud Pond in East Lee suddenly failed. (See Figure 1.1) Icy floodwaters gushed into Greenwater Stream in East Lee, drowning seven sleeping citizens in their beds, their names listed officially as Mr. A.N. White (48), Mrs. A.N. White (43), their two daughters Alice (9) and Ida (11), along with Simeon Dowd (60), Mrs. Theodore King (50), and Mrs. Charles King (20).[66] The more fortunate, but surely bereaved, son of the devastated White family survived by climbing a tree. Along with these tragic human losses, the flood resulted in extensive destruction of East Lee homes, mills, and businesses.

Figure 8.1 *Mud Pond dam after its failure, 1886.*
Courtesy of Lee Library Historical Collection.

Later that year, Edward S. Rogers published an exhaustive investigation of this devastating dam failure in *A Complete Account of the Terrible Disaster at East Lee, On Tuesday, April 20th, 1886*. Included in that book is a chapter about the nearby Goose Pond dam, which he determined to be sound, in which he wrote the excerpt seen in Figure 8.2[67].

We will shortly learn that, in 1886 when Rogers wrote this report, Goose Pond's dam had been built forty-seven years earlier in 1839. According to Rogers, this 1839 dam had itself been constructed directly on top of an even older dam that was twelve feet wide and built seventy-five years before that, which would have been circa 1764 (when we were a British colony), and then strengthened (and/or raised) in circa 1799 (when we weren't). The original 1764 dam had been built for a single sawmill on the Goose Pond stream and raised the water level by only eighteen inches.

Mills build dams to gain control over their source of hydropower. Water flow through streams can fluctuate widely during seasonal changes, as well as periods of drought or heavy rainfall. By placing a dam at a stream's source, mill owners gain control of the water flow and also the opportunity to store excess water in the millpond for use during dry seasons. In 1839, Edward and

> When the present dam was built it was not thought best to disturb the foundation already laid, which was of huge boulders deeply and firmly imbedded, so that the foundations have undoubtedly been in place at least 75 years and the upper portion of the dam about 40 years. The bottom of the stone work was made 12 feet wide, but some time after it was built the owners fancied they saw a slight bilge on one end and accordingly it was faced with another wall 12 feet wide, also of large heavy mountain stone. When the dam was repaired a few years later an opening in the wall was made a short distance from the rear and a row of long, heavy planks were driven down and tightly fitted. The wooden tube, 40 feet in length, which furnishes the outlet was also puddled and cemented so that the dam is water tight. There was some talk a few years ago of replacing the wooden tube by an iron one and estimates were secured, but for some unacountable reason the project was not

Figure 8.2 Excerpt from A Complete Account of the Terrible Disaster at East Lee, On Tuesday, April 20, 1886, *by Edward S. Rogers, describing the origins of the Goose Pond dam.*

Sylvester May collaborated with other Goose Pond paper mill owners to enlarge the small twelve-foot wide dam already on the pond, thereby increasing Goose Pond's water level by thirteen feet and prompting a shortlived change in the lake's name to "Lake May."[68][69]

The May brothers soon thereafter purchased the lone, original sawmill (from 1764) and converted it to their Middle Mill, which can be seen on maps to be located about 1/3 mile from the bottom of the Lake May stream.[70] While the May brothers' dam underwent other modifications over the years, these have been limited to enhancing the dam's strength and safety, without any further increase in the lake's water level.

Rogers also wrote another passage, also in relation to the Goose Pond's 1839 dam construction, solving yet another little mystery, this one surrounding the origins of Sucker Brook:

> was formerly called, is in reality two large ponds, the lower being a mile and a half long and three fourths of a mile wide. The upper pond is something over half a mile in length. The two had no visible natural connection but a small opening was made to augment the supply from the lower pond. Formerly the power was used only for driving a saw mill at the mouth of the pond and the water could not be drawn more than a few inches. The land in the vicinity was

Figure 8.3 Excerpt from A Complete Account of the Terrible Disaster at East Lee, On Tuesday, April 20th, 1886, *by Edward S. Rogers, describing how Goose Pond was originally two distinct ponds with no visible natural connection and that a "small opening" (i.e. Sucker Brook) was manually dug when the dam was enlarged in 1839, thereby significantly increasing the volume of water stored behind the dam. Without the dam, Sucker Brook – which is much shallower than thirteen feet – would even today be completely dry.*

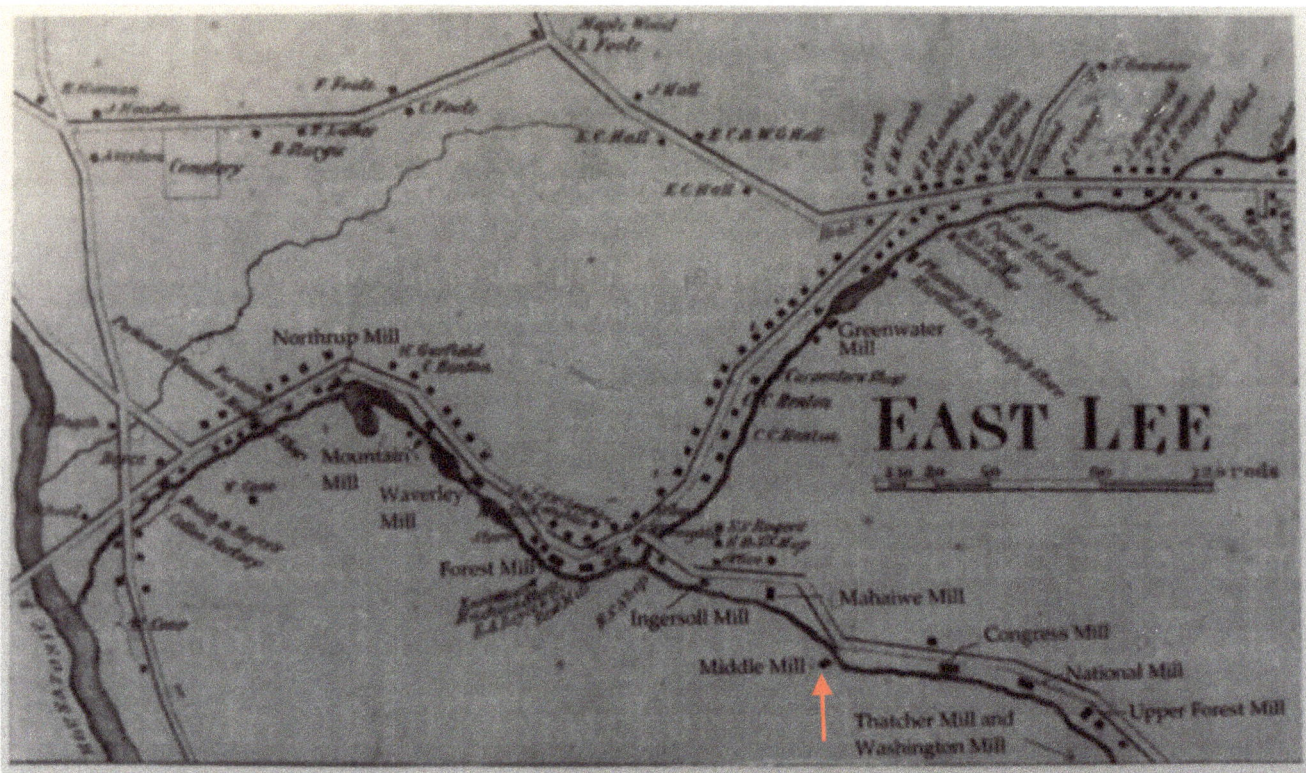

Map of East Lee, Mass., depicting paper mills. This region had the highest concentration of paper mills in the nation prior to 1860 (adapted from Henry F. Walling County Map of Berkshire County, Massachusetts, Smith, Gallup & Co., publishers, 1858).

Figure 8.4 Map of East Lee showing the location of the Middle Mill (red arrow). The Middle Mill is known to have replaced the original eighteenth-century sawmill, which was not truly "at the mouth of the pond" but instead located 1/3 mile from the bottom of the Goose Pond Stream. The owners of this original sawmill built the first dam on Goose Pond in the late 1700's. Modified, from Henry F. Walling County Map of Berkshire County, Massachusetts, Smith, Gallup & Co. publishers, 1858.

Although the 1886 Rogers investigation had affirmed the safety of Goose Pond's dam, sudden rumors of its impending failure nevertheless prompted a local scare in 1887 — a scare put to rest when inspections once again confirmed the dam's soundness.[71] But Goose Pond's dam did come close to actual failure during the Great Hurricane of 1938, a catastrophic Category 5 hurricane, which devastated New England. During this massive storm, the rapidly rising waters of Goose Pond overwhelmed the dam's limited spillway, ate a sixteen-foot diameter hole in the wall of the dam, and led to the evacuation of over 100 people downstream of the dam. Fortunately, emergency repairs by sixty workers were successful in restoring the dam's integrity.[72] The spillway was subsequently enlarged and lined with concrete.

The failed Mud Pond dam was rebuilt in 1965, and the lake's name changed, temporarily as it turns out, to Lake Lee, all for the purpose of a planned residential development. It was not to be. On March 24, 1968, the Mud Pond/Lake Lee dam failed yet again, this time with two fatalities: Edward Gage and Olive Cordonirer, whose East Lee homes were caught in yet another flood. An investigation revealed serious deficiencies in this dam's construction and non-conformity to the engineering plan. Plaintiffs won a major lawsuit. The Lake Lee dam was never rebuilt.[73][74] The lake was renamed, once again, this time to Basin Pond, which can now be —quite safely— explored on a lovely hiking trail maintained by the Berkshire Natural Resources Council.

From 1839 to 1992, Goose Pond's dam was owned and operated by an ever-changing set of industrial entities related to the paper mills and hydroelectric power plant on the Goose Pond stream. During these years, lake levels varied widely at the whim of these mills, a source of consternation for lakeside residents. In 1992, the Lake May Power plant and its associated Westfield Paper Mill ceased operation and sought to abandon the dam, which would have resulted in the dam's destruction and a thirteen-foot drop in the Pond's water level.

Concerned about the loss of the dam, lakeside homeowners formed the Save Goose Pond Association and explored their options. This effort led to the official formation of the Goose Pond Maintenance District (GPMD), which was officially established by the Massachusetts State Legislature as a "municipal overlay". After the several years of complicated, and often contentious, negotiation that followed, the GPMD ultimately acquired ownership of the dam on October 1, 1997, receiving the deed, at the cost of one dollar, from the Lake May Power Company.

The GPMD, financially supported by the taxation of several hundred Goose Pond-adjacent property owners, currently provides for dam oversight, control over water flow, periodic safety inspections, insurance, and emergency action plans as required by the Commonwealth. Regulators required that the GPMD undertake certain dam improvements including the expansion of the overflow spillway and making the downstream face of the dam less steep, with much of the cost covered by a grant from the Commonwealth. This work was completed in 2000.[75]

Figure 8.5 *Spillway on Goose Pond's dam in 1938. The great hurricane of 1938 overwhelmed this spillway and threatened the dam's failure. The spillway was later enlarged and lined with concrete. Courtesy of Lee Library Historical Collection.*

Figure 8.6 *Downstream face of Goose Pond's dam, in the 1960s. Note how steep is the downstream face's vertical drop in the 1960s. Courtesy of Bruce Walton.*

Berkshire County and state officials walk across the Goose Pond dam in Tyringham last week. The Goose Pond Maintenance District now has ownership of the dam.

Figure 8.7 *Downstream face of Goose Pond's dam in 1994. Notice the extremely vertical face of stones at that time, which has since been made more sloped. From The Berkshire Eagle, 1994. Courtesy of Tyringham Historical Commission.*

Figure 8.8 *Upstream face and control house of the current Goose Pond dam.*

Figure 8.9 *Downstream face of current Goose Pond dam. Notice how the vertical stone face seen in 1994 has since been modified into a more gradual slope.*

Figure 8.10 *Goose Pond Maintenance District sign on the Goose Pond dam. Sign designed by Tim Puntin.*[76]

The dam currently measures 287 feet in length, rises twenty-seven feet above its outlet pipe, and raises Goose Pond's water level by about fifteen feet. Regulators have classified the dam as a "large dam", based on the volume of water behind it and the resultant downstream flood risk. An annual six-foot drawdown each autumn is mandated by regulators to protect the dam's integrity during winter months when the Pond's frozen surface would prevent lake lowering to occur. Ongoing scientific and regulatory analyses at the University of Massachusetts might lead to a future reduction in this seasonal drawdown to as little as three feet because of the impact of lake drawdowns on marine life and climate change. The dam's management is overseen by several agencies, including the Massachusetts Department of Conservation and Recreation, the Massachusetts Office of Dam Safety, as well as Lee and Tyringham Conservation Commissions. It undergoes a safety inspection every two years.

It is interesting to consider our dam as a giant device designed for the storage of *potential* energy, and with the ability to convert this into the *kinetic* energy needed by dozens of downstream paper mills and hydroelectric plants. Upper and Lower Goose Ponds together cover 324 acres. Because our dam elevates the water level by about fifteen feet, this would translate to the dam holding back 4280 acre-feet (1.4 billion gallons) of water. With the knowledge that our dam stores this 1.4 billion gallons of water at a height of 500 feet above the valley, we can roughly calculate that the dam holds back the equivalent power of 2.2 gigawatt-hours of electricity.[77]

One way to understand this energy is to remember that Doc Brown's DeLorean Time Machine, in the movie *Back to the Future, Part II*, reportedly required 1.2 gigawatts to travel through time. A less fanciful way to understand this is to imagine the dam's total power storage as *one hour's output* from any one of the following: 5.5 million solar panels, or 682 utility-level wind turbines, or 2.86 million galloping horses.[78]

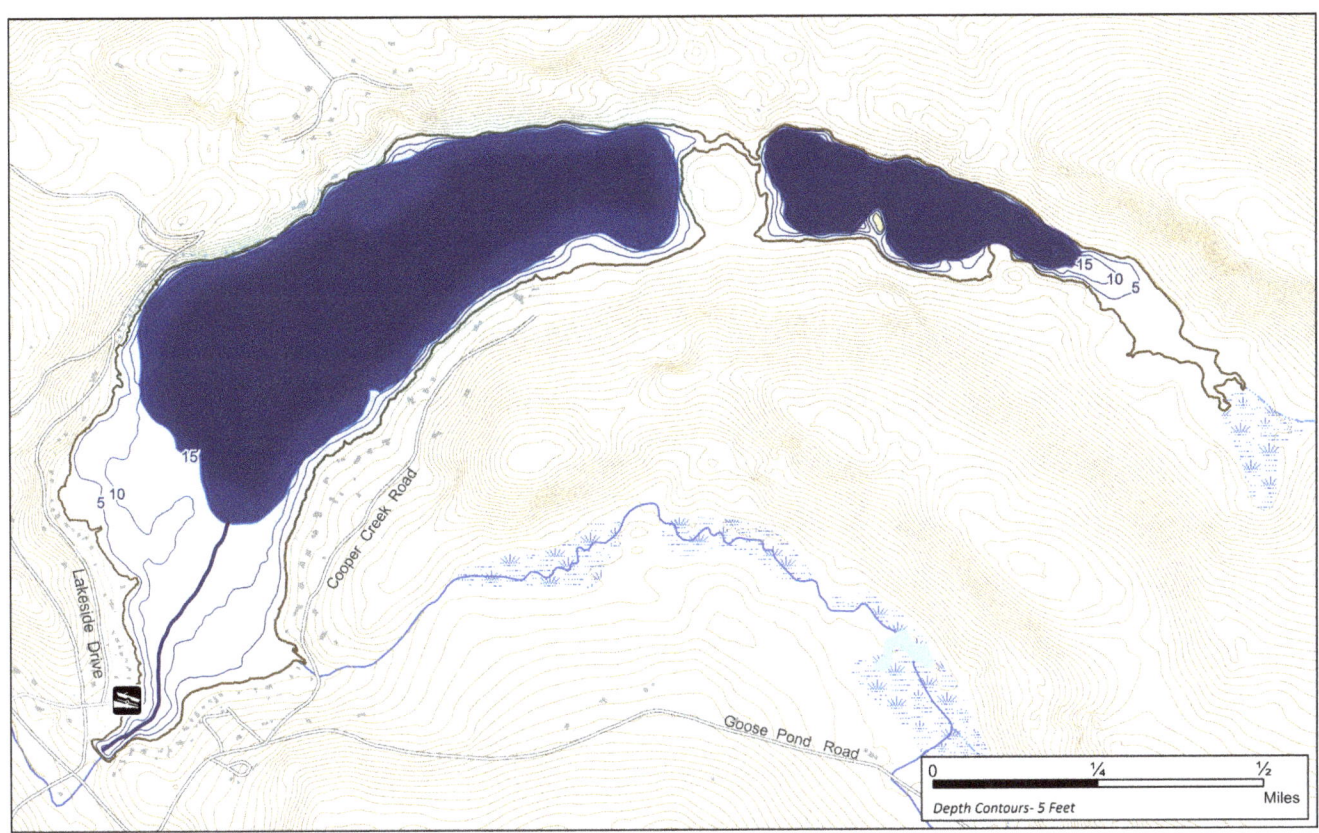

Figure 8.11 *A common question is what Goose Pond would look like without its dam. The solid blue area indicates the shape and size of Goose Pond if its water level was lowered by fifteen feet in the absence of any dam. Note that Sucker Brook would be dry and the two ponds disconnected. The redrawn blue line connecting the smaller Lower Goose to the location of the current dam represents the hypothetical course of the Pond's draining stream in the absence of the dam. Modified, courtesy of the Commonwealth of Massachusetts, Division of Fisheries and Wildlife.*

Mountain Laurel on Lower Goose

CHAPTER 9

LAKE MAY POWER

*A*LL THAT REMAINS TODAY of the storied Lake May Power company is a small, classically proportioned brick building, now standing empty, abandoned, and mostly roofless. It is set back a bit from Route 20 in East Lee, by the base of the Goose Pond stream, and still displaying an engraving on its stone lintel reading, "Lee Plant - Tayford Company."

Figure 9.1 *Lintel over Tayford Company / Lake May Power building.*

We can trace the origins of Lake May Power back to its formative meeting, held on Monday, August 26, 1895, attended by "capitalists", owners of several mills on the Lake May stream, electrical experts, and engineers. The meeting's attendees agreed to procure water rights to the Lake May stream and to form a stock company with the goal of constructing a hydroelectric plant on the Lake May stream.[79]

> **LAKE MAY POWER FOR LEE, MASS.**
>
> A special dispatch of Aug. 26 from Lee, Mass., says: The initiative steps are being taken by parties interested to procure the water privileges on the Lake May stream, form a stock company and put in a $75,000 electric power plant that will run some 18 or 20 mills and factories in Central Berkshire. The following firms are interested: Smith Paper Company, Eaton, May & Robbins Paper Company, Hurlbut Paper Manufacturing Company, and the following paper firms: Benton Bros., G. K. Baird & Bro., Eaton, Dikeman & Co., Forest Mills, and the other investors are Clark & Spencer's, Dowd's and McLaughlin Machine Shops, and a number of smaller flour, wire and shoddy firms. The scheme is somewhat novel, and has not been tried in New England before, though it has worked successfully in Nevada and California. The lake, which is high in the mountains, is to be drawn through a conduit 18 inches at the beginning and 4 inches wide at the foot of the mountain. It will be a little over two miles long, and by the connection of a Pelton water wheel and electric machinery is expected to give a horse power exceeding 3,000, or sufficient to run all the mills within a radius of 10 miles, the power being transferred, of course, by wire.
>
> The scheme will furnish power at one-quarter the present cost per horse power to the paper industries of the western part of the State, which are at present somewhat handicapped, because of the shortage of water in summer, and the excessive charges of freighting coal. The charges on coal are much higher than in any part of the State east of Springfield, and even in the north part of Berkshire the price is $1.50 per ton less.
>
> A meeting of the capitalists has been held, and the scheme laid before them by Mr. Upton, an electric expert, and a committee consisting of G K. Baird, A. W. Eaton and E. S. Rogers was appointed to see what could be done with the present owners of mill privileges on the stream. Mr. Upton says it is the only location in the State where an almost direct fall of 600 feet can be obtained, and it will be a boon to the manufacturing interests of Western Massachusetts.

Figure 9.2 Description of the formative meeting of the Goose Pond hydroelectric power plant. From The Electrical Engineer, *September 11, 1895.*

With an expenditure of $150,000, which was twice the cost anticipated in 1895, the Tayford Company, of New York, built the Lee power plants in 1920, a time when many other small hydroelectric plants around the country had already ceased their operations because of prohibitive economic pressures largely arising from their expensive staffing requirements. However, the designers of the Lee plants, civil engineers Henry Taylor of New York and Arthur Palme of Pittsfield, avoided these financial challenges by including newer methods of automation and by integrating with local grids.

These innovations were explained in the March 25, 1922 issue of *Electrical World* (bracketed content added):

"These economic obstacles can be removed to a great extent...by installing automatic induction-generator stations and tying them in with a larger station or system. Recently a

practical application of this suggestion has been made by the Tayford Company, Inc near Lee, Mass, where two induction-generator stations are interconnected with the Lee and Pittsfield service systems…A watershed with a total area of about 15 square miles is utilized, the two generating plants operating under gross heads [vertical water drop distance] *of 437 feet and 68 feet. The former or main head is associated with a pond* [Goose Pond/Lake May] *representing 225 days of storage, and the latter head [lower plant] is utilized below the first station and in hydraulic series with it."*[80]

Tayford Company's Lee hydroelectric project involved the construction of, not one, but two adjacent power plants, working in series, and receiving their waterpower from the fifteen-square-mile combined watersheds of Goose, Greenwater, and Mud (now Basin) Ponds.

The larger, upper plant, whose brick building still stands, received only the water draining from Goose Pond. The Goose Pond stream's flow was first subjected to an "intercepting dam", which can still be seen by the side of Forest Street, at the Lee-Tyringham border. From this intercepting dam was run a 7300-foot long, 24–28-inch diameter, machine-wound, wooden penstock (i.e. pipe) which dropped 437 vertical feet to the larger power plant. Remnants of this penstock can still be found in the woods surrounding the stream. The water entering this upper plant turned three 350hp Pelton waterwheels which, in turn, powered three 300hp General Electric induction generators which ran at 600 RPM and generated 2,300 volts of electricity.

After first powering the generators in the upper power plant, the water would then drain into a small holding pond, which also received the additional water flowing out of Greenwater and Mud (Basin) Ponds. The combined water from all three ponds would then enter a second penstock, this one measuring forty-two inches in diameter, 1650 feet long, dropping sixty-eight vertical feet, and leading to the lower, smaller power plant, therein powering its two 200-hp wicket-gate-type turbines, each connected to a 200-hp induction generator. The electrical output from these two plants was interconnected with the Lee and Pittsfield electrical service systems.

Figure 9.3 *Tayford Company main power plant building in 1922 (left) and in 2023 (right). The 1922 photograph is courtesy of Lee Library Historical Collection.*

Figure 9.4 *Remains of the Tayford Company/Lake May Power "intercepting dam" seen today beside Forest Street at the Tyringham-Lee town line.*

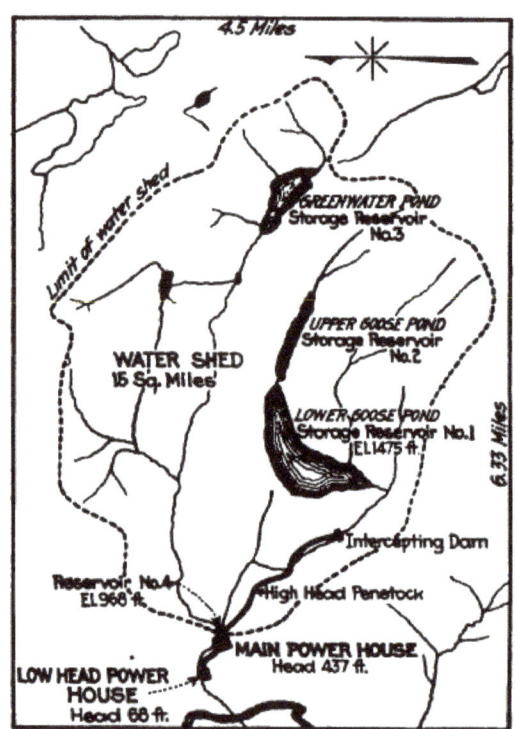

Figure 9.5 *The fifteen-square-mile watershed of Tayford Company included Lower Goose Pond (Storage Reservoir No. 1), Upper Goose Pond (Storage Reservoir No. 2), Greenwater Pond (Storage Reservoir No. 3), and Mud Pond (unlabeled). From* Electrical World, *March 25, 1922.*

In 1922, the paired Tayford plants could be operated by a single on-duty mechanic working alone. The day shift mechanic worked 10 a.m. to noon, 1:30 to 6 p.m., and 7 p.m. to 10:30 p.m. The night shift mechanic worked from midnight to 8:30 a.m. The two plants would run without any attention during the mechanic's breaks. A general supervisor was available on call as needed. Labor costs, in 1922, were only $2500/year. The enhanced automation and efficient staffing requirements of the Tayford plant overcame many of the challenges faced by other hydroelectric plants, providing for its technically successful and financially sound operation for seventy-three years.

Figure 9.6 *Corresponding photographs of the interior of Tayford Company, in 1922 (on left) and in 2023 (on right). Older photographs are from* Electrical World, *March 25, 1922.*

Figure 9.7 *Interior of the smaller lower plant at Tayford Company (1922) (left). Remains of bridge across from the East Lee Package Store, likely originally built to access the lower Tayford Power Plant (right). 1922 photo is from* Electrical World, *March 25, 1922.*

Lake May Power took over the Tayford Company's Lee plant in 1926 and operated it continuously until 1993. In 1941, the plant had a generator capacity of 900kW, an annual production of 966,100 kWh, and one customer (which was presumably the Mountain Mill)[81]. In 1968, the power plant had a generator capacity of 700kW and an average annual production of 1,800,000 kWh of electricity.[82] At our current electrical rates ($0.35/kWh) the annual revenue from this plant today would be $630,000.

During the years of the power plant's operation, the residents on Goose Pond contended unhappily, and quite helplessly, with dramatic changes in the lake's water level, experiencing severe flooding alternating with marked receding of the shoreline. When we think about a dam, common sense would understandably lead most of us to assume that water flow through it would typically be increased during rainy seasons and reduced during drier conditions. However, in real life, common sense doesn't always rule the day, and it didn't here either.

Because Lake May Power owned Goose Pond's dam and had firmly established its legal rights to the water stored behind it, it could exercise complete control over the flow rates through the dam. Embedded in the design of these two linked plants was an unusual water management paradigm: the flow through Goose Pond's dam would actually be *reduced* in rainy seasons and *increased* in drought conditions, a counter-intuitive regime that would clearly explain the exaggerated swings in water levels seen on the lake during the plant's years of operation.

This technical rationale for this unusual protocol is outlined in the 1922 *Electrical World* article (bracketed content added for clarity):

> *"During spring flows and after rainstorms a quick run-off is received from the lower shed [Greenwater and Mud Ponds] and is used at the lower-head [lower power] station. At such times this [lower power] station does the greater part of the work, the wheels at the high-head [upper power] plant being partly shut down [Goose Pond dam's flow reduced], thus saving water [flooding] in the ample storage [Goose Pond flooding] above. Under the reverse [drought] condition ... the high-head [upper power] station does most of the work, drawing on storage [opening Goose Pond dam]"*

Once the Lake May Power plant ceased its operations in 1993, life for residents on the Pond improved; the dam's flow rates, and hence the lake's water level, coming under the control of the Goose Pond Maintenance District. My father no longer needed his 2'x6's to reach the family barbeque.

After the plant's closing, the plant's machinery was salvaged by William K. Fay, of the French River Land Company, who described his salvage as follows:

> *"These machines come with three runners, three pelton cases, six bearings, six bearing pedestals, three pelton deflectors, three complete pelton nozzles, three high pressure valves, three high pressure pipe flanges, two Pelton and one Woodward governor, two induction*

Figure 9.8 *My father cooking on Pinepoint during a typical Goose Pond flood, c1972.*

generators, and one synchronous generator."[83] They appear to have inadvertently omitted listing the partridge in a pear tree.

It saddens me a little that the waters draining Goose, Greenwater, and Basin Ponds now flow freely into the Housatonic River without turning a single waterwheel or generating so much as a single watt of power. It seems a little wasteful these days, what with climate change and the cost of electricity. Generations before us understood something important that we appear now to have forgotten. Maybe someday the unused power of Goose Pond's water can once again be harnessed, for the good of the planet -- and our wallets.

Goose Pond Reservation

CHAPTER 10

THE HUCKLEBERRY TROLLEY LINE

$\mathcal{S}$HORTLY AFTER MAKING THE TURN onto Forest Street from Route 20 (in East Lee), on your right, you will see the Goose Pond stream flowing through a 1911 concrete trestle, and just past that on your left, remnants of a concrete wall on the side of the road. These are remains of the Huckleberry Line, a short-lived railroad trolley line running through East Lee and onto a railroad bridge over Forest Street and the Goose Pond stream, and then alongside Silver Street. The trolley line, running in an East-West direction, had stops in Lee, Becket, Otis, North Blanford, and Huntington.

Figure 10.1 *Huckleberry Trolley Line trestle over Forest Street being demolished after the line ceased operation. Courtesy of Lee Library Historical Collection.*

Figure 10.2 *Remnants of the Huckleberry Trolley trestle over Forest Street and the Goose Pond stream as they appear today (upper left and bottom). Some stairs climbing up the wall suggest that a train station may have existed here. Other remnants of the railroad can be seen as the visible railbed just north of Silver Street (not shown), as well as a large concrete retaining wall opposite the streambed south of Route 20 (upper right). Above the concrete retaining wall can be seen the path of the railbed (upper right, red arrows).*

In the early 1900s, before the widespread availability of the automobile, local farmers, workers, and students faced many unmet local transportation needs. Therefrom arose the plan to build a railroad trolley line starting in East Lee, proceeding along the side of Route 20 through Becket, Otis, Blandford, and finally to Huntington. The line was built by the Western Massachusetts Contracting Company for the Berkshire Street Railway, which was itself owned by the New York New Haven and Hartford Railroad. While the line's name was officially the "Springfield and Berkshire Street Railway" it soon became widely known as the "Huckleberry Line," a reflection of the abundant huckleberries that could be picked alongside the railway. Construction, involving 1,000 workers, was started on April 17, 1911, and the last spike was driven on November 29, 1913, at the cost of $3 million and sadly the lives of two workers.[84]

The beginning of operations on the finished trolley line was delayed for another four years because of anti-trust court battles enveloping its parent company, the New York New Haven and Hartford Railroad. The first through-trip on the line did not take place until 10:05 a.m. on August 15, 1917. From the day it started service, the trolley's schedules were poorly planned and inconvenient for the local population. A few months after starting, operations were briefly suspended because of the impact of World War I and then restored in April 1918. By the spring of 1919, towns serviced by the line refused to cover the line's $8000 operating deficit and the New York New Haven and Hartford Railroad subsequently declared the end of its obligation to the trolley line. A post-war labor strike in the fall of 1919 and then the increasingly widespread arrival of the automobile dealt the line's crippling blows. The rails were salvaged starting in 1920.

"The Huckleberry Trolley Line was a blunder of mammoth proportions, ambitiously conceived, laboriously built, and reluctantly operated for just two years. The Huckleberry Line can be seen as a pawn in the great national contests of the day."[85]

Figure 10.3 *First run of Huckleberry Line. The woman on the left is seen to be holding two buckets, likely full of the huckleberries often picked alongside the railbed. Courtesy of Western Mass Hilltown Hikers.*

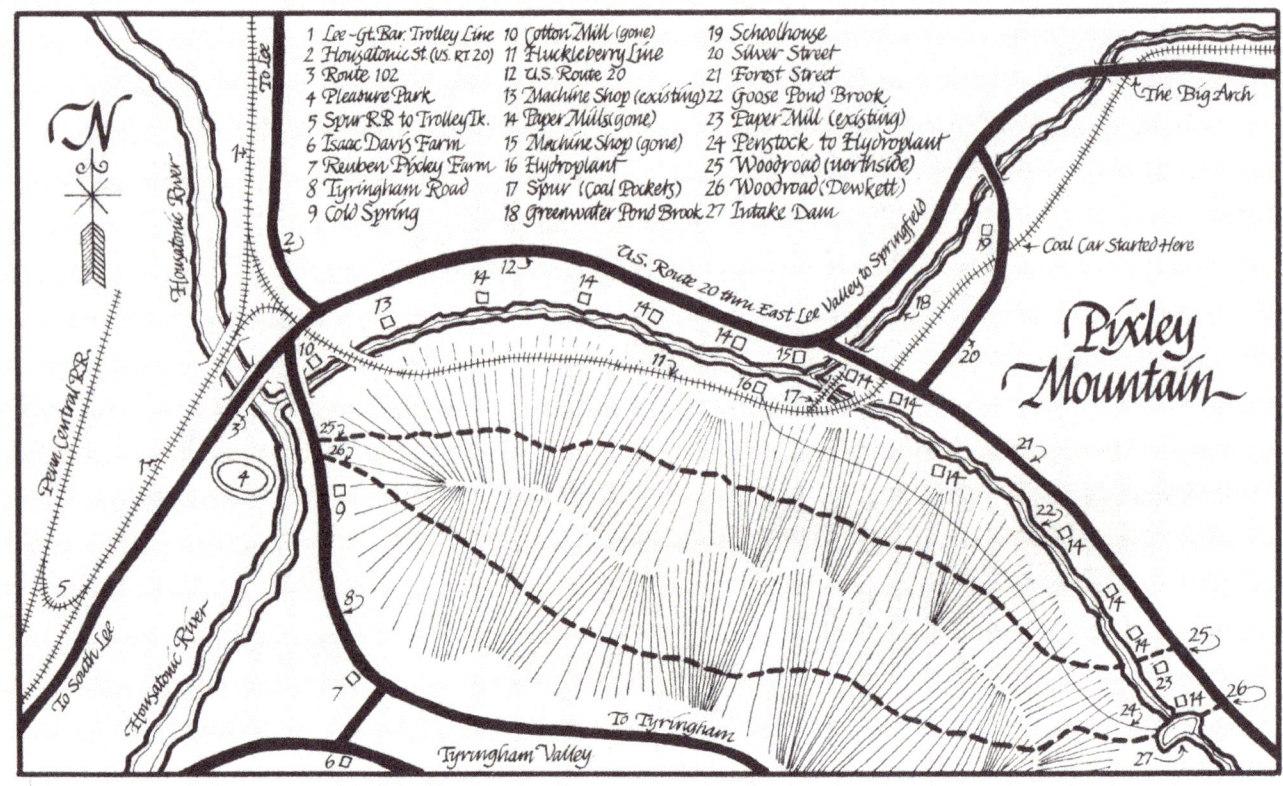

Figure 10.4 Illustration showing the route of the Huckleberry Trolley Line near the Goose Pond stream. From Three Thumbnails *by RW Smith. Courtesy of Flint Smith.*

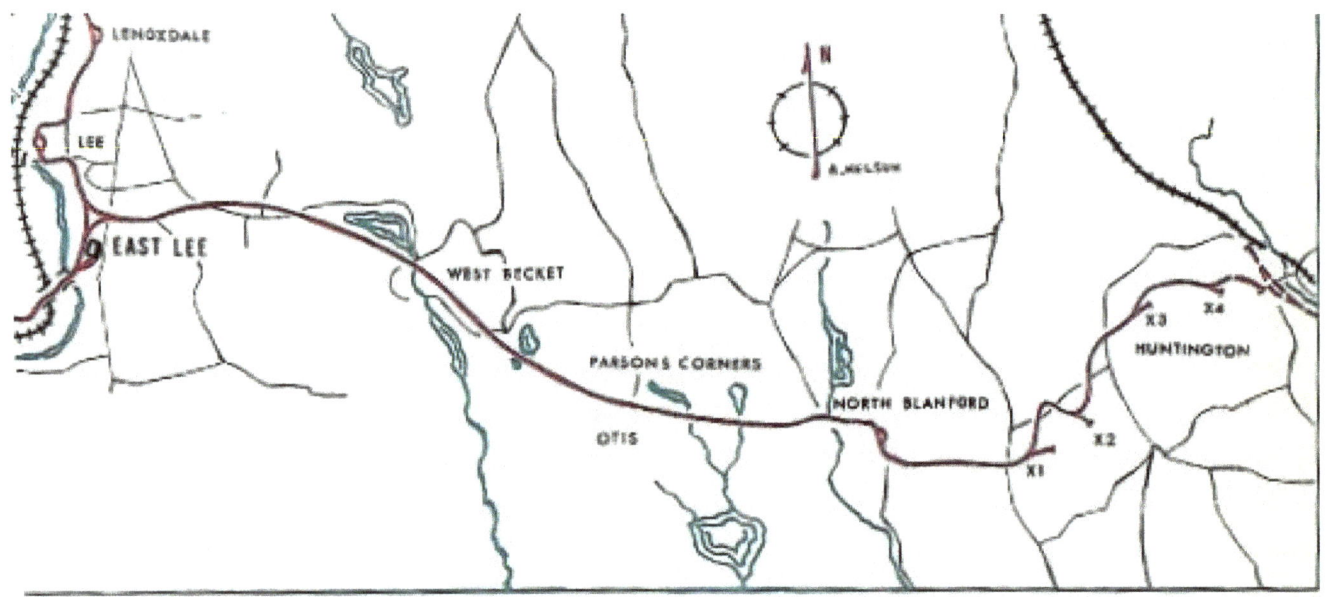

Figure 10.5 Huckleberry Line route. Courtesy of the Western Mass Hilltown Hikers.

LEE CENTER TO:	Miles	Hr.Min.	Fare
East Lee Junction	.69		
Jones' Crossing	2.51		.05
Chestnut Street siding	2.88		
Broga's Crossing	3.89		.10
Houston's Crossing	6.39		.15
Phelan Road	7.88		.20
Lincoln Road	10.25		.25
Newell Quarry, Becket	11.35		
Otis Substation	12.66	50	.30
Algeree Bridge	13.95		.35
Gibbs Farm			.40
North Blandford (Waite Pond)			.45
Lee's Farm			.50
North Street, Blandford	18.97		.55
Peck's Farm			.65
Ripley's Farm Road			.60
Lesage Road			.70
County Line			.75
Huntington Village	23.86	1 25	.80

Figure 10.6 Huckleberry Line fare schedule. Courtesy of the Western Mass Hilltown Hikers.

There is a funny little Huckleberry vignette — well, funny in hindsight anyway — described in great detail by RW Smith, in *Three Thumbnails*. The Mountain Mill, like many of the Lake May paper mills, would use Huckleberry trains to take coal deliveries. Two of this mill's employees, Charlie Vreeland and Charlie Jones, were tasked with unloading the coal from a Huckleberry coal car. This particular coal car had been mistakenly parked further up the hill on Silver Street than it should have been. Eager to avoid more work than was absolutely necessary, the two Charlies devised the plan of releasing the coal car's brake and letting the coal car glide down the rail closer to Forest Street, thus reducing the distance they needed to move the coal. But first, they had so strategically placed some railroad ties across the rails intended to halt the car exactly where they wanted it. Their ingenious plan did not work out as hoped, the coal car blowing right past their oh-so-clever railroad ties, quickly becoming a runaway rail car, speeding fully loaded and uncontrolled, down the hill into East Lee, following the track's sharp turn into Lee itself, derailing on Park Street, and finally crashing into a maple tree near the home of Mr. and Mrs. LeRoy Hubby as they were eating their lunch. There were no reported injuries except for the maple tree. It seems rather likely that the two Charlies were thereafter busy seeking alternative employment. [86]

Today, much of the old Huckleberry railbed has been added to the multi-use, recreational Housatonic Heritage Trail which stretches from the Connecticut border to Adams, Massachusetts.

Spring Ice Melt

CHAPTER 11

THE MACDARBY FARM

MONDAY, 22 FEBRUARY, 1932, was George Washington's Birthday. Joseph "Hooker" Moore, forty-two, was enjoying some afternoon coffee, warming himself by the wood stove, and gazing out of his window at Goose Pond, its frozen surface blinding in the bright winter sun. With the old MacDarby homestead perched on the gentle rise just above the lake's dam, Hooker's window had a commanding view of the lake, which, on this fateful morning revealed a strange, black column of smoke rising in the distance over Upper Goose Pond.

Born in Saugerties, New York, Joseph "Hooker" Moore (1890-1963) was the grandson of Michael MacDarby (1841-1890) and Hannah Cahalan MacDarby (1841-1920), both born in Ireland and the parents of at least nine children. After Michael and Hannah emigrated to the United States, Michael served in the Union Army during the Civil War. After the war had ended, they purchased a 175-acre plot of land in Tyringham on the northern shore of Lower Goose Pond, its 3,500 feet of waterfront extending from the dam to just past the Lee town line. They founded a dairy farm, widely known as the MacDarby Farm. For their large family of nine or more children – one of which was Hooker's mother Elizabeth, born in 1867 -- they built a ten-room farmhouse just above the dam, the first structure built on Lower Goose Pond. After Michael's death at the age of fifty-one, Hannah ran the farm for another thirty years. In the early 1900s, Rose MacDarby was the schoolteacher for the Lake May School District, holding her classes in the MacDarby home.[87]

Figure 11.1 MacDarby family in front of their farmhouse on Goose Pond. Courtesy of Tracie Schneyer.

Figure 11.2 MacDarby farmhouse. Courtesy of Tracie Schneyer.

Figure 11.3 Aerial photograph of MacDarby Farm and Lower Goose Pond in 1955, showing the MacDarby farmhouse (red arrow), the dam (green arrow), Pinepoint (yellow arrow) and construction of the Mass Pike (blue arrow). The clearing (white arrow) likely represents the extent of Chanter's "Snow Farm." The extent of the fields surrounding the MacDarby farmhouse indicates the size of their farm. Modified, courtesy of Pamela Margaret Haskell.

Hooker would later work as a steam engineer at the Mountain Mill, down the street, where he earned himself the nickname "Babe Ruth of steam-shovel operators."[88] When he wasn't busy excavating at major construction sites, he ran Goose Pond's only boat livery for fifteen years. The Moore Boat Livery, located at the spot occupied now by the public boat ramp, would provide its customers with one of his green, flat-bottom rowboats for a daily fee of fifty cents. By 1958, he had thirty boats available for rent as well as some nearby picnic tables (also for rent).

Figure 11.4 Hooker Moore with his rowboats at the Moore Boat Livery.
Courtesy of Pamela Margaret Haskell.

Figure 11.5 *Hooker Moore (right) with a nice day's catch. Courtesy of Pamela Margaret Haskell.*

So, on that frozen afternoon in 1932, Hooker found it curious to see that plume of black smoke rising from over Upper Goose Pond and felt inclined to investigate it further. There not being any roads to Upper Goose, he evidently considered it a good idea to drive his car over the ice to find the fire. Whether bringing his fourteen-year-old son Robert along for the ride was for the sake of his son's shared sense of adventure or to provide another pair of helping hands isn't clear. He also made the fateful decision to bring along his two dogs on the expedition. They never made it to the fire.

As their car reached the far end of Lower Goose, in the middle of the lake, with forty feet between the ice and the bottom, and just opposite the old Henry Smith cabin on the south shore, the car crashed through thin ice and dropped into the icy water below. Hooker managed to push Robert out of the car, along with one of the dogs, before the car submerged. Robert was dragged out of the icy water to safety by nearby ice fishermen who had formed a rescue chain. The car sank, front first, to the bottom, taking Hooker and his other dog down with it.

Trapped inside the car, with only a small air pocket near the roof, Hooker was unable to break the front window. He climbed into the back seat and was able to open a rear window and emerge from the car, along with his second dog, swimming up through forty feet of freezing water to the surface. Hooker was dragged to safety by the same ice fishermen who had rescued his son. Both dogs drowned. Hooker and Robert ran across the frozen lake to get home and warm up.[89]

Hooker and Robert were treated for exposure by Dr. George Wickham. However, Hooker subsequently developed blood poisoning from an infection on his right arm, was hospitalized at St. Luke's Hospital in Pittsfield, and underwent surgery by Dr. John A. Sullivan. Penicillin had not yet been discovered, so Dr. Sullivan must have been an ace surgeon because Hooker recovered. What Hooker regretted most from the whole incident was that he had lost his treasured Elk's Lodge button, which had been torn from his vest during the sinking.

A week after Hooker's car sank, an East Lee garageman named Arthur Dewkett attempted a salvage operation to retrieve it from the lakebed using "a rigging of blocks and tackles and huge poles"[90] Dewkett, apparently undeterred by any rational fear of the thin ice, successfully erected his rig around the ice hole and somehow attached his large grappling hooks to the submerged car. He must have been quite excited as he raised the car fifteen feet above the bottom, but his excitement quickly evaporated when the hooks gave way. Dewkett subsequently made some improvements to his rig, with the intention of making a second salvage attempt, but thin ice and high winds evidently prohibited any further efforts.

Figure 11.6 *Montage of newspaper headlines relating to the sunken Moore car in 1932. Clockwise from upper left:*
The Berkshire Eagle *February 23, 1932;* The Berkshire Evening Eagle *March 7, 1932;*
The Berkshire Eagle *March 1, 1932;* The Berkshire Eagle *February 29, 1932;*
The Berkshire Evening Eagle *March 7, 1932 (center);* The Berkshire Gleaner *March 4, 1932;*
The Berkshire County Eagle *February 24, 1932.*

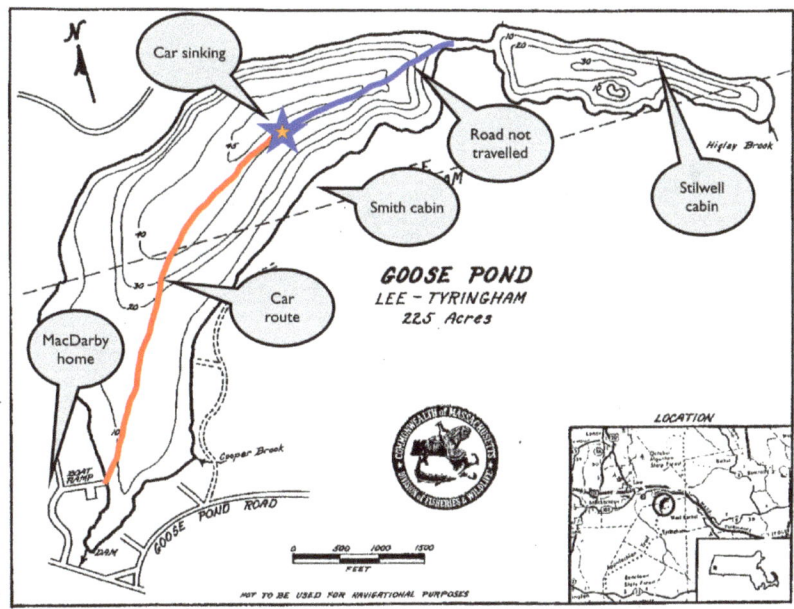

Figure 11.7 *Postulated route (solid red line) of Hooker's car on the Goose Pond ice and approximate location of its sinking (blue star). According to newspaper stories, the sinking occurred in 35-40 feet of water, directly offshore from the "Henry Smith" cabin, and in "the middle of the lake." The car's route strongly suggests that Moore was headed for the channel to Upper Goose Pond (blue line). Modified, courtesy of the Massachusetts Division of Fisheries and Wildlife.*

Now I have always assumed that operations by the United States Navy were generally confined to ocean waters and always with the purpose of ensuring national security, but it appears there can be exceptions or at least maybe one exception. There was, in fact, a United States Navy operation on Goose Pond, and, judging from the photographs of this operation, it probably occurred in the 1930s. Since these photographs were discovered in the possession of Hooker's family, it is likely that the photographs were taken by Hooker himself or his family. Everything suggests that the expedition was an attempted naval salvage of his sunken car.

The photographs show a U.S. Navy truck and Hooker himself near his dock, several uniformed sailors, some uniformed officers, a towed raft laden with what appeared to be equipment suitable for an underwater salvage operation, and a navy diver in a diving suit complete with air hose ready to leap from the raft into Goose Pond.

Figure 11.8 *Truck at the Goose Pond boat ramp with "U.S. Navy" emblazoned on the door. Courtesy Pamela Margaret Haskell.*

Figure 11.9 Hooker Moore (standing on dock) with sailors preparing their raft.
Courtesy of Pamela Margaret Haskell.

Figure 11.10 U.S. Navy sailors preparing raft on Lower Goose Pond ramp.
Courtesy of Pamela Margaret Haskell.

Figure 11.11 Navy diver getting prepared for dive into Lower Goose Pond. Courtesy of Pamela Margaret Haskell.

A careful study of the background topography, in these photographs, confirms that the Navy dive operation itself took place near the center of Lower Goose, in about forty feet of water, and directly offshore where the old Henry Smith cabin was located. This is precisely where Hooker's car was reported to have sunken. It would appear that Hooker managed to convince the United States Navy that it was in the national security interests of the United States of America to get his sunken car out of Goose Pond.

Figure 11.12 A review of the background topography (red outline) in the diver photograph (left) matches the unique background topography on Lower Goose Pond as seen from the likely location of the Moore car sinking (right). The water depth at this location is 35-40 feet, also corresponding to Hooker's account of the location of the sinking. It therefore appears likely that the Navy operation was aimed at salvage of the sunken car. Left photo, courtesy of Pamela Margaret Haskell.

Certainly, a small raft would not have adequate buoyancy for the lifting of a sunken car, so perhaps the plan was to cable the car to a shoreline tree and winch it to shore. I don't know the Navy's plan, nor if any salvage was actually successful, but I would have expected that a successful operation would have been memorialized with some prize photographs of a recovered car, or at least some newspaper stories, neither of which have surfaced. A recent search of historical archives of the U.S. Navy for any records of this operation was unsuccessful. I think it likely the car still rests on the bottom of Goose Pond.

The allure of sunken treasure, and the irresistible drive to search for it, runs deep in human history. While a Chevy or Oldsmobile submerged for almost one hundred years may not rank up there with Blackbeard's Treasure, treasure hunters have to take what they can get. Accordingly, we carried out a detailed sonar map of the lakebed over the area thought likely to encompass the site of our sunken treasure. The sonar findings were largely featureless and flat with only a few local elevations suggesting a possible sunken car close to shore. With the quest for sunken treasure still running strong, we launched a scuba expedition in the areas of interest, sending our fearless diver into thirty-five feet of pitch black, fifty-five-degree water, only to find a mostly featureless lakebed, a few large rocks, and some shells. Perhaps a broader search area and a stronger underwater light will someday be more successful.

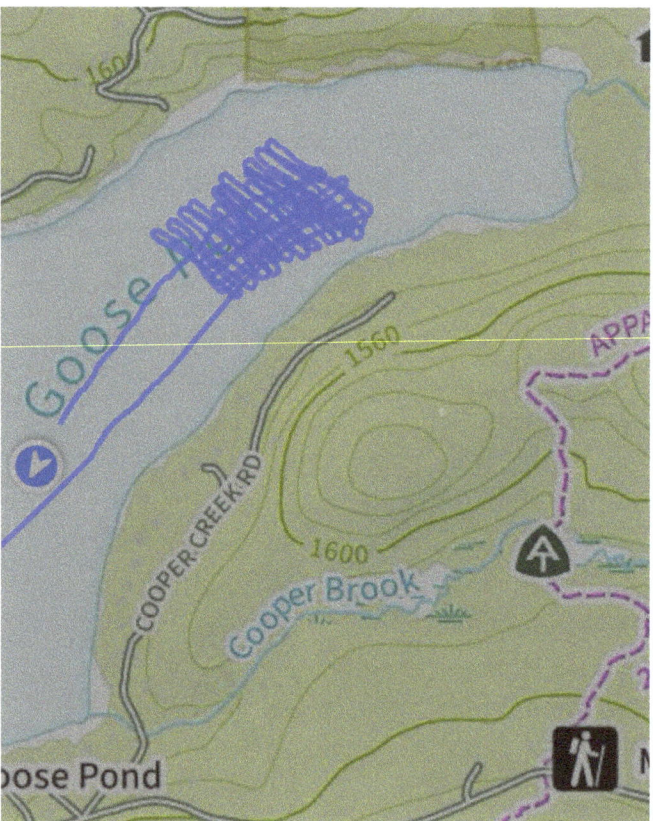

Figure 11.13 *Map tracing the location of our sonar survey done to search for Hooker's car. Only a few signals suggesting a possible sunken care were identified and a scuba investigation of these areas found only large rocks. It is entirely possible that the car is by now covered in silt, undetectable by sonar, and invisible to divers. Modified, from Topo-Maps. Courtesy of Roger Brown.*

Broken ice, a sunken car, a brazen rescue, a nearly frozen father and son, two drowned dogs, a U.S. Navy operation, a case of blood poisoning, a surgical procedure, a lost Elk's Lodge button, and a scuba expedition over a hundred years later, are all events arising purely from some smoke rising from Upper Goose Pond. Despite the havoc caused by this smoke, or perhaps because of it, no one at the time seemed at all curious about the culprit smoke's origins. Historical records do not indicate any cabins burning down nor any forest fires on that day. However, it turns out that the Stilwell family kept a meticulously maintained guest logbook for their Upper Goose Pond camp dating back to the day their cabins were built. Their logbook does in fact offer an answer to the smoke Hooker had seen. An entry on February 22, 1932, the very day Hooker's car broke through the ice:

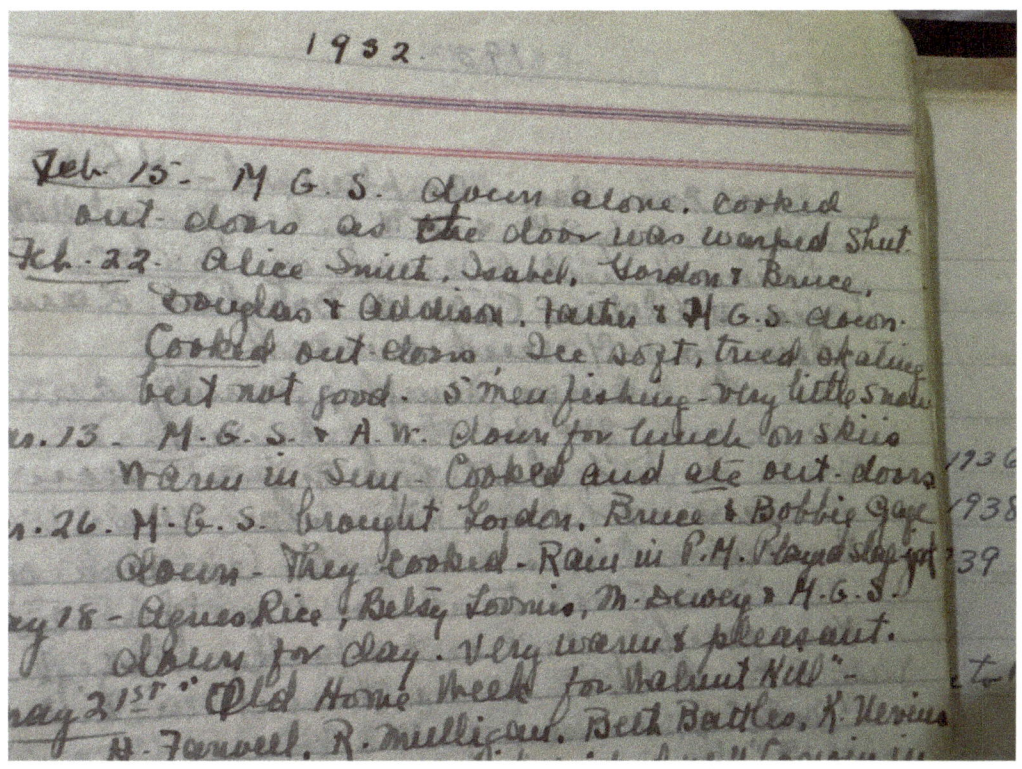

Figure 11.14 An entry for February 22, 1932, in the Stilwell cabin guestbook, corresponding to the date of the sinking of Moore's car, recorded an outdoor cookout — a cookout which likely produced the very smoke that lured Hooker out on the ice that fateful day and led to all the subsequent events. The Stilwells and their guests evidently never learned of the chaos that resulted from their afternoon cookout. (And Hooker, it appears, was not the only person to experience soft ice that day.) Courtesy of David Stilwell.

In 1958, the MacDarby Farm was sold to the Goose Lake Development Company, which intended to subdivide it into residential lots. Hooker, who was then retired to Florida, decided that same year to purchase back the 4.8 lakefront acres with his old farmhouse, move back into the house, and re-open his boat livery for a few more years. The rest of the land was subdivided and became the Lakeside Drive neighborhood that stretches today from the boat ramp to the Lee town line.

After Hooker's passing in 1963, his son Robert, who inherited, among other things, the nickname "Hooker", lived on the old MacDarby-Moore property in a small trailer for several

Figure 11.15 Newspaper advertisement (unknown year) for "Moore's Boat Livery." Hooker's son, Bob Moore was then the proprietor, after taking over the livery following his father's passing in 1963. The "Sandwich and Cold Drink Stand" was called the "Chuck Wagon." Courtesy of Pamela Margaret Haskell.

years, and outside his trailer hung a sign which read "Hooker." Hooker Jr. had been a fighter pilot in the Army Air Corps during World War Two, completing sixty-five missions and 870 combat hours. Robert continued to operate the livery service, augmented by the addition of a lakeside trailer he named "Chuck Wagon" for selling hot dogs, hamburgers, beverages, and fishing gear.[91]

Today, there is a public boat ramp running through the old MacDarby-Moore property. In 1957, the Berkshire County Commissioners passed legislation granting themselves the authority to provide a right of way for public access to Goose Pond. In 1958, Berkshire County obtained an easement through the Moore property and opened the public boat ramp. After the ramp opened Hooker continued to rent his boats to those who didn't bring their own, but the fee had increased to four dollars a day.[92]

The MacDarby-Moore homestead, then on 4.8 acres, was later purchased by Virginia "Ginger" and George Van Zandt of Lee. George and Ginger lovingly converted the old farmhouse into a lakeside restaurant they called the G&G Restaurant. The G&G opened in 1972 and operated for a few years with a simple menu. There was music and dancing on Wednesday nights. I recall eating at the restaurant in the early 1970s and found it quite cozy and delicious. We didn't dance, so I'm guessing it wasn't on a Wednesday. The G&G didn't run for long and was later to become the "Golden Goose" restaurant and inn, also with a short run of operation.[93] The MacDarby homestead was subsequently demolished in 2015, but its stories live on.

Century-Old Farmhouse Converted to Restaurant

By RALPH CONROY

TYRINGHAM — The G & G Restaurant will have its grand opening tomorrow from 1 to 7 p.m. in what was formerly the Robert "Hooker" Moore boat livery near the dam on Goose Pond.

There will be a buffet featuring 26 different varieties of food including "seafood newburg," baked beans, barbecued chicken, meat balls in sauce, ham and roast beef.

Chef and manager of the new restaurant, which will cater mainly to private parties and snowmobile groups, is John "Mickey" McCormack. Mickey was chef at Eastover in Lenox for 17 years. He, his wife Theresa, and their seven daughters and one son will live at the restaurant.

Bought Last Year

The restaurant is owned by Ginger (Virginia) and George Van Zandt of Lee, hence the name, G & G. It is situated upon 4.8 acres with 470 feet of lake frontage. George and Ginger bought the property last year for $30,000, and since then have spent about $15,000 more in renovations. The couple razed a large barn which sat off from the house about 200 feet and used the barn siding to decorate the main dining room.

Above the five-feet of barnboard siding there is a copper shelf and then a red colonial wallpaper with eagles and bugles extending to the sand-painted ceiling. Three walls were removed in the old house to make the dining room which is about 25 by 16 feet.

Beams Exposed

There is another adjoining room approximately 16 by 16 feet. This room is papered in a light green and has light and dark green curtains sewn by Theresa and Ginger. The floor is of wide boards fastened with square headed nails.

While removing the three walls in the main dining room the Van Zandts exposed a chimney and overhead beams. They shellacked the bricks of the chimney after finding they could not clean them even with muriatic acid and installed more overhead beams salvaged from the barn. The result is rustic early Tyringham.

The walls of the restaurant are decorated with antiques which Ginger found in the old barn and the house. There is a large oxen yoke, old skates, enormous ice tongs which may have been used to haul ice chunks up from the pond and a large ice saw.

Other items, the Van Zandts are hoping will be identified by the customers. There is a large copper bucket with a thermometer attached to the outside and a long spear with prongs, appearing to be a frog or an eel spear.

Seats 40

Interestingly, about four weeks after George and Ginger had settled on the name "G & G" for their restaurant, the former owner, Robert Moore, found a wrought iron plaque which is believed to be from an old stove, with the initials, "G & G." The plaque now hangs over the door.

The restaurant will be able to seat about 40. There are two large tables in the main dining room and a long 10-stool, stainless steel counter. There is no liquor license. Lights are overhead suspended from wagonwheels.

In one corner there is a player piano "antiqued" in "Olé red," which Ginger bought from a man in Dalton who had advertised it in The Eagle. The piano had formerly been in the old Raoul Club in Lee.

The restaurant will be open to the public Friday and Saturday from noon till midnight and Sundays from noon until 10 p.m.

The old farmhouse which is now a restaurant is believed to be nearly 100 years old.

SPECIALIST in the restaurant field in Berkshire County will be Mickey McCormack and his wife, Theresa, who will be operating the new G&G Restaurant in Tyringham. The newest eating place was created in a 100-year-old farmhouse on the site of Hooker Moore's boat livery on Goose Pond. Many antiques have been used to emphasize the age of the building which once was a farmhouse.

Figure 11.16 Opening of the G&G Restaurant. From The Berkshire Eagle, *January 8, 1972.*

Figure 11.17 *Menu of the "G&G Restaurant" From the* The Berkshire Eagle, *1976.*

A Winter Sunrise on Pinepoint

CHAPTER 12

A PRESIDENTIAL VISIT

THE GILDED AGE, running from the 1870s to the early 1900s, and named after Mark Twain's satiric 1873 novel by the same name, was a period of dramatic American industrialization and economic growth. Riding high on that age's transformational waves were Richard Watson Gilder (1844-1909) and his wife Helena de Kay Gilder (1846-1916), who lived at the epicenter of New York City's cultural and artistic scenes. Helena was an artist, an advocate for artists and women, and founder of the Art Students League and the Society of American Artists. Richard was the Editor-in-Chief of the *Century Monthly* magazine, the founder of several educational institutions, an activist for social causes, a player in Washington politics, and a poet — who read his poem, *The Dead Comrade,* at the 1885 funeral of Ulysses S. Grant:

Come, soldiers, arouse ye!
Another has gone;
Let us bury our comrade,
His battles are done.
His sun it is set;

He was true, he was brave,
He feared not the grave,
There is naught to regret.

Bring music and banners
And wreaths for his bier—
No fault of the fighter
That Death conquered here.
Bring him home ne'er to rove,
Bear him home to his rest,
And over his breast
Fold the flag of his love.

Great Captain of battles,
We leave him with Thee!
He What was wrong, O forgive it;
His spirit makes free.
Sound taps, and away!
Out light, and to bed!
Farewell, soldier dead!
Farewell—for a day.

Figure 12.1 *Richard Watson Gilder. Courtesy of Reese and Linda Gilder Palmer, the Fourbrooks Farm Collection.*

Figure 12.2 Funeral for Ulysses S. Grant in New York City 1885. Richard Watson Gilder is walking in front, in lower right corner, and seen holding a printed copy of his poem. Grover Cleveland is standing hatless, behind the folded coat just behind Gilder. Courtesy of Reese and Linda Gilder Palmer, the Fourbrooks Farm Collection.

To escape the stifling heat of New York summers, the Gilders purchased Tyringham's Four Brooks Farm in 1899, constructing a house and gardens on the property, which incorporated architectural elements designed by the famous architect, Stanford White. At Four Brooks, which still stands at the base of George Canon Road, the Gilders entertained many of their prominent friends, including Mark Twain, Henry James, Daniel Chester French, Winslow Homer, naturalist John Burroughs (who spent much time exploring Goose Pond), Cecelia Beaux, Edith Wharton, and Theodore Roosevelt.[94]

Among the many nationally known figures who visited the Gilders in Tyringham was also the former (twenty-second and twenty-fourth) President Grover Cleveland (1837-1908), accompanied by his wife Frances Folsom Cleveland, and their young children. Grover had married Frances in the Blue Room of the White House on June 2, 1886, in an intimate ceremony attended by only thirty-one invited guests. The Cleveland family visited the Four Brooks Farm in 1901, four years after Grover's second term had ended.

Cleveland, born in Caldwell, New Jersey, had been elected mayor of Buffalo in 1881 and governor of New York in 1882. When he was elected the twenty-second President in 1885, he was the first Democrat elected to the office since the Civil War. He was one of only two presidents in American history elected to two non-consecutive terms. Cleveland was a pro-business President known for his passions for political reform, fiscal conservatism, and "Classical Liberalism," which fostered free markets, civil liberties, rule of law, and individual autonomy. He was an ardent anti-imperialist and had called for the restoration of Hawaiian Queen Lili'uokalani's rule after her overthrow in 1893, and he was opposed to Hawaii's annexation. Because of severe economic events, by the end of his second term in 1897, he was deeply unpopular, even among Democrats. Today, he is ranked by historians in the upper tier of American Presidents in terms of honesty and integrity. Following his presidency, he served a few years as a Trustee at Princeton University.[95]

During his visit with the Gilders, Grover Cleveland, an avid fisherman, tried his sporting luck, first in Hop Brook (Tyringham's widely touted trout fishing stream), and then, yes, on Goose Pond. It was on July 13, 1901, with Frances Cleveland sitting peacefully on Goose Pond's rocky shoreline alongside her friend Cecelia Beaux, a much sought-after portrait painter, when the unsuspecting bass, trout, perch, and pickerel of Lower Goose were plied with bait dangled from the rod of a (twice) former President of the United States who was fishing from a rented wooden rowboat, joined by his good friend, Richard Watson Gilder.

In Gilder's later biography of Grover Cleveland,[96] he described what it was like fishing with the former President:

"It was a strange experience, when off alone with the ex-President in a rowboat on some secluded sheet of water, to hear one's fishing companion, while skilfully getting ready his tackle, talk with inside knowledge, and in phrases as graphic as they were homely, of great international events in which he was himself a leading actor, and naming unostentatiously some of the leading living characters of the world. When he fell into reminiscences of this sort, it was apparently without any sense whatever of his own historic importance. I have never seen such unconsciousness."

Gilder added that "Mr. Cleveland was immoderate in only two things – his desk work and his fishing. Over and over he sat up till near morning at his desk in the White House, and he was always eager to begin fishing, and never appeared to be quite willing to stop." And then this, "when fishing, he [Cleveland] limited the number of fish caught with a view to some reasonable use, and he killed his fish as soon as they were caught."

In an 1898 letter, penned to an unknown recipient, the former President shared his own amusing, and rather atypical, interpretation of the ubiquitous "fish stories" universally told by fishermen throughout the ages:

'And then too I am a fisherman and never doubt a fish story that another fisherman tells.'[97]

During their outing to Goose Pond, the Clevelands also visited Madge and Haywood Cavarly, who were camping on Pinepoint, and enjoyed some hard cider at the MacDarby farmhouse, later spending the night there in a spare bedroom down the hall from young Hooker who was 10 at the time.

Anyone exploring Grover Cleveland's presidential archives would likely find precious little about his luck with the rod and reel that fine summer day in 1901, nor any mention of the (totally true!) fish stories he himself may have told. However, we do have a few treasured photographs of Goose Pond's presidential visit which have survived the passing years...

Figure 12.3 Grover Cleveland fishing from a boat on Lower Goose Pond, just off Pinepoint in 1901. Courtesy of Reese and Linda Gilder Palmer, the Fourbrooks Farm Collection.

Figure 12.4 Richard Gilder (left) and Grover Cleveland (right) fishing on Lower Goose Pond in 1901. This card, and also the cards shown in Figures 12.5 and 12.6 were apparently inscribed and created by the Clevelands, the Gilders, and Cecelia Beaux to be used as handmade Christmas cards to their children.[98] Courtesy of Reese and Linda Gilder Palmer, the Fourbrooks Farm Collection.

Figure 12.5 Frances Folsom Cleveland (left) and Cecelia Beaux (right) seated on Pinepoint rocks in 1901. These particular rocks can still be identified on Pinepoint. Courtesy of Reese and Linda Gilder Palmer, the Fourbrooks Farm Collection.

"Au hasard!"
Cecilia Beaux

Tyringham – Sept 16.

Figure 12.6 *Cecelia Beaux (left), Richard Gilder (standing in center), Frances Folsom Cleveland and Grover Cleveland (seated) on Pinepoint, Lower Goose Pond, c1906. Grover Cleveland had lost much weight by this time because of a gastric condition. "Au hasard" translates from the French to "haphazardly, randomly, wild." This photograph was taken on Pinepoint from a vantage point similar to that of the winter scene shown at the top of this chapter. Courtesy of Reese and Linda Gilder Palmer, the Fourbrooks Farm Collection.*

Postcard of Pinepoint

CHAPTER 13

PINEPOINT

*W*HAT FOLLOWS IS THE MEMOIR of Madge Cavarly, born Margarita "Madge" Bartholf in 1871, telling us the story of her early years on Goose Pond. Madge and her husband, Haywood Cavarly (1871-1941), started camping on Pinepoint in 1898. When they built their cabin there a few years later, it was the first cabin on Goose Pond, other than the MacDarby farmhouse by the dam and the Griffin homestead on Upper Goose. This memoir was written in 1954 when Madge was eighty-two years old. (Reproduced courtesy of Charles Mecklem)

THE GOOSE POND STORY

Madge Cavarly

CAVARLY COTTAGE IN 1905

THE GOOSE POND STORY

After we had been married a few months in 1898, my husband came home one night with the trilling news that we were going to have a wedding trip after all. We had only one weekend when we were married. I had been badly bitten by the green-eyed monster when my chum, who was married about the same time, announced she was going on an extended European trip for her honeymoon. My envy was turned to pity, when on her return, I learned she had been most unromantically seasick all the way over and back.

Now the question of where to go occupied us completely. We wanted to go where we could tour the country on our tandem. We decided on the Berkshire Hills. Lee, Mass. sounded less demanding on our slim purse, so one Friday morning we loaded our tandem on the Pittsfield express, jumped aboard and disembarked at Lee. We asked a friendly looking man at the station if he could tell us where we could find a not too expensive boarding house. He pointed over his shoulder to a house about two miles up the road where he said he believed they took boarders. We manned our tandem, pedaled up there and asked for a room. Mr. Warren, the owner, looked us over suspiciously and said, "Well, I reckon you want two rooms, don't you?" "This lady is my wife" Haywood said proudly, "One room will be enough". He took us in. At supper the boarders scrutinized us carefully even to my new wedding ring and decided we were honest to goodness newlyweds. We stayed there two weeks.

One day we met Major May. I was greatly impressed by a real major and pictured him charging up San Juan Hill, facing death with brave Teddy, but subsequently I found that he had only served in the commissary. He was fat and pudgy and showed signs of an over-filled stomach. He promised to take us up in the mountains and show us a beautiful lake called Goose Pond, that was filled with Black Large Mouth Bass, just waiting for someone to drop a

fat worm in their mouths. There were no humans around except an old half-breed Indian who was a woman hater. The Major said that the road up to the lake was very difficult to travel. However, the Major never fulfilled his promise to take us to the lake, but Goose Pond seemed to be calling us, so one fine morning we decided to tramp up to it. We did, and when we stood on the big rock over-looking the lake, the beauty of it was breath-taking. We so loved it that for fifty-six years, our children, grandchildren and now our great-grandchildren have loved Goose Pond. Throughout the changing years of our lives it has always beckoned to us to come up and rest awhile in its peace and quietness.

The next day we found a man who would drive us up, so up we went again taking the Major with us. I doubted if he could make it up the hill with all that avoir-du-pois to carry. But such fishing! We caught eighteen or twenty good sized bass. Toward evening Haywood caught sight of a little white tent being pitched about half-way down the lake. His eyes just gleamed, as he said, "That is what I would like to do," then turning to me he said, "But you wouldn't like roughing it like that, would you?" I cast my eyes timorously on the darkening pines on the shore and thought of the half-breed woman hater in the woods, but being a new little bride I just gulped and said, "I would like it if you would". So it was decided then and there to come up camping the following summer.

The whole winter long we planned for it, and all winter the whole Atlantic Works of the National Lead Company devoted all their spare time at lunch hour assembling our camping supplies. We collected two army cots, blankets, folding card table, two chairs, fishing tackle, Klondike Stove and innumerable little things, any of which would have been tragic to forget in the mountains with the nearest store four miles down the mountain. It was my job to order the food so I went to A & S's and ordered a barrel of canned baked beans, ham, bacon, sugar, salt, canned fruits and coffee.

MacDarby Farmhouse

It took two lumber wagons to haul our tent and equiptment up the mountain, stopping over each "Thank you ma'am" to rest the panting horses. One horse fell down and refused to budge, so we had to go back to Lee to replace him. Finally we made it, and we came to an old farm house near the lake and consulted with the best friend we ever had up there, Mrs. MacDarby, as to the best place to pitch our tent, which would be in her cow pasture. We wanted a spot where we could get a good view of the lake spread out before us, but the lady with the practical good judgement of the pioneer woman, advised a little knoll jutting ou on the lake, covered with pine trees. Good sense lost, and we insisted upon the lake view, pitched the tent there and put up the cots, not taking account of the fact that we would have to climb a fence everytime we went around the tent. But oh, I will never forget that night! Most of our things were stored underneath those canvas cots and every time we moved we would roll against a table leg, trunk, bait pail or other gear. The frogs croaked all night, the whipporwills whipped and an industrious hoot owl hooted. At last morning came and when we could disentangle ourselves from our belongings we got up.

With the dawn came the jingling of cow bells. The cows were investigation this curious contraption anchored on their favorite breakfast table. We opened the tent flaps thinking to get that glorious view of the lake but such a comotion! The cows just kicked up their heels and stampeded down to the lake. The next disturbance which interfered was Old Man Jones swearing at his cows as he drove them out to pasture. I heard such profanity as I didn't know existed in any language. One D—— followed another as it echoed through the mountains. Now hunger began to call us. Mrs. MacDarby had told us the night before we could get milk and cream at her house so Haywood fished out two pails and started for the farm. A chorus of dogs, big and little, greeted him when he arrived so I knew he had arrived there safely. When he came back my eyes just popped out when he showed me a pan of hot biscuits just out of the oven. We quickly set up the klondike stove, gathered some wood, made a fire

and brewed some coffee to eat with the bisquits. The cream was so thick we had to spoon it out. Now we had to consider washing our face and hands, and there was the matter of washing the dishes. Haywood found two pails among the junk which had been digging my ribs all night and again set forth, this time for the lake. A geologist told us later that the lake was probably a burned out volcano, as there was old volcanic rock all around, and the lake was probably the extinct volcanic crater. This accounts for the steep pitch down the hill to the lake.

When Haywood came steaming back with the pails full of water, he just set them down and said, "Well, today we move the camp." I just gasped, "Well where do we go from here?" Haywood just pointed to the pails and to the lake— I got my answer. Mrs. MacDarby loaned us a bobsled which they used to carry logs through the snow in the winter. We hitched old Daisy to the sled and she dragged our things down to the knoll, which Mrs. MacDarby had first advised. We found it an ideal spot under the pines. We had plenty of water for washing and swimming and a good spring for drinking water.

I followed the bobsled to retrieve the leftovers dropped off the sled. When I got down to the lake I found the cows had eaten all the flowers off my hat. I brushed a tear off my cheek which was struggling for egress when I thought of all the glamorous hotels I had passed on the way. It was just a passing thought and in time we got accustomed to the little animals walking across our beds at night. We never knew what they were, nor cared. We just drew the covers over our heads thinking it may be a bat which we might find imbedded in our hair in the morning. We got used to seeing the cats being driven out of the milk room every morning wiping off their mouths and the chipmonks which stole my dishcloth every morning and scurried up the tallest pine tree with it.

One night I was wakened by the most unearthly screams. It sounded as if someone was being murdered. Haywood said what I feared he would, "I am

going to take the boat and see what that noise is, will you stay here or will you go with me?" I looked at the black pines over the tent and then across the lake where the murderer probably was and I said tremblingly, "I will go with you." We armed ourselves with shovel and rake and set forth. The screaching stopped when it heard the noise of our oars, then it kept up till morning, just keeping a little ahead of us. Finally we went back to a troubled sleep until morning dawned. Later we went over and searched the ground carefully but found no corpse nor any signs of a struggle. Later we read in the paper that a panther had strayed from its pack in the Maine Woods and had been heard in the mountains around Lee making horrible noises until the farmers in the vicinity tracked him down and shot him. I slept easier after that.

Now I became the heroine of Goose Pond for I caught the largest bass ever caught in that small lake, four and one-half pounds. The story grew and grew, "Did you know that woman in the camp at Goose Pond caught a huge bass which weighed eight pounds!" Many people braved the mountain road and came up. Even R. W. Gilder came up with his guest Grover Cleveland, but no one ever did outdo me. I was beginning to like life in the mountains. We even became good pals with the livestock in the pasture. The cows became our friends, commissioned to wake us up in time for the good fishing early in the morning. One morning old bossy cow came for breakfast and with one lap of her tongue swept the whole pound of butter off the table. Another morning I heard a noise in the dish closet. We peeped out and found a big skunk eating all our bacon. We quietly ran inside and sat down to consider the best way to attack that problem. We borrowed a gun and waited until the nest morning. In the meantime Haywood put up a target to represent the skunks head and bided his time practicing on the target. Sure enough the skunk came back and Haywood shot him squarely in the head. That was the end of the skunk. The word got around in atdome that there was good nibbling in the Cavarly camp so we had to cover up everything after that.

We never had a rainy day while we were there. The days were heavenly but the nights were cold as we were nearly two thousand feet high. Haywood took big rocks and put them in the stove to heat before we went to bed until one night the bed caught fire. So we stopped that and just froze.

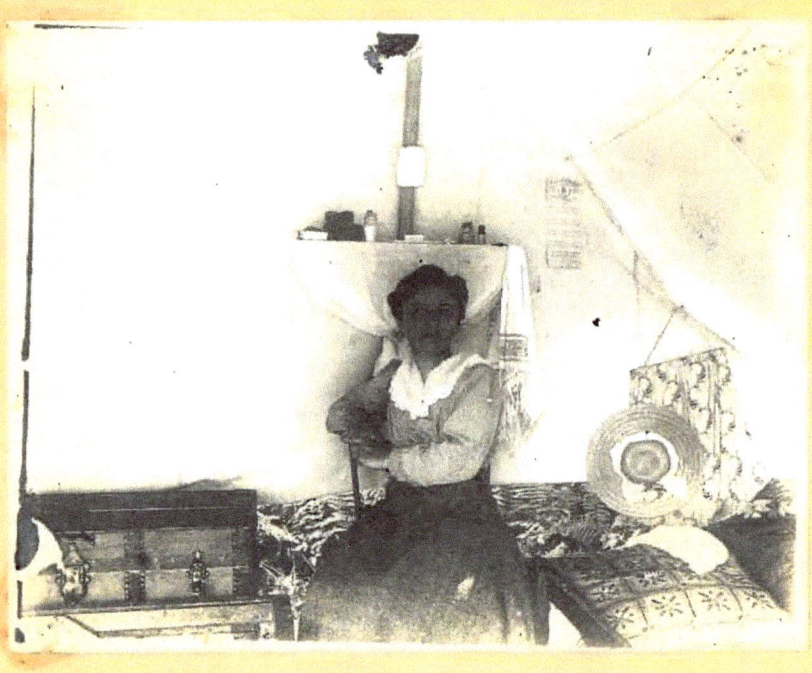

SECOND SUMMER

Haywood had lived with a group of young bachelors before he was married. Now that he had taken the final plunge, they followed us to Richmond Hill where we had rented a house. Every Sunday they came in full force. They built a tennis court up the street, left their clothes in our guest closet and they occasionally stayed overnight. They announced that they would provide and cook supper every Sunday night when the maid was away. Fine! But the mess the next morning. Occasionally they dropped a plate of toast on the floor and in the exuberance of youth, dishes broke and scared the cat so that she jumped up on the mantel piece and broke Mamie's antique vase. But we had fun. When they heard about our camping trip nothing would do but they must go too. So the next summer we went up with the whole gang in tow, including Dina Shaw, the puppy dog whose habit was to carry off each morning a shoe or piece of intimate underwear which must be found before emerging from the tent. We ate fish until we hated to hear them jump in the water.

Now I'm ashamed to say I got mad, so mad the fur flew. The dogs barked, the cows stampeded, the crows flew to the tallest pine. "Just look at you", I scolded the men. "You boys are a sight to behold - hair long enough to braid, clothes not fit for a tramp, and smelling to high heaven of dead fish." They stood in a row like bad schoolboys in front of me. "What do you want us to do, go home?" they said dolefully. I said, "No, but take a good bath with that good dog soap, shave, and get into your go-home clothes, and go down to Lee if they will admit you anywhere and get a haircut. Then take me to the best hotel in the Berkshires for lunch somewhere among civilized people. I want something to eat beside fish and baked beans. I held my point even though the weather had cleared beautifully and the "wind was in the West when the fish bite best."

I relented about the best hotel in the Berkshires and began to feel sorry for them. So then on my own initiative I led them into an owl wagon at the foot of the hill. After lunch we walked around Lee a little to cool off my ire and to see the sights of civilization, which consisted mainly of farm implements, house dresses, kitchen ware and fishing tackle. Then back to camp. They showed their appreciation of the owl wagon lunch by suggesting we ride back which I imagine was one good mark for me and two for them. They were pretty well exhausted by the walk down in their unaccustomed cleanliness but Haywood, who was ever my champion, had kept them walking to the bitter end, even if they were inwardly swearing at me and hating me besides. But now it was over, off with collars, shirts, ties, and all the nuisances of civilization. Back to the smelly clothes, fish and baked beans. They collected underwear hung around the trees and were thankful the day was over. The cows sauntered back, the dogs slept, the crows came out of hiding. Mother was pacified and all was happy again.

No one liked to clean fish. Some of the men had sore fingers that wouldn't heal, and Brother Billy declared he never ate fish, didn't like them and wouldn't clean them. So many of them were incapacitated, some valid reasons and some imaginary, that it fell to John and Haywood to clean fish. This was done on a little island out a few rods from camp, to the delight of the crows. When I caught John and Haywood exchanging glances I knew some deviltry was afoot. There was no more discussion about fish cleaning until one night I saw Haywood and John disappear over the mountain. They had gone up to Mrs. MacDarby's and asked if they could buy a chicken. She said of course they could, to just go out to the hen house and take anyone you wanted. They went out, lifted every one until they found the fattest and heaviest hen on the roost. They chopped off its head and brought it back to camp and dangled it dripping with blood in front of Billy's nose and said, "Here is a chicken, I know you can clean a chicken for you used to do it up on the farm." He was game and all the next

Tents on Pine Point

day he picked, cleaned and cut up that bird ready to fry while the boys were out fishing and jeering at him. My but that was good and such a welcome change from fish.

It was the custom among the farmers around Goose Pond to make hard cider. It was very gratifying after a hard days work in the hay field to take a drink of it, and it was very potent. One day Frank was out in the hay field and thought to try it. He did and feeling too frisky, jumped over the wood pile and landed squarely in a hornets nest. I was sitting under the pines placidly reading when I saw Frank running down through the fields jumping and bouncing. He never stopped until he reached the lake and jumped in clothes and all. Horrors, I thought, one of my boys has gone wild. One of the hornets stopped on the way to call on me and when I realized what it was that caused all that leaping, I spent the rest of the day plastering mud all over Frank.

One morning a group of girls appeared on the hill in back of our tent and beckoned me to them. They wanted to know if there would be any objection to their putting up a tent near us. I said I would go up and ask the boys. I did, and such a chorus of "no's" went up that I had to go back and tell them as gently as I could what the answer was. I think I had spoiled them by undertaking to stay in bed until they took their early morning dip in the lake in the altogether.

And now it was nearly the first of September and sorrowfully we began packing up our things to go home. But jobs must be considered and all good things must come to an end. We commissioned our good friend Charlie MacDarby and he hitched up old Daisy to the lumber wagon and began to pile things aboard. I positively refused to pack up any of those old smelly clothes to take home but made a bonfire of them while the boys looked on dejectedly. Many things, including the tents, we put into the MacDarby's barn, hoping the next summer we could come again. Charlie calculated we could make it down the Hill, but I will never forget that ride. It took two of them to

hold me from bouncing off as I sat on the top of the trunk. We finally caught the train as it began to pull out. They held it a few minutes while we loaded our stuff and we were on our way home. As the years have intervened, and I begin to look back on it, I forget the discomforts and realize what a good time we had.

Bonfire on Point

THIRD SUMMER

It was our third summer that we took Mr. Failor with us. He was an enthusiastic fisherman and with him came his wife and two daughters. But after one night sleeping under the pine trees, with a thunderstorm for good measure, they decided to go back home until a camp was built for them. After their cottage was built they were much happier there. With the Failors and the Hubbards we had quite a good time. The men and boys with us broke their backs carrying stumps and fallen limbs to feed the campfire which we built every night on the point, to get through to our shivering bones before sleeping.

Every night about ten o'clock our friendly ghost came out for his nightly stroll. Never a word did he speak, never a sound did he make, but just walked quietly up and down the beach on the other side of the lake, and then quietly disappeared into the woods. Haywood determined to find out what the mystery was. He found it was a "Will-o-the-wisp" which appeared like a man carrying a lantern.

ANOTHER SUMMER

We had been accustomed to leaving Perry with his grandmother Cavarly for the two weeks and Sister stayed with her grandparents in Pompton. We found according to reports we had better take them with us so it was decided. We took Bertha, their nurse, with us too. We went up with that crowd to live in two extra tents with floors to keep the children off the damp ground.

One day a telegram came for Haywood making it necessary for him to leave the next day for Brooklyn. So now there was nothing for this pioneer woman to do but stay with Bertha and the two children in those tents over night alone. There was a rumor around that the boys in a tent near us had ordered an old man who lived in the mountains alone to bring them some of his whiskey or else! The old man was never seen again. Haywood went up to the boys camping near us and found they were very nice boys and came from good families in Lee. Night came and we stayed alone but not to sleep much. Haywood had given us a huge bell to ring if anything went wrong. The boys came down about ten o'clock to see if we were all right and promised to come right down if the bell sounded an alarm. The night proved without incident or accident and when morning came we were glad to know Haywood would be back on an early train.

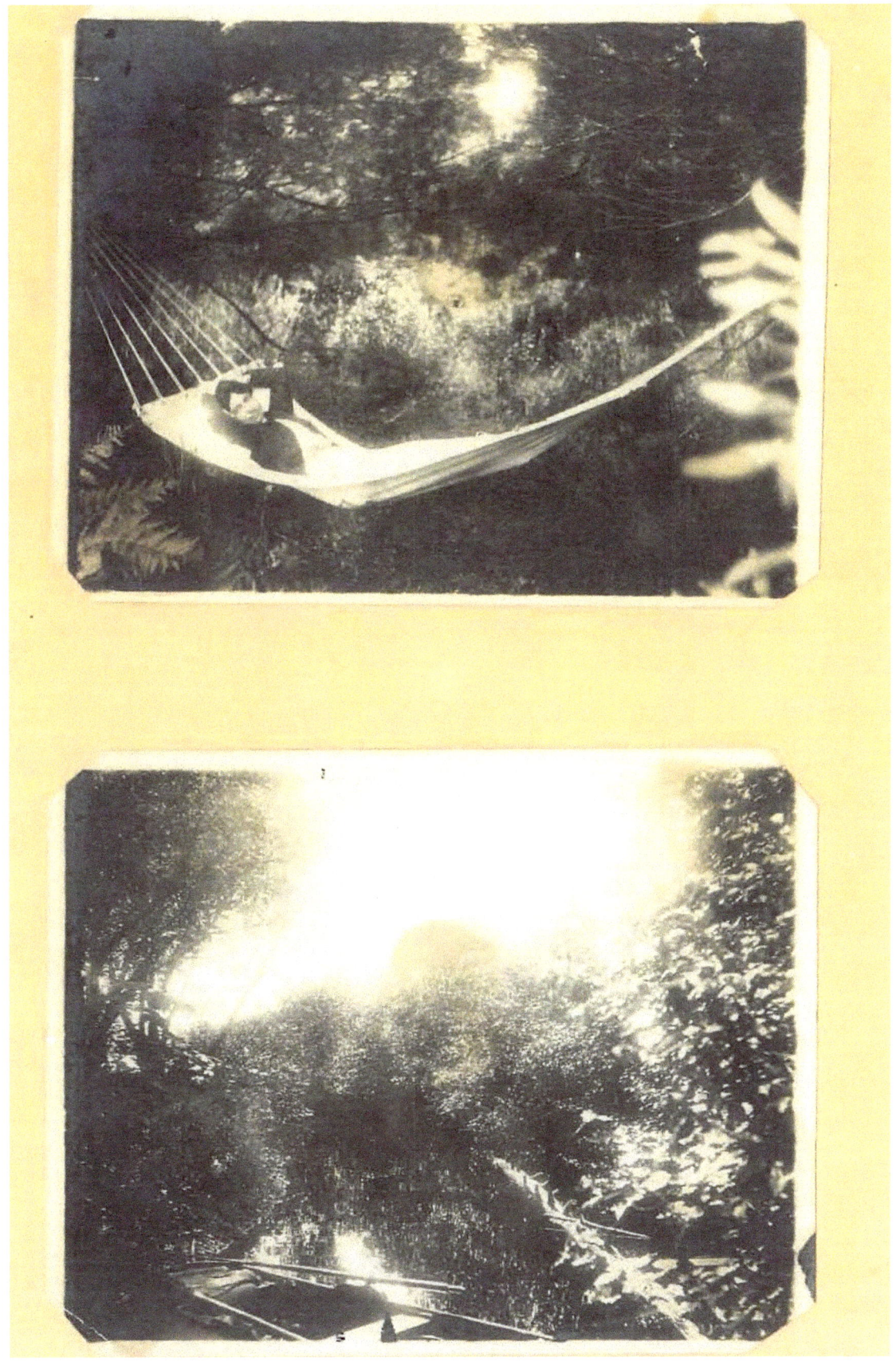

FOURTH SUMMER

Another year had rolled around and I had a plan seething in my mind all winter. Came February and I spoke my piece clearly and deliberately, with no if, ands or buts. "Boys, I have decided, now that we have two children, that I will never go up to Goose Pond again without a house to live in. You may go up where and when you wish but count me out. I am staying home with my children." Dead silence. I had thrown a bomb in their midst, but I suspected Haywood was with me. He never said a word but the next night when he came home he showed me a plan of a little camp to be built on our same point. It had a living room, two tiny bedrooms opening off it and an attic with a ladder up to it, which we always called the "Shizzel-post," and that was designed to keep the trunks and spare bed if necessary.

All winter I haunted second hand junk shops. I raided my own and my mothers attic. I accumulated furniture which was enough to start with. We were to take Bertha, the children's nurse with us, and go up with them the third of July. Haywood was to come up the following Friday Night and during those few days we would get the camp ready for occupancy. The third of July dawned a beautiful clear day and delightedly I got the children ready for the great adventure. I had made all kinds of sandwiches and a fried chicken to take with us on the train. Haywood took us and our belongings to the station in Richmond Hill. From there we took a trolley car across New York, then aboard the Pittsfield express for the long ride into the Berkshire Hills. About eleven o'clock the children began clamoring for food. I produced the lunch box while the children stood by expectantly. A terrible stench greeted my nostrils. The chicken had turned bad and had to thrown out the window. Fortunately we knew a man on the train who volunteered to get out at Danbury and get some more sandwiches for us. Finally we got to Lee and Mr. Daily's three seated rig was there waiting for us, so after a hard days journey we

arrived at the lake. As Mr. Daily never drove through the fields down to the camp we had to walk it. The furniture had come up by Mr. Doolittle's truck the day before, and it was all dumped on the front porch. Such a pile of junk I never saw anywhere except in the junk shop. We unlocked the door and encountered a house full of nothing. First we found some nails which Bertha drove in the walls with a stone to hang our hats on. We had nothing to open our barrels with. The Failors had come up to their cabin the week before so we borrowed a hammer and other tools from them. We dragged the beds inside but had no idea how to put them together. The stove was an equal enigma to us. One of the barrels we fortunately were able to open had a can of cocoa in it, which we mixed with some lake water to appease the children's hunger. About that time Mr. Failor came down and layed a string of fish, on the porch, proudly saying, "I thought you would like this for supper." Cleaning fish was something quite beyond our knowledge, so we buried them in the ground and drank some more cocoa. About eight o'clock those blessed MacDarby boys came down to see what they could do for us. We told them if they could put up the beds so we could take a much needed sleep it would be such a help. Mr. Failor had tried to put them up but couldn't do it. The boys put them up in a hurry and then tackled the stove which they got all ready for our breakfast. So with blankets for the cold we snuggled down blissfully, but about ten o'clock such an all night thunderstorm as I had never experienced drove through those pines and threatened to uproot our cabin. With every clap of thunder we felt ourselves to see if we were still alive. The children were freightened and so were we, but at last morning came, clear and beautiful as Goose Pond can be. We lighted the stove hopefully but it smoked so bad we nearly chocked to death, but at long last we got some hot coffee and started to work. In all those beautiful castles scattered through the mountains, I don't think there was ever a woman so happy as I was arranging that little cabin. When Haywood came up Friday night we had it all decorated with ferns and wild flowers. We had no place to

put the gorgeous steak, butter, and other perishable things, so Haywood went to work and dug a hole lining it with stones to keep things comparatively fresh. It was our first ice box.

The winter's conversation had been on fish; the best places to fish, and the best bait to use. Haywood had heard from someone that the best bait would be shiners from any pond. He brought some with him but what was his chagrin when he liberated them to find them all dead. In walking around the lake he met a small boy who had just pulled in a good sized bass with a bent pin and a worm for bait. The bass they found were so fussy they would only eat bait caught at Goose Pond so we had to make a bait net. They also insisted the bait must be caught early in the morning. So be it, and at break of day we had to sally forth to bring their breakfast to them.

ANOTHER SUMMER – KITCHEN BUILT

We put up the kitchen which was a great help and bought a new stove which didn't smoke so badly. Haywood insisted that Uncle Frank Stevens, who had bought the Failor cabin that year, put a kitchen on his cabin too. They both worked very hard on it. It rained all night and Haywood decided to go up to see how Uncle Frank's kitchen was doing. He found their maid in the new kitchen with an umbrella held over her head trying to cook breakfast with tears blending with the rainwater. They went to Lee and bought some tarpaper to keep Gerta from going home.

ANOTHER SUMMER

Grandpa and Nana offered to go up to camp to stay with the children for two weeks while I went down to Brooklyn to see a little civilization. I think they had a high time. Jerry wrote me a letter which ran something like this, "Dear Mother, We are having a good time, we are all right except that I ran into a tin can in swimming and cut my leg to the bone, but

We hoisted the rain barrel up on the roof and rolled it off to scare Nana and Bampa. It was such fun to see them jump. Love, Perry."

When Bampa consented to go up with us, the children were clamoring for their Rassie Cat which they could not dispense with. Bampa shook his head and positively declined to carry the cat in the basket, no matter how carefully sealed up it was. When we started for the train the basket was standing on the platform and no one but poor Bampa dared to carry it. So he found himself climbing aboard with the basket on his arm. When the train started the cat went wild. It got itself out of the basket and ran across a woman's bare shoulder leaving a big scratch. The woman screamed and the cat ran to the door but saw the scenery rushing past and decided not to jump. We got it back and quieted in its basket, but when we got into the station we saw a little stream trickling out of the basket and needless to say Bampa balked in earnest when it came to carrying it further.

The MacDarby dog had a daily fight over our cats breakfast. We put the cats milk just about two inches under the house so when the dog came to get it he couldn't reach it. Every time he stuck his nose in, the cat would strike him with a paw and off he would go howling for help.

IDYL OF GOOSE POND

Little lake in the heart of the Berkshire Hills- I salute you and the cottage on your shore, which a great man built, the like of whom I shall never see again in this world. The camp has been a haven for the Cavarly clan and their friends for many years. You are old now, but younger and loving hands have renewed your life. Once you were the lone dweller on the lake and of the feet that trod those pine needles there are few left, perhaps only mine. The joys which we knew in this little cottage are still graven in our memories. The camp fires on the point in the evening under the stars while we all gathered around to our banjo accompaniment, gave the first Berkshire Music Festival, fifty years ago with only the mountains to applaud. The thrill of welcoming Dad when he appeared over the hill Friday nights with untold good things from the city. The way we slept after the days spent in the mountain air. The murmer of the pines to lull us to sleep, but when the wind rose the pine trees seemed to grow impatient with us for not understanding their whispered message. The memory of the roar they made raging down the mountain still makes me shiver. When morning came how wonderful it was to waken to the smell of bacon sizzling in the pan mingling with the odor

of the pines while we drank our coffee. Daisy, the horse, would come lumbering through the woods and stick her head in the window for a lump of sugar. The glory of the laurels outlining the lake as we came up in the spring was always such a glad welcome. The outstanding achievement of the summer vacation was climbing Becket Mountain. We took our lunch with us as it was an all-day trip. The trail was hard to find as it led through brambles waist high, also loose stones and hidden snakes, but we always reached the top eventually and when at last we stood on the great rock at the summit, the beauty that burst upon us was overpowering. There were mountain peaks rising in majesty to greet us, little lakes sparkling like diamonds in the hollows. I think whether we realized it or not, we all felt the Hand of God.

But now, my children, an automobile road has been built to within a

few yards of the top, and you can reach the great monument with little effort. But, my dears, you will still have your mountains to climb and when I think of the future for you some of them may be very difficult indeed, but those of you who persevere through the hidden brambles and evils in your path will reach the top where you will touch the Hand of God. So I salute you, my children, grandchildren and great-grandchildren to whom I dedicate these memoirs of long ago with love in my heart.

                                                       Madge Cavarly

Written in 1954 at age 82

Upper Goose Pond Swamp in Autumn

CHAPTER 14

THE MOHHEKENNUCK CLUB

SITTING NEATLY in its Long Island driveway and shimmering in the August heat, the White family car was loaded up with a week's worth of supplies. The year was 1954, and Warren Rapelye White, then nine, and his little brother Bill, could not even finish their breakfasts, bubbling over as they were with the anticipation of their annual adventure at the Mohhekennuck Club. Sleeping bags, board games, innumerable cans of beef stew, fishing gear, and bags of marshmallows were, as they were every summer, essential components of the packed gear.

Warren's father, a music teacher who always took his vacation during the last two weeks of August, would eagerly sign up each spring for the White family's annual time slot at "camp." The Whites were long-standing members of the Mohhekennuck Club, a benefit passed down from Warren's grandfather Warren Rapelye, who had been one of the Club's founders back in 1909.

The club's story officially began on March 30, 1909, when Lee Judge Bart Bossidy signed off on the incorporation papers of a non-profit called Mohhekennuck Club, Inc. with the designated purpose "for fishing, boating, and general recreation." On August 18, 1909, the club's founders, mostly from East Lee and Brooklyn, New York, purchased thirteen acres of Upper Goose

Figure 14.1 Warren Rapelye White (right) and his family in their Long Island driveway prepared for their trip to the Mohhekennuck Club c1954. Photograph courtesy of Warren Rapelye White, Reno, NV. All rights reserved.

shoreline from William and Bell Davol for the price of one dollar. One of the club's founding members, Wolcott Hamblin, was related to the Davols, which might have something to do with the affordable selling price. Although the Mohhekennuck Club derived its official name in honor of the local Indian tribe, it has, over the years, been called by other names including "The Clubhouse," the "Men's Club," and "The Chimney Club," the last derived from the club's only visible remains after its fiery demise in 1971. Given the consistent presence of girls and women on the club's premises, the term "Men's Club" is clearly a misnomer.

Within weeks of purchasing its property, the club's members quickly hired Lee carpenter Nick Carter, who, using oxen to haul the chestnut logs up the logging road, built their two-story log cabin with the help of "twelve Brooklyn and Lee men."[99] The cabin had a large stone fireplace and chimney and sleeping quarters for ten to twelve campers in three upstairs bedrooms. Just behind the cabin was the old Griffin homestead, now just a faintly visible cellar-hole.

Each year members would sign up for their time at the club and weekly rotations progressed throughout the summer, with members enjoying swimming, hiking, music, dancing, fishing, boating, hunting, and plenty of spirited camaraderie. Heartier members would sign up for winter deer hunting. Wolcott Hamblin was a local Boy Scout leader and would often bring his Boy Scout troupe for visits, sometimes during winter months for skiing, tobogganing, and skating.

Having driven to the local train station, the White family boarded the first of several trains, gradually making their way to East Lee where they stayed overnight with Warren's grandmother, Charlotte Rapelye. Although they would sometimes reach camp in a rowboat rented from Moore's Boat Livery on Lower Goose, this particular summer they planned to hike in from East Lee. The next morning, they headed out on the hot, buggy trek up to "camp," Warren and Bill bristling with excitement, and everyone carrying their share of the week's gear. They would cross a series of farmers' fields, follow a section of the extinct Huckleberry trolley railbed, climb the mountain's

Figure 14.2 This remarkably beautiful postcard, mailed on March 5, 1907, was sent from "Nick" (in Lee) and addressed to Parks Hamblin (in Brooklyn). Parks Hamblin was to become one of the founders of the Mohhekennuck Club in 1909. The signer might conceivably be Nick Carter who was the carpenter who built the Mohhekennuck Club in 1909. The handwriting on the card reads, **"Dear Parks, Have just sent one of these to Paul. Doesn't this look natural tho? Can you picture yourself with a rod & line from the rocks and a box of crickets? Nick."** *The photograph was taken from the mouth of Sucker Brook looking east at Upper Goose Pond -- the island is on the right in low water. The boat's name, only partially visible here, is probably "The Madge" which would have belonged to Madge Cavarly, the original owner of Pinepoint, in which case the photograph was likely taken by someone in the Cavarly family. This postcard is the only example I have ever found showing BOTH names: "Goose Pond" and "Lake May" on the same document. The card reflects Hamblin's involvement with Goose Pond a full two years before founding the Club. Parks Hamblin is likely one of the "Brooklyn men" (see Figure 14.3) referenced among the founding members. This would not have been the only postcard created by the Cavarly's: there is another one showing Pinepoint cottage which can be seen at the top of Chapter 13. Courtesy of Edward Habermehl.*

Young Men Break Camp.

The Hamblin camp on the upper end of Upper Goose pond, built by twelve Brooklyn and Lee young men last fall and which has been in continual use this summer, closed for the season Monday, the Brooklyn parties returning to the city. This is by far the largest and finest camp on our local waters. It is built of logs and the name of the club taken from one found by Wolcott C Hamblin in the Lee history is Mohhockenneck.

The following guests have been entertained there this month by Harry and Parks Hamblin—Mrs. Wolcott C. Hamblin, Miss Mildred Hamblin, Jack Hamblin, June Hamblin, Harry A Reybert, R. M. Agar, Ed Doyle, S. S. May, Harold May, E M Ryder, Brooklyn; Miss Florence McLaughlin, Hartford, Miss Helen Carr, Manchester, Conn. Charles F. Wagner, Boston, Leon Foote, Lee, H. S. Carter, Lee, Mrs. C. H. Chaffee, Miss Florence Chaffee, Louis Chaffee, East Lee.

Figure 14.3 The "Hamblin Camp," aka Mohhekennuck Club, opened in 1910. Guests S.S. May and Harold May were the sons of S.S. May (Sr.) who was the builder of Goose Pond's dam in 1839. From The Berkshire Gleaner, *September 14, 1910.*

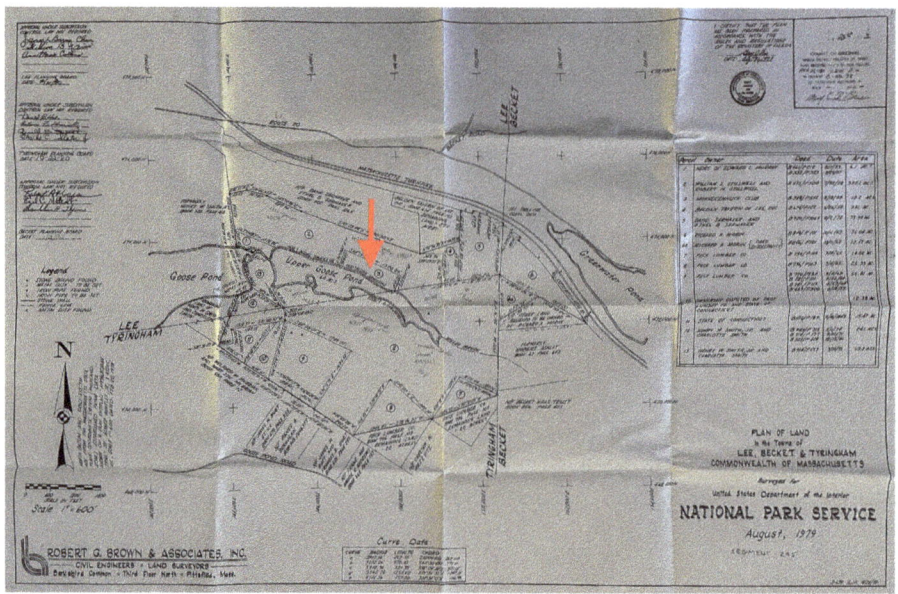

Figure 14.4 *Map of Upper Goose Pond from National Park Service, August 1979. Lot #3 (red arrow) is the Mohhekennuck Club property. Courtesy of David Stilwell.*

old wood roads, and finally descend into the serene coolness of Upper Goose Pond and the tree-shaded Mohhekennuck Club nestled on its northern shore. By the time the Whites arrived, the camp would already be bustling with activity as the previous week's campers were busy packing up and making room for the new arrivals.

Warren White, now seventy-eight, recalled how his family would traditionally stake out their four iron cots in the common room on the first floor, leaving the three upstairs bedrooms for other arriving campers. He loved this big main room with its enormous fieldstone fireplace, the giant snapping turtle shell hanging on the wall, and all the hunting trophies hanging on the walls, their eyes always watching. By the time the White family had settled in, the sun would be sinking over the horizon and the coolness of evening descending. Kerosene lamps would be lit, and a warming fire set ablaze in the fireplace. It would not take long for someone to wind up the phonograph and start up the musical festivities -- a guest might pull out a banjo, and dancing often followed. The music floated up the pond and could surely be heard in the Stilwell and Murphy camps too and likely continued long after the stars came out.

Warren's dinner that first night was the usual: canned beef stew warmed over the fire, and tasting, as always, far more delicious than anything *ever* cooked in his family's modern Long Island kitchen. After dinner, marshmallows would be toasted over the fire and the night's fireside board games would commence. Warren and his brother would spend their days playing around the lake, often "fishing for guppies" using a pail (with limited success), and other times using rod and reel (with more success). Warren recalls, now with more than a little horror, how his mother, fearful that his little brother Bill would drown in the lake, would often tie her youngest son to a tree. Soon the boys' best week of the summer would seem over in a heartbeat.[100]

Figure 14.5 *Mohhekennuck members on the club's front steps. The man smoking the pipe, seated on the right, and holding a rifle is young Warren's grandfather and club co-founder Warren Rapelye. Courtesy of Edward Habermehl.*

A huge, 53-pound snapping turtle, believed to be 190 years old, is captured by Dr. Parks Hamblin and Roy Dowd in upper Goose Pond, East Lee, after a terrific battle. Dr. Hamblin plans to mount the head and feet and preserve the shell.

Figure 14.6 *The shell from this snapping turtle was mounted on the wall at the Mohhekennuck Club, and fascinated young Warren White. It was Parks Hamblin who received the 1907 postcard (see Figure 14.2). I wonder if Roy Dowd might have been related to Wolcott Dowd who rented out his rowboat at Lee Landing and/or to Simeon Dowd who drowned in the 1886 Mud Pond dam failure. From* The Pittsfield Berkshire Evening Eagle, *October 18, 1955.*

Figure 14.7 Mohhekennuck Club co-founder Warren Rapelye (Sr.) and his daughters (Audrey, left, was Warren White's mother) hiking to the cabin. Photograph courtesy of Warren Rapelye White, Reno, NV. All rights reserved.

Figure 14.8 The Mohhekennuck Club cabin. The image on the right shows deer carcasses hanging from the porch ceiling. Photograph courtesy of Warren Rapelye White, Reno, NV. All rights reserved.

Figure 14.9 Mohhekennuck Club members on front steps. Photograph courtesy of Warren Rapelye White, Reno, NV. All rights reserved.

Figure 14.10 Bruce Walton (right) and his friend Jon Bauer (left) standing on the Mohhekennuck Club cabin in 1968. Courtesy of Bruce Walton.

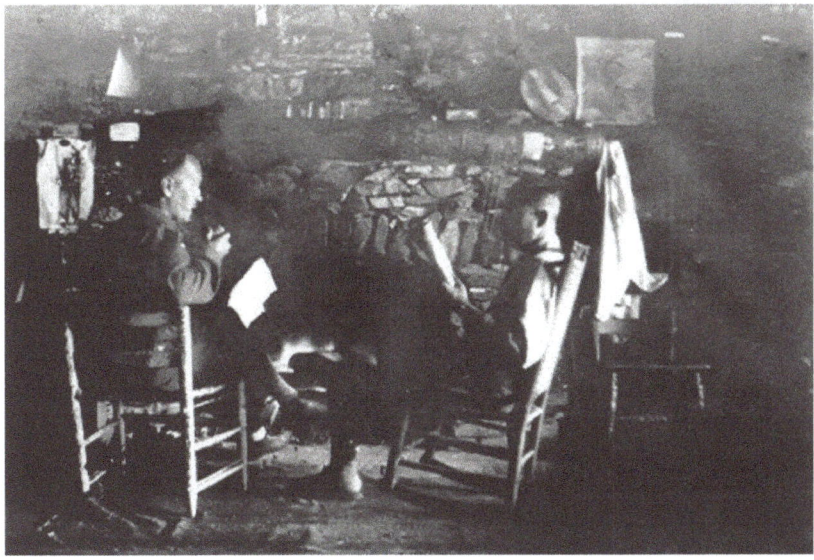

Figure 14.11 Interior of the Mohhekennuck Club cabin. The glow of a nice fire is seen in the bottom image. This is the fireplace whose remains still stand near Upper Goose. Photographs courtesy of Warren Rapelye White, Reno, NV. All rights reserved.

Figure 14.12 Joyful Mohhekennuckers enjoying their time on Upper Goose. Photographs courtesy of Warren Rapelye White, Reno, NV. All rights reserved.

The club's membership began to diminish in the 1960s, the Upper Goose social scene declining into an ongoing party scene rife with unregulated camping, litter, vandalism, and cabin break-ins. The Mohhekennuck Club cabin burned to the ground on Patriots Day, April 19, 1971[101], reportedly the consequence of a poorly managed fire in the lodge's fireplace.[102] The insurance claim payment of $5000 was insufficient to rebuild, and the cabin was never resurrected.

Despite the loss of their lodge, the club's membership remained committed to its founding mission. When the National Parks Service purchased the club's property on October 17, 1981 (a consequence of the Appalachian Trail Act), the club's members pledged $12,000 from the sale proceeds to the local chapter of the Appalachian Mountain Club for the purpose of maintaining the hiker cabin on Upper Goose. To this day, these funds continue to cover the operating costs of the hiker cabin.

In recognition of the club's contribution, an engraved bronze plaque commemorating the Mohhekennuck Club was created by the Appalachian Mountain Club, mounted on granite, and, in cooperation with the National Parks Service, installed beside the remaining chimney during a 1982 ceremony (See Chapter 18). However, local vandals had other plans, and the monument subsequently went missing.

The missing plaque was re-discovered on the lake's bottom by a fisherman, who dutifully retrieved it from the lake floor and delivered it to the Lee police station. The plaque was relocated from the police station to Linda Cysz's basement. Sometime later, this same fisherman was seeing his local physician, Dr. Peter Rentz (an interventional radiologist in Pittsfield), and when the conversation drifted into non-medical topics, the patient shared the story of the recovered plaque with his doctor. As it turned out, Rentz, who was active in the Appalachian Mountain Club, would soon retrieve the plaque from Linda's basement, mount it more permanently on a much heavier stone, and re-install it, safely anchored in concrete, adjacent to the old chimney -- where it continues to sit securely, reminding us of the legend of this storied club and thanking its members for their generosity.[103] [104]

Sometimes, I wonder if the Mohican Indians themselves would have been happy having this club named after them. After some reflection on the Mohhekennuckers' deep love of nature, of each other, and of Goose Pond, I think the answer is likely yes.

Figure 14.13 Mohhekennuck Club fireplace, before and now.
Left photograph courtesy of Warren Rapelye White, Reno, NV. All rights reserved.

Figure 14.14 Plaque at the site of the Mohhekennuck Club (left).
Dr. Peter Rentz of the Appalachian Mountain Club (right) whose patient discovered the missing plaque.

Snow on Goose Pond Shore

CHAPTER 15

THREE GOOSE POND FAMILIES

LINE TWO WAS RINGING at the Boston offices of The Trustees of Reservations, a Massachusetts conservancy dedicated to the preservation of many of the state's most pristine properties. It was 1985, and the caller, Henry Wilds Smith Jr, a Professor of Forestry at the University of the South in Tennessee, explained to the receptionist how he had inherited the 112-acre Annie B. Foote Tree Farm on the shores of a little lake high in the Berkshire Mountains called Goose Pond. And he wanted to donate the land to The Trustees.

Some fifty years before making this call, Henry Wilds Smith, Jr. (1923-2002) had spent timeless boyhood summers on, in, and around Goose Pond, hanging out with his like-minded lake buddies, Bob Stilwell and Ted Murphy. Barefoot all summer, these three boys would row, run, paddle, fish, swim, dive, hike, explore, horse around, sail around, joke around, poke around, occasionally commit a little mischief, and once or twice dance with the girls at the Mohhekennuck Club.

Henry's grandmother, Annie Butler Foote Smith, and Ted's grandmother, Nellie Foote Bassett Murphy, were first cousins, making Henry and Ted third cousins, descended from many generations of Foote's, traceable even further back than Jonathan Foote (1715-1803), one of Lee's earliest citizens.[105] At the time of these dreamy summers on the Pond, Ted and Henry were not, however, related to their co-conspirator Bob Stilwell. A marriage would later change that.

Jonathan Foote, with the American Revolution raging about him, had built for his family a large colonial-style home on Maple Street in Lee, a house that stands even today as the Maple Hill Farm. Quite a few generations later, and quite a few generations ago, cousins Annie and Nellie Foote would spend much of their childhoods in this Foote household which, because of its proximity to Goose Pond, exposed them at an early age to the magic of this little lake -- magic which would, much later in life, lead them to build their own homes (cabins really) on its tranquil shores. These early Foote claims on Goose Pond would prove to have an enduring and profound impact on not just the childhoods of young Henry, Ted, and Bob -- but on the future preservation of the lake's surrounding hills as well.

The combined good fortunes derived from the Foote family's own means and her marriage to Augustus Smith, the president of the Smith Paper Company, later acquired by Kimberly Clark Corp, provided Annie Foote Smith (1865-1947) with the resources to make a series of land purchases on the shores of Goose Pond in the early 1900s. Her accumulated land holdings included the most eastern section of Lower Goose's southern shoreline, extending along the southern side of Sucker Brook to Upper Goose's southwestern shore. She also purchased the so-called "Garfield Tract", which sits along the most eastern part of Lower Goose's northern shore – a tract which, many years later, was the subject of her grandson Henry's phone call in 1985.

In 1916, the Smiths built their large log cabin on the far southern shore of Lower Goose; with its oversized kitchen, heated with a large Franklin stove, fieldstone fireplace, and long, covered, lake-facing porch, the cabin was, for many years, the beating heart of the Smith family life on the Pond. Here is where Annie, quite the artist, would create wonderful sketches of the lake while her daughter Lucile (Henry's mom), in her artistic hand, would pen her celebratory poetry. It was from this cabin, after finishing his morning's breakfast, that young Henry would commence (on foot or by boat, depending) his daily adventures with Ted and Bob.

Figure 15.1 *Annie Foote Smith on the shore of Lower Goose Pond. Courtesy of David Stilwell.*

Figure 15.2 *Annie Foote Smith's sketch of Goose Pond. Courtesy of David Stilwell.*

Figure 15.3 *The three daughters of Annie Foote Smith: Juliet (left), Elsie (middle), and Lucile (right). Lucile was the mother of Henry Wilds Smith and Caroline Wilds Smith. Photograph taken at the Smith camp in 1911. Courtesy of David Stilwell.*

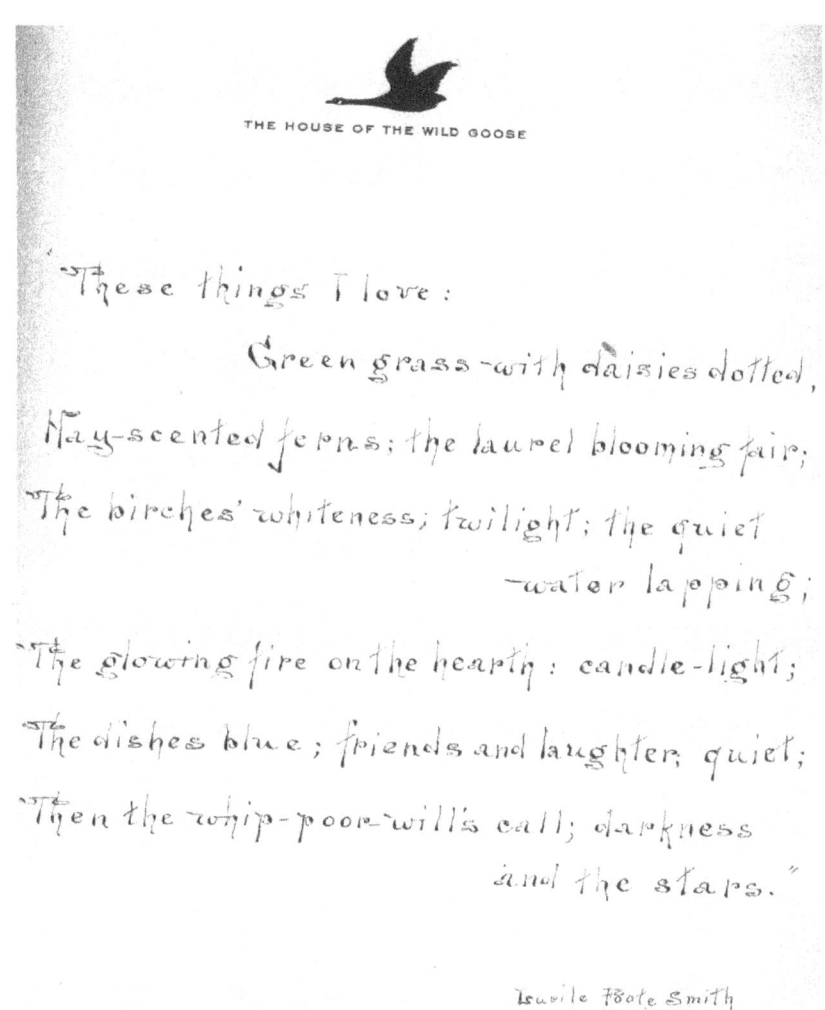

THE HOUSE OF THE WILD GOOSE

"These things I love:
    Green grass – with daisies dotted,
Hay-scented ferns; the laurel blooming fair;
The birches' whiteness; twilight; the quiet
    –water lapping;
The glowing fire on the hearth; candle-light;
The dishes blue; friends and laughter, quiet;
Then the whip-poor-will's call; darkness
    and the stars."

Lucile Foote Smith

Figure 15.4 *Poem by Lucile Foote Smith. Courtesy of David Stilwell.*

Figure 15.5 Smith family cabin on Lower Goose Pond. Courtesy of David Stilwell (left). Courtesy of Ellen Apfel (right).

Meanwhile, Annie's first cousin Nellie Foote Murphy (1872-1947) and her husband, Edward L. Murphy, purchased their own Goose Pond lots, theirs on the north side of Sucker Brook abutting both Lower Goose and Upper Goose and (temporarily it turns out) extending along much of the northern shore of Upper Goose. By 1916, they had built their log cabin on the Upper Goose shoreline just north of the channel's entrance, thereafter the base of operations for their future grandchildren Margueritte, Duncan, and Ted.

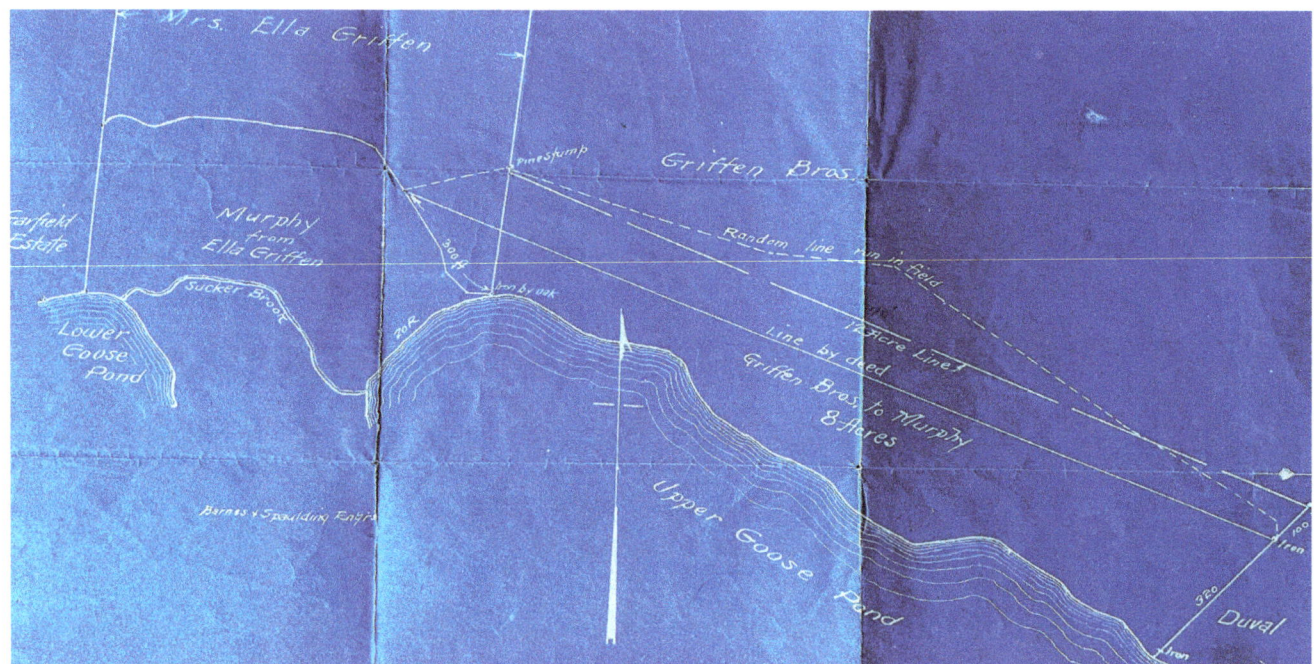

Figure 15.6 Survey of Upper Goose Pond in 1908 showing the Murphy plots purchased from the Griffins. Also note the so called "Garfield Estate" on the far left which had been purchased by Annie B. Foote. Courtesy of David Stilwell.

Figure 15.7 Murphy cabin on Upper Goose Pond. The photograph on the left shows Ted and Duncan (Jr.) Murphy in the doorway. On the right is the view of Upper Goose Pond from inside the Murphy cabin. Courtesy David Stilwell.

Back in 1910, the Mountain Mill, the remains of which still stand by the roadside on Forest Street, had, like many businesses then and now, a board of directors. Sitting on this paper mill's board was Edward L. Murphy, who spent his days as a local banker when he wasn't camping on Upper Goose, and William Chipman Stevenson, the owner of the Stevenson Insurance Company in Pittsfield. During their board meetings, Murphy and Stevenson would naturally be deep in discussions about paper output quotas, equipment investment, raw material supplies, shipping costs, payroll, profit and loss statements, and other considerations necessary for the operation of a successful business. But once the board meetings were adjourned, the two men would talk about their true love, which was nature and wilderness.

Stevenson, yet unaware of his future as the patriarch of Upper Goose Pond, surely did not hesitate to accept his friend's repeated invitations to visit the Murphy camp, which, in those early days, was limited to a tent on the water's edge. Stevenson, like the Murphy's and Smiths before him, was quickly stricken by the lake's allure, and soon found himself inviting his employees to annual company picnics at the Murphy camp. His employees would hike up to the lake, dressed up smartly in their white shirts, ties, and dresses, and enjoy a lakefront picnic with the boss. After a few years, when the Murphy's had built their cabin in 1916, the picnics got just a little bit fancier.

Figure 15.8 Duncan Murphy (Sr.) carving a roast at the Murphy camp in 1935. He was the son of Edward and Nellie Murphy and the father of young Duncan (Jr), Marguerite, and Ted (Edward). Courtesy of Edward G. Murphy.

Figure 15.9 William Chipman Stevenson on Mt. Greylock, 1906. Courtesy of David Stilwell.

Having by now contracted a serious case of the Goose Pond Bug, Stevenson proceeded to make his own series of land purchases around Upper Goose Pond, ultimately acquiring almost its entire shoreline -- except that which already belonged to the Smiths, the Murphy's, and the Mohhekennuck Club. He even purchased some of Murphy's land on the northern sure of Upper Goose. It was on this land acquired from Murphy that Stevenson and his son-in-law (Winfred Stilwell) built their cabins in 1926. The chestnut tree blight had by then left stands of dead chestnut trees in the Berkshire woods, resulting in an abundant (although not long-lasting) supply of lumber. Using his oxen to haul hewn chestnut logs up the hill, the builder, a Mr. Durkee, erected the Stilwell cabins which still stand today. It was from these cabins that Bob Stilwell (Helen and Winfred's youngest son), maybe without even waiting for *his* breakfast, would embark on his daily escapades with Ted and Henry.

Figure 15.10 William Chipman Stevenson (seated on left) at his insurance company picnic at the Murphy Cabin, c1920. Standing, second from left is Stevenson's daughter, Mary. Courtesy of David Stilwell.

Not long ago, Ted Murphy, just weeks shy of his 100th birthday and still winning track and field gold medals in the Senior Olympics, ("It's competition by age group. All I have to do is show up"), shared with me an amusing boyhood story about his rather mischievous, and perhaps not entirely politically correct, older brother Duncan.[106]

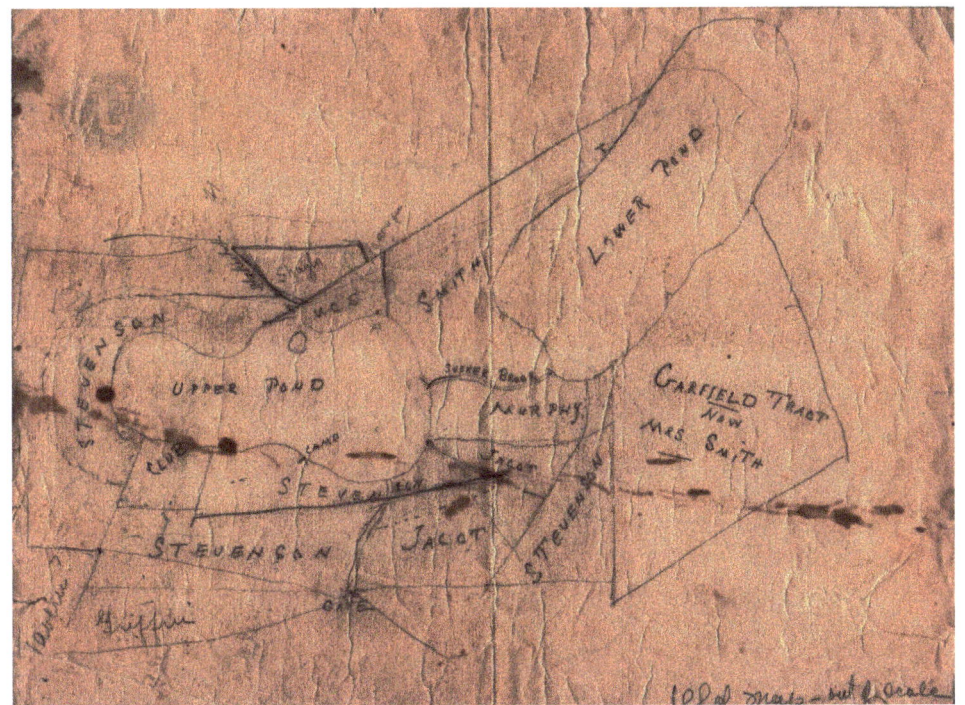

Figure 15.11 *Map drawn by William Chipman Stevenson on the back of his insurance company letterhead. I can envision Stevenson drawing this in his office as he daydreams about Upper Goose Pond. The so-called "Garfield Tract" later became the "Annie B. Foote Smith Tree Farm," and then the Goose Pond Reservation of the Trustees of Reservations. The "Club" property refers to the Mohhekennuck Club. Courtesy of David Stilwell.*

Figure 15.12 *Stevenson's cabin on Upper Goose Pond, shortly after being built in 1926. Courtesy of David Stilwell.*

The story has to do with the fishermen who, back in the 1930s, would quietly row their rented wooden rowboats up to Upper Goose on dark summer nights hoping to catch a few nice bass or trout, perhaps to be fried up for the next day's breakfast alongside some hash browns and eggs. Duncan, with a scheming mind rather typical of many teenagers then and now, decided there was way more fun to be had here than he could ever reasonably be expected to resist. Having previously purchased some phosphorescent white paint in town, he proceeded, one windless, moonlit night, to brush it onto his face and a big stick. All painted up, he lurked in the darkened woods, patiently waiting for the evening's fishermen to row their boats to their choice spots on the glassy lake, toss in their anchors, and drop their fishing lines down into the tranquil black depths. Once the fishermen were all nicely settled in, Duncan ran to the shoreline, face glowing white in the dark, and commenced whooping, jumping up and down, and brandishing his painted stick, imagining himself an Indian "on the warpath." Ted recalled how the fishermen predictably panicked, how their boats immediately descended into utterly hysterical chaos with oars banging, anchor chains dragging loudly over gunwales, more than a little cursing, and fishing poles being thrown all over the seats, their lines tangled and hooks flying every which way. The fishermen rowed feverishly back through the channel as fast as ever they could. Needless to say, Ted, Bob, and Henry immediately considered Dunc a world-class hero. Me, I wonder how his parents felt the next morning about all the paint on his face and how long it took to get it off.

And now, of course, I can picture a wide-eyed, spellbound little girl somewhere, sitting on the floor, her mouth agape, as she listens for the umpteenth time to her dad's most excellent retelling of her all-time favorite (and totally true) story, passed down faithfully through many generations, about how her super-brave great-great-grandpa Willy, while fishing one windless, moonlit night on Upper Goose Pond, a hundred years earlier, barely escaped from a most terrifying attack by a whooping and jumping Indian with a big stick and a painted face.

Figure 15.13 *Photographs of Bob Stilwell with Ted (Edward G.) Murphy on Upper Goose Pond. Bob is the younger boy. In the canoe picture, Bob is the paddler. Courtesy of Edward G. Murphy.*

Figure 15.14 *Fun on the Stevenson/Stilwell dock on Upper Goose. Courtesy of David Stilwell.*

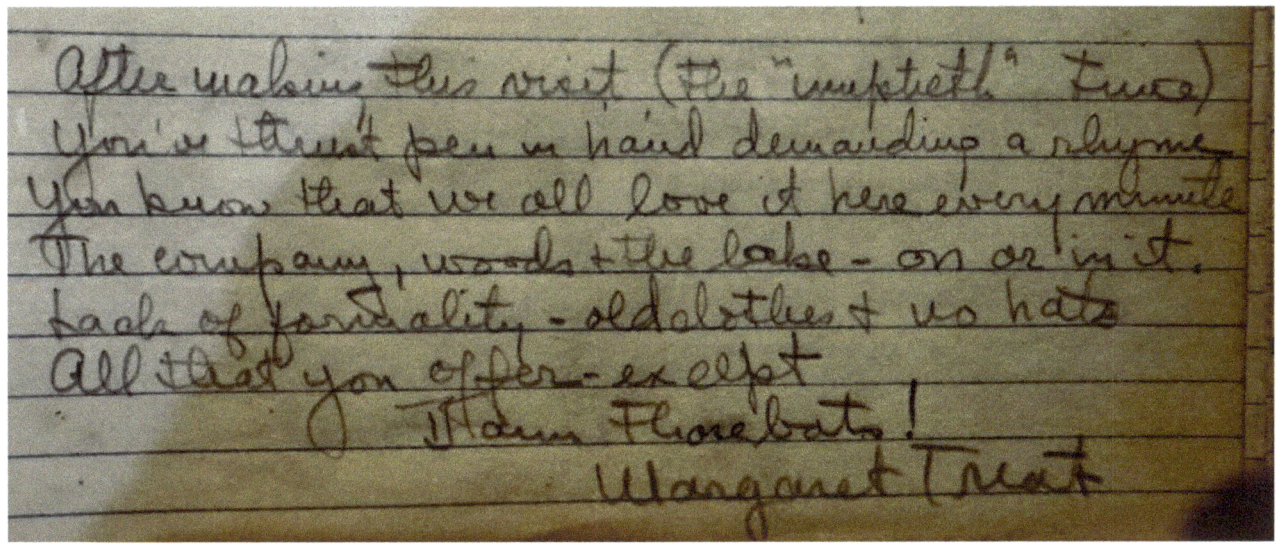

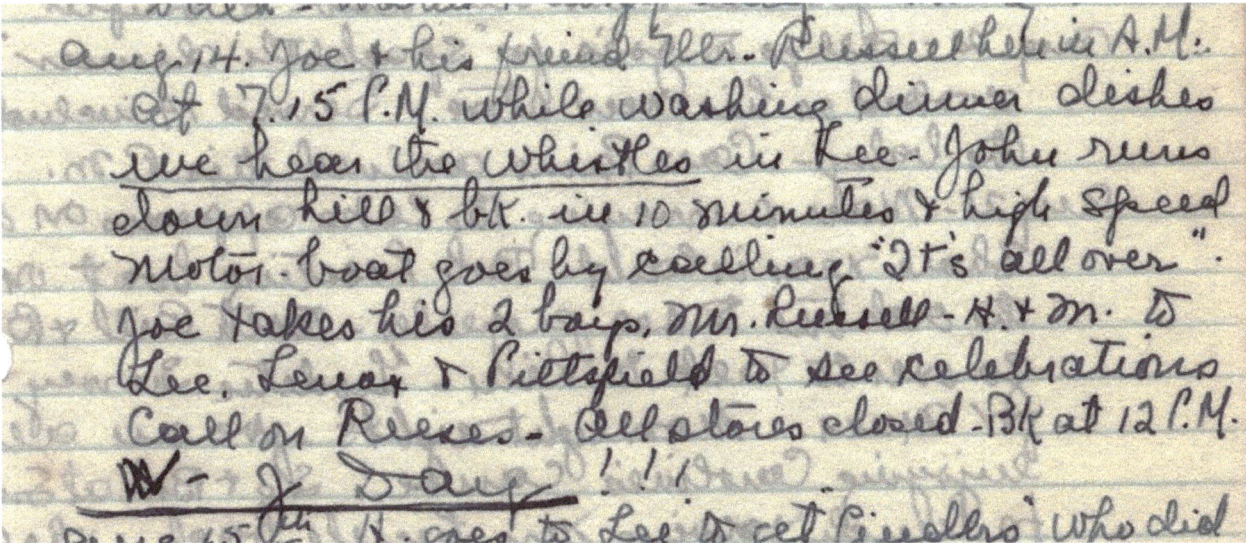

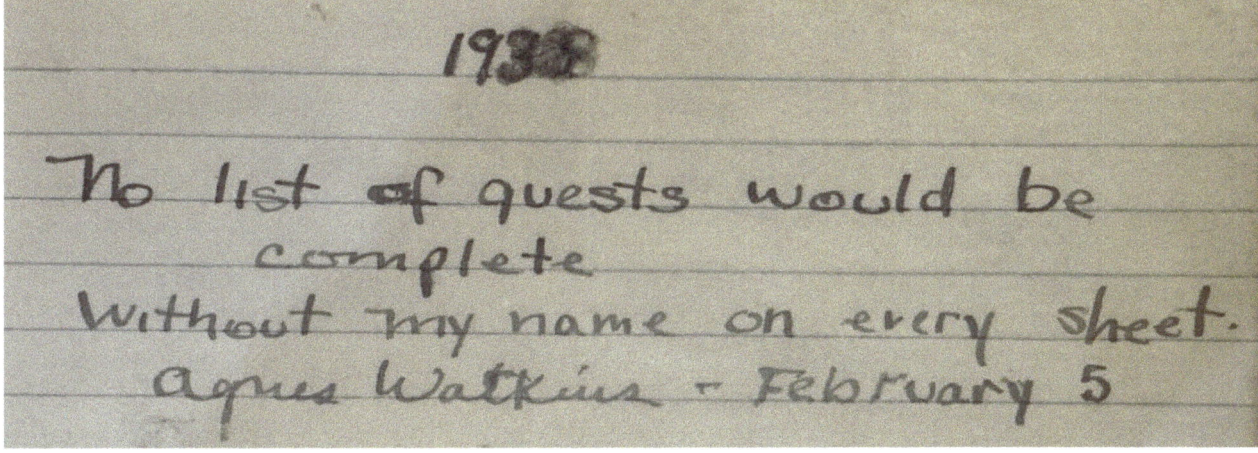

Figure 15.15 Sample entries in the Stevenson/Stilwell cabin guest logbook. The middle entry from August 14, 1945 describes the events of "VJ Day" on Goose Pond, the day Japan surrendered in World War II. Courtesy of David Stilwell.

Bob Stilwell had an older brother Bill, whose romantic life, with more than a little help from Henry's older sister, Caroline Wilds Smith, would forever merge these three pond families. Spending numerous summers on Upper Goose Pond, Bill naturally had become neighborly friends with Caroline. But it was not until quite some years later when Bill and Caroline had both grown up and gone off to college, each still embracing the outdoor life, and Bill having joined the outing club at Wesleyan University and Caroline having joined hers at Vassar College, did their friendship rise to a whole new level. With Wesleyan being an all-boys school, and Vassar an all-girls school, it makes some sense (socially speaking) that their outing clubs might have arranged for combined outings. Perhaps it was a bit of a surprise for Bill and Caroline to meet again this way, but now the chemistry was different than before and, when they married in 1942, they merged not only the Pond's iconic Stilwell and Smith families but by extension the Murphys' also.

Figure 15.16 Caroline Wilds Smith in a rowboat at the Smith camp. Notice the goose drawing on the bow. Courtesy of David Stilwell.

Figure 15.17 Caroline Wilds Smith (left), Bob Stilwell (middle), and Henry Wilds Smith (right) skiing on Lower Goose Pond. Courtesy of David Stilwell.

Bill and Caroline's predictably rustic honeymoon plan, which was to sequester themselves at the Stilwell camp on Upper Goose Pond, quickly ran amiss when in the darkness their car became mired in mud before even reaching the Smith cabin. After hoofing it to Sucker

Brook, they waded into the channel's chilly water (it was the month of May), swam across it, hiked, now soaking wet, through the lightless woods to the Stilwell cabins, launched the canoe, and paddled back to the car for their supplies (and probably some dry towels) – not the start typical of most honeymoons. The rest of their married days went smoother. It remains a mystery if these dripping wet events would have played out any differently had the car avoided getting stuck in the mud – what with no bridge over Sucker Brook, it would seem swimming across it might have always been part of the plan. Regardless, it was with this marital merger that Bill's brother Bob (and Bill too for that matter) finally became related to their boyhood friends, Henry and Ted.

Figure 15.18 Caroline Wilds Smith (right) and her cousin Ann (left) at the Smith camp. Courtesy of David Stilwell.

Figure 15.19 Caroline Wilds Smith and Bill Stilwell in 1941. When they wed in 1942, they merged the Stilwell, Smith, and Murphy families. Courtesy of David Stilwell.

Studying these family stories, popping up everywhere was the name Griffin. A photograph of the Stilwell camp from the 1920s shows "Wilbur Griffin and his oxen" delivering ice to the Stevenson icehouse.

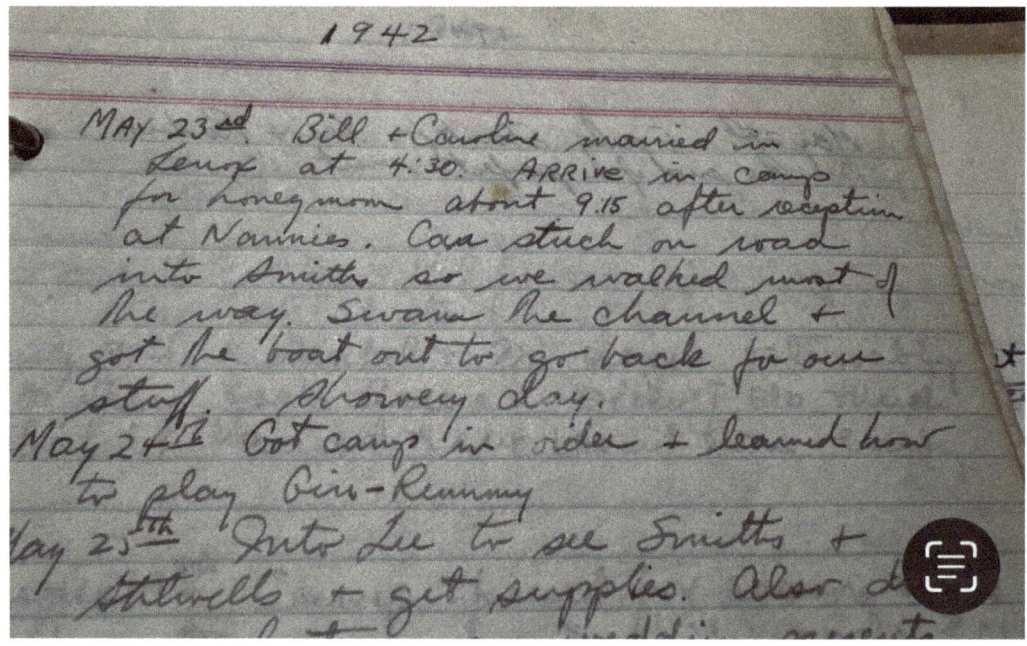

Figure 15.20 Entry in the Stilwell guest logbook describing Bill and Caroline's honeymoon adventure. Courtesy of David Stilwell.

Figure 15.21 Wilbur Griffin with his oxen at the Stevenson cabin in the 1920's. Griffin would cut ice and use the oxen to deliver ice to the Stevenson's icehouse, seen here in the background behind the main cabin. Courtesy of David Stilwell.

Many of the land purchases made by the Upper Goose families show the seller to be named Griffin. When the land was sold to the Mohhekennuck Club in 1909, the deeds mentioned a Griffin "homestead" and a Griffin "right of way" to the Griffin sawmills, and the club's members

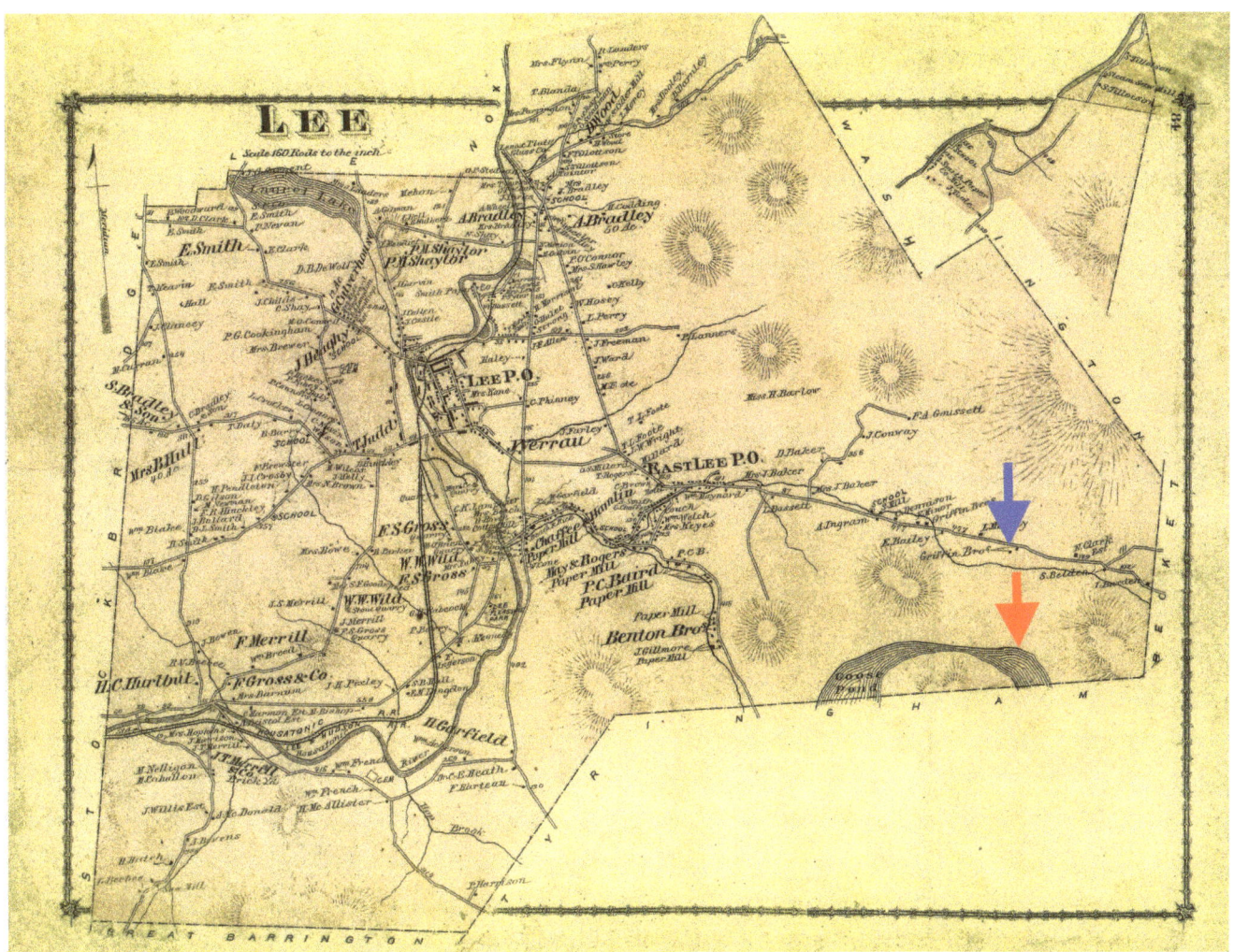

Figure 15.22 *Map from 1876 showing the Griffin Bros. mills (blue arrow) and their proximity to Upper Goose Pond (red arrow).*

would hike across the Griffin Farm to reach the club. A map of East Lee dated 1876 shows a pair of mills on the Greenwater stream, just over the mountain from Upper Goose Pond, called "Griffin Bros".

Ted Murphy recalls that a man named Griffin built the Murphy's cabin, icehouse, and their first boat. It was, in fact, from the Griffin family that many of the Smith, Stevenson, and Murphy land purchases were made. After these sales, Wilbur Griffin's presence on Upper Goose continued as he provided the new landowners with his various services: home building, ice harvesting, boat building, oxen hauls, what all. It appears that his homestead on the far northern shore of Upper Goose may actually have been the first on either Pond, almost certainly built no later than the early-mid 1800s. As difficult as it might be to imagine today, it is entirely likely that, in those early years (even before Chanter Road), access to Upper Goose was easier than to Lower Goose, given the Upper Pond's closer proximity to the main road and the presence of many rough wood roads accessing Upper Goose – the remnants of which can still be found winding through the woods.

Meanwhile, on Main Street in Stockbridge stood a jewelry shop owned by a Charles Jacot, himself the son of a Swiss jeweler. Jacot purchased his lot on Upper Goose in 1929, his wedged between the Murphy and Stevenson holdings, and then built his "Jacot Cottage" in 1930 just up the hill from the shoreline, sporting bright red paint and kitchen dishes supplied from his jewelry shop. Likely as a consequence of the challenges presented to the jewelry market by the Great Depression, Jacot sold his cottage to Stevenson in 1935. Jacot and his wife died suddenly on a rainy day in 1941, their car broadsided by a jack-knifed tractor-trailer on Pittsfield's Snake Hill Curve. The Jacot Cottage was used by the Stevensons-Stilwells as an overflow guest house until 1982 when it was purchased by the National Parks Service and converted to the Appalachian Trail Hiker Cabin, which still operates today.

Figure 15.23 Charles Jacot's cabin, in 1979, on Upper Goose Pond. At the time this photo was taken, the cabin belonged to the Stilwell family. This photo was taken for the survey by the National Parks Service. The cabin became the hiker cabin for the Appalachian Trail a few years later.
Courtesy of the National Parks Service.

There exists a curious pair of eloquently worded letters written in by William Chipman Stevenson in 1929, one addressed to Annie Foote Smith, and the other to his good friend Edward Murphy, both outlining his desire to pass on ownership of his Upper Goose Pond property to his two daughters (Helen and Mary) and requesting Annie's and Edward's consent. While these letters certainly appear unusual on the surface, they suggest a pre-existing, informal "pact" between these three to mutually preserve the natural state of their lands – a pact that would prove prophetic.

Prophetic because the joys, the curiosity, the good humor, the art, the poetry, the passionate embrace of freedom, of friendship, of family, fun, and nature, of the Pond life, the manifest love that Bob, Henry, and Ted -- and their families -- brought into our world during those summer idylls have transformed Goose Pond forever. Today, 770 acres surrounding Upper Goose are protected by the National Parks Service while the 112 acres that comprised the Annie B. Foote Tree Farm is under the wing of the Trustees of Reservations. It was the love that these three families had for Goose Pond, and their deep desire to preserve its natural essence, that made these enduring protections a reality, and stands as a reminder to us all, of the power that resides in our dreams.

WILLIAM C. STEVENSON
PITTSFIELD, MASSACHUSETTS

Jan. 25, 1929.

Mrs. Annie F. Smith,
Lee, Massachusetts.

My dear Mrs. Smith:

It is my intention to deed to my daughters Miss Mary G. Stevenson and Mrs. Winfred N. Stilwell the property I own around Goose Pond. I would like them to keep it in the family, and feel sure that they will take as much interest in it as the rest of us do. Also that no harm is done to anyone that is interested in the developement of the lake.

I trust that you have no objections to my doing so as that was in accordance with our understanding.

Very kind regards.

Yours very truly,

WCS:MO'D

Figure 15.24 *Letter from William Chipman Stevenson to Annie Foote Smith. A similar letter was sent to Edward Murphy. Annie and Edward both granted their consent. Courtesy of David Stilwell.*

Figure 15.25 *Henry Wilds Smith Jr. sitting on Stump Island. In the background is the Lower Goose Pond shoreline (red arrows) that, many years later, he would donate to the Trustees of Reservations and become the Trustees' Goose Pond Reservation. Courtesy of David Stilwell.*

Snow dusting on Pinepoint

CHAPTER 16

CHANTERWOOD

ONE OF THE RECIPES in Eva Bender's 1965 cookbook, *Chanterwood Favorites*, instructs us to beat four egg yolks and three tablespoons of water until thick and lemon-colored, and then to add one teaspoon of almond extract. Once the remaining steps are completed, we pour the batter into a greased and lined 11"x7"x2" cake pan and bake at 350 degrees for thirty minutes. After it cools, and the cake is sprinkled with sifted confectionary sugar, we will have baked "Miss May's Sponge Cake," a popular Chanterwood favorite during a time when the prevailing taste in dessert ran, it appears, somewhat simpler than it does today.

Although this particular sponge cake was a Sunday specialty at Chanterwood, its recipe was actually created earlier by a champion ice skater named Miss May (or really Mary) Morse, who was the owner and operator of Chanterwood's predecessor, Camp Morse, an eleven-acre lodge nestled on Lower Goose's northern shoreline, opened by Miss May and her sister in 1925, both hailing from New Jersey, and both rumored to have been descended from Samuel Morse, the inventor of Morse Code.

Camp Morse, consisting of a spacious central lodge, several rustic guest cabins, a large dock, and a floating swim platform (complete with diving board), entered the modern era shortly after it opened when, in April 1928, the Lee Electric Company ran electric lines to five of its buildings, making it the first property on Goose Pond to have electric lights.[107] Camp Morse was very likely a beneficiary of the "Roaring Twenties," a period marked by a substantial growth in disposable family income, the increasing mobility brought by automobiles, and dramatic growth in entertainment and leisure activities.

Goose Pond Developing.

A. F Viale has sold for Mary and Edward H. Kline their property at Goose pond to Miss Mary Morse o New York city. This property is situated on the side of the pond known at Lee Landing and consists of 11 acres of land and a cottage Contractor Edward X. Mougin will begin in the spring the erection of seven buildings there, which, when finished, will make this shore one of the most thickly settled of any resort pond in this section. Mr. Viale has in the past sold several properties greatly benefiting the town. Miss Morse, who will spend the summer at the pond, is known as the champion lady skater of the country.

Figure 16.1 Sale of property to Mary Morse in a newspaper clipping dated January 23, 1925. Courtesy of Edward Habermehl.

Figure 16.2 Postcards of Camp Morse. Courtesy of Sophie Sterling.

Rustic Cabin overlooking Goose Lake, Chanterwood, Lee, Massachusetts

A contented guest has caught our "hideaway" deep woods setting with this sketch of one of our cabins. You have received our literature in the past. But if you want to know more about our ideal lake, perfect swimming, all sports, Hi-fi, good food, Loafing Patio — EVERYTHING to make your short vacation congenial, "different" and moderate, send for our Folder P, Box M, Lee, Mass. A truly unique lakeside resort near Tanglewood, Jacob's Pillow and all Berkshire Hills attractions.

J. Grigo, Mgr.

Figure 16.3 *Postcard (front and back) of Chanterwood under J. Grigo, Mgr. Courtesy of Sophie Sterling.*

When the Morse sisters retired in 1949, the lodge was purchased by Joseph Grigo, who added additional cabins to the resort, renamed it Chanterwood, and had the good sense (or good luck) to hire Eva Bender, also from New Jersey, to be his chef, manager, and host, positions she held for the next twenty years. When Grigo himself retired in 1968 to Coconut Grove, Florida, it was Eva's turn to buy the resort and thereby become promoted to owner -- while still also filling the positions of chef, manager, and host, mind you -- positions she held for yet *another* fifteen years.

Providing fifteen private and semi-private cabins, each with its own name such as "Moonrise," "The Greenery," "Robin's Nest," and "Pine Cone," and each cabin with one to four bedrooms, Chanterwood could host up to sixty guests at a time. Open from Memorial Day to Columbus Day, the resort would provide its lodgers with three home-cooked meals daily, eaten family style at long tables in the main dining room, a large dock for swimming, sunbathing, and fishing, tennis and volleyball courts, quiet reading rooms, shuffleboard, evening dances, card games, campfires, chess boards, evening theatricals, all-day classical music piped to the patio -- starting with chamber music each morning and growing to symphonies by afternoon -- along with the use of a small fleet of rowboats and canoes, each painted with a large green "C" at the bow.

One of these Chanterwood canoes sported its letter "C" painted backward, a curious consequence of my younger brother Ron, employed as Eva's teenage foreman for a few summers in the 1970s, having been tasked with painting the "C" on this particular canoe while it (the canoe) was upside down. And Ron — always the genius and apparently (over)thinking that an upside-down but correctly painted "C" would for some strange reason manage to become backward upon the canoe's righting — proceeded to deliberately paint the letter backward, imagining that the cleverly reversed letter would thus become normalized when the canoe was subsequently turned right side up. To be fair, Ron, I had to think this through a bit myself. The canoe's reversed letter "C" was never corrected.[108]

Figure 16.4 *A Chanterwood brochure. Courtesy of Sophie Sterling.*

Figure 16.5 A Chanterwood brochure. Courtesy of Sophie Sterling.

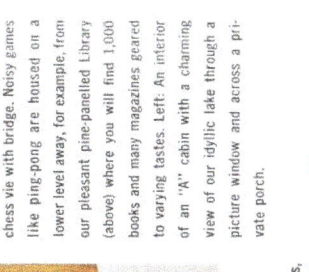

Chanterwood is Unique

WHY? It's hundreds of little things like vases of wild flowers everywhere (often guest arranged). It's feeding Leo, our pet chipmunk—generations of him now. It's the house-party atmosphere of a well mixed crowd (55-60) of all ages, mostly professional and business people who return to our "hideaway" for its honest back-to-nature way of life avoiding the garish, the hectic, the "organized". It's our "unsophisticated" activities, our wonderful meals, our comfortable Lodge, our separate living quarters. It's the informality, for example, of a guest-sponsored Community Chip-in Cocktail Party in the Patio before dinner. Volunteers collect, buy, mix, serve. It's getting together for an outdoor dance on the spur of the moment. It's our college and high school staff—youthful, friendly, courteous. Anyway it's SOMETHING we have acquired in small ways since 1925 in a place always under Owner-mgt. One guest told us: "It's habit forming!" You really have to try it once to know why we are called UNIQUE.

Informality and Variety

OUR cheery, tree-top Dining Room, enclosed with large windows overlooking our ever admired lake is completely informal. Tables of 6-8 mean easy mixing. No separate tables or assigned seats—join new companions each meal, if you wish. Shorts and slacks always O. K. Three delicious meals daily—abundantly served with care for variety, taste, imagination —no doubt account for our many, many returnees. Features: buffet service at breakfast; help-yourself late breakfast; weekly lakeside cookouts; outdoor buffet lunches or suppers; packed picnic lunches on 24 hrs. notice except on weekends.

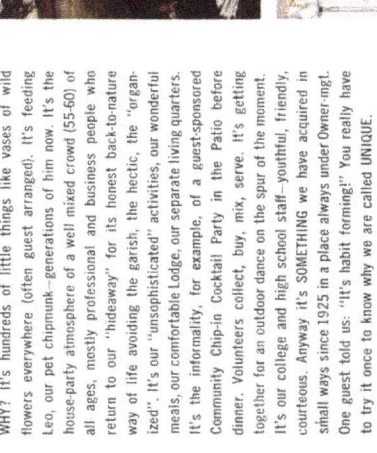

What About Evenings?

If you are not "out" to Tanglewood, ballet, theater, there's plenty to do. Maybe join a square dance outdoors on a clay court which some nights becomes our Concert Grove for requested stereo concerts. There's always a table or two of bridge, scrabble, chess. The Game Room downstairs for ping pong and such draws some. Romantic ones go canoeing or rowing by moon or star light. Maybe someone starts a fireside sing either indoors or down at the lake. Anyway, no social director will "coax" you into anything if you prefer reading by the fire, say!

Plenty of Play & Rest Areas

You often wonder where 50 or more people disappear to after breakfast. Besides the indoors, there are five courts, the Musical Patio, the Lakeview Terrace, the Morning Sun Spot, the many trails, the floats, the boats and canoes. See our Campus Map in the Rate Sheet.

TOP: Cozy corner of our cheerful Card Room where scrabble and chess vie with bridge. Noisy games like ping-pong are housed on a lower level away, for example, from our pleasant pine-panelled Library (above) where you will find 1,000 books and many magazines geared to varying tastes. Left: An interior of an "A" cabin with a charming view of our idyllic lake through a picture window and across a private porch.

Figure 16.6 A Chanterwood brochure. Courtesy of Sophie Sterling.

Figure 16.7 A Chanterwood brochure. Courtesy of Sophie Sterling.

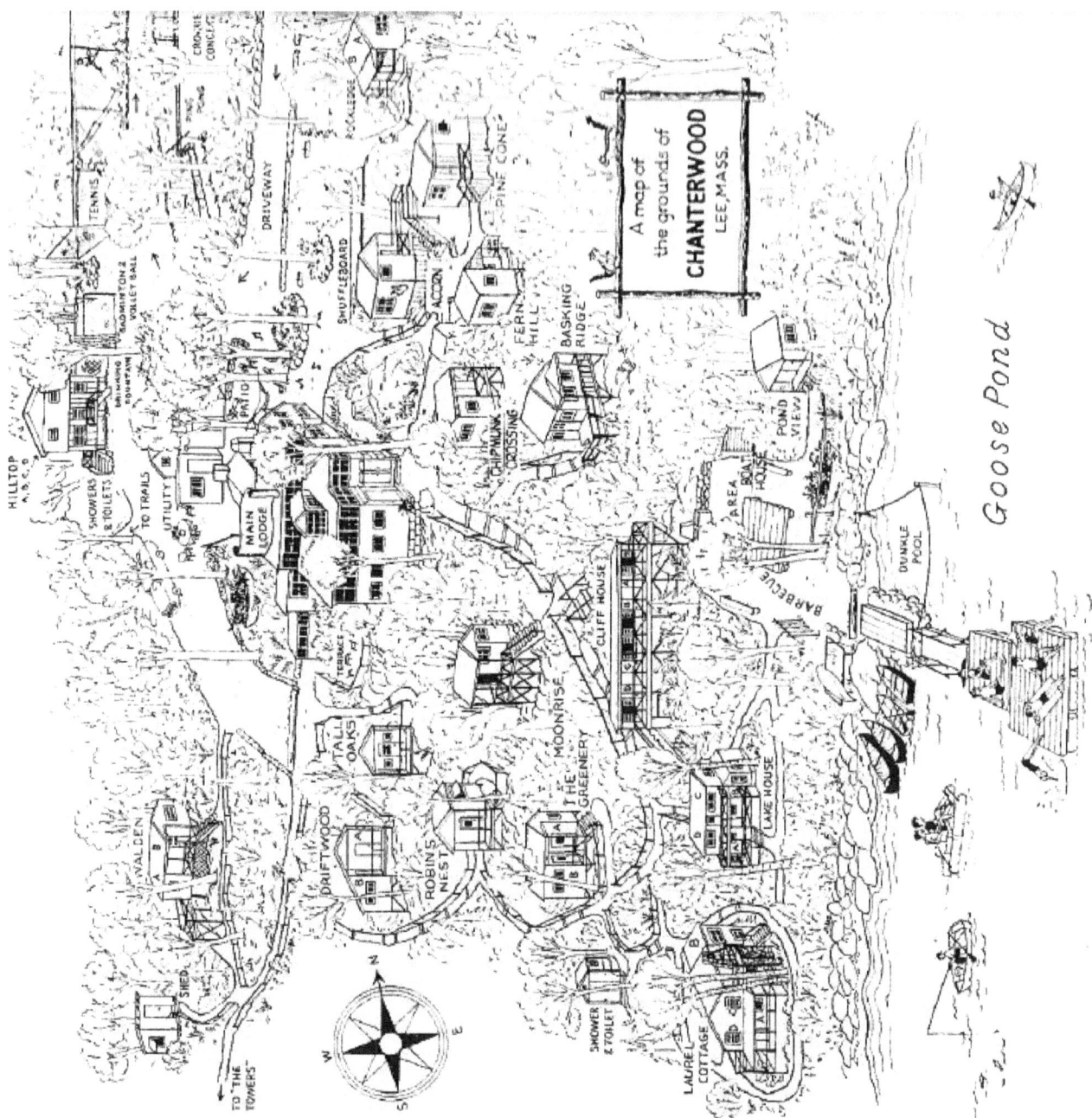

Figure 16.8 Map of Chanterwood showing cabin names. Courtesy of Sophie Sterling.

Figure 16.9 Postcards showing the lodge and a cabin at Chanterwood. Courtesy of Sophie Sterling.

Ron had this to say about his former boss:

"She was a quiet and serious person and had a great impact on me. Her work ethic was incredible. She would get to Chanterwood (alone) before Memorial Day and never leave until November. She was the first one there and the last to leave - and in between she ran the business, 30+ cabins, and oversaw everything - while cooking 3 meals every day for 60 guests and a staff of 15. She never took a day, an hour or one meal off. She never left the mountain. Even though I was just a teenager when I started there - she trusted me implicitly and gave me tremendous responsibility. (I quickly learned managerial skills and had management responsibility over most of the other kids working there.) I particularly remember in early spring when I would get there around Memorial Day and she and I would be the only people there for several weeks. She would sometimes talk to me a little about the business and her life. I don›t think she ever mentioned any family members - she was never married. And once the summer rush began - she would default to her no-nonsense demeanor.

"Although I do recall her smiling once: one afternoon after lunch was over, Eva had left the kitchen, and I was helping the other kids clean up the dining room and I decided to show-off and juggle some hard-boiled eggs. As I made a fancy move of lifting my leg to juggle under my knee - I accidentally kicked over a large tray with all the milk and juices from lunch. Everything ended up on the floor including me. Just then Eva walked back in. She tried not to smile but I saw it! She said nothing and just turned away and walked out. I knew she approved of the way I 'entertained the troops.'"[109]

Figure 16.10 *Postcard showing Chanterwood Reading Room. Courtesy of Sophie Sterling.*

When Eva K. Bender passed away on June 24, 1983, Chanterwood closed its doors. After this, a short-lived restaurant opened on the premises, and when this too closed, a much-treasured era on Goose Pond came to an end. But Eva's legacy can live on through her illustrated, 1965 *Chanterwood Favorites* cookbook. (Courtesy of Sophie Sterling) Her otherwise serious persona loosens up a bit in these recipes which feature her own folksy witticisms and humorous sketches. Maybe we should let the smell of some of Eva's recipes waft over Goose Pond from time to time.

Figure 16.11 Eva Bender. From Family Sketches: The Albert F. Bender Family, *by Edward J. Bender.*
Courtesy of Sophie Sterling and Gary Bender.[110]

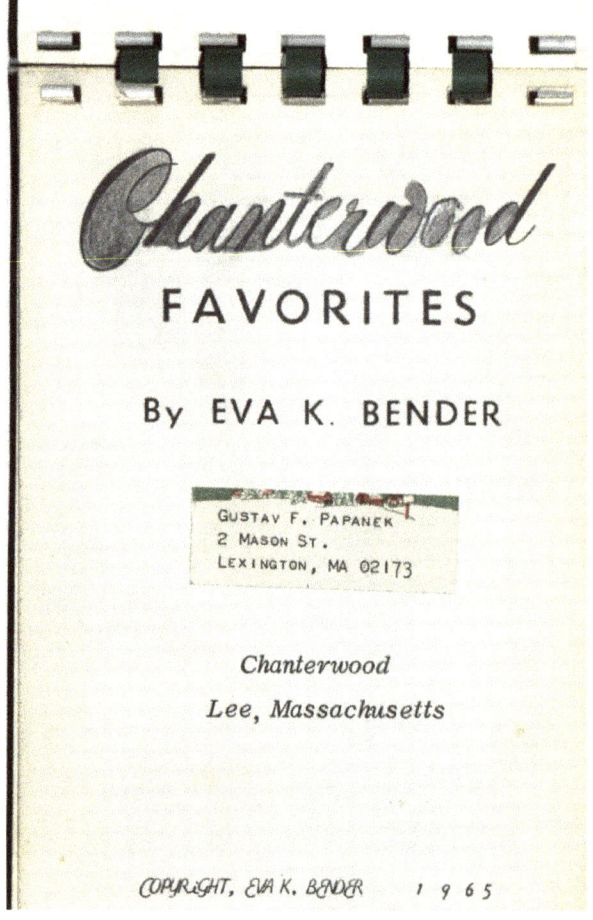

"FAVORITES"

A new addition to our home-baked "goodies" file, which can be clipped and inserted in your "Chanterwood Favorites" recipe book.

Sherry Almond Crisps

- 1 cup butter or margarine
- 1 cup sifted confectioners' sugar
- ½ tsp. vanilla
- 3 Tbsps. sherry
- 1½ cups sifted all-purpose flour
- ¼ tsp. salt
- ½ cup finely chopped almonds, toasted

Cream together butter (or margarine) and sugar till fluffy. Stir in sherry. Sift together flour and salt and add. Stir in almonds and vanilla. Drop by teaspoonful on ungreased cookie sheet. Bake in 375° oven for 10-12 mins. until lightly browned. Store in tightly covered container. Makes about 36 delicate and delicious cookies.

Chanterwood

FAVORITES

By EVA K. BENDER

Gustav F. Papanek
2 Mason St.
Lexington, MA 02173

Chanterwood

Lee, Massachusetts

COPYRIGHT, EVA K. BENDER 1965

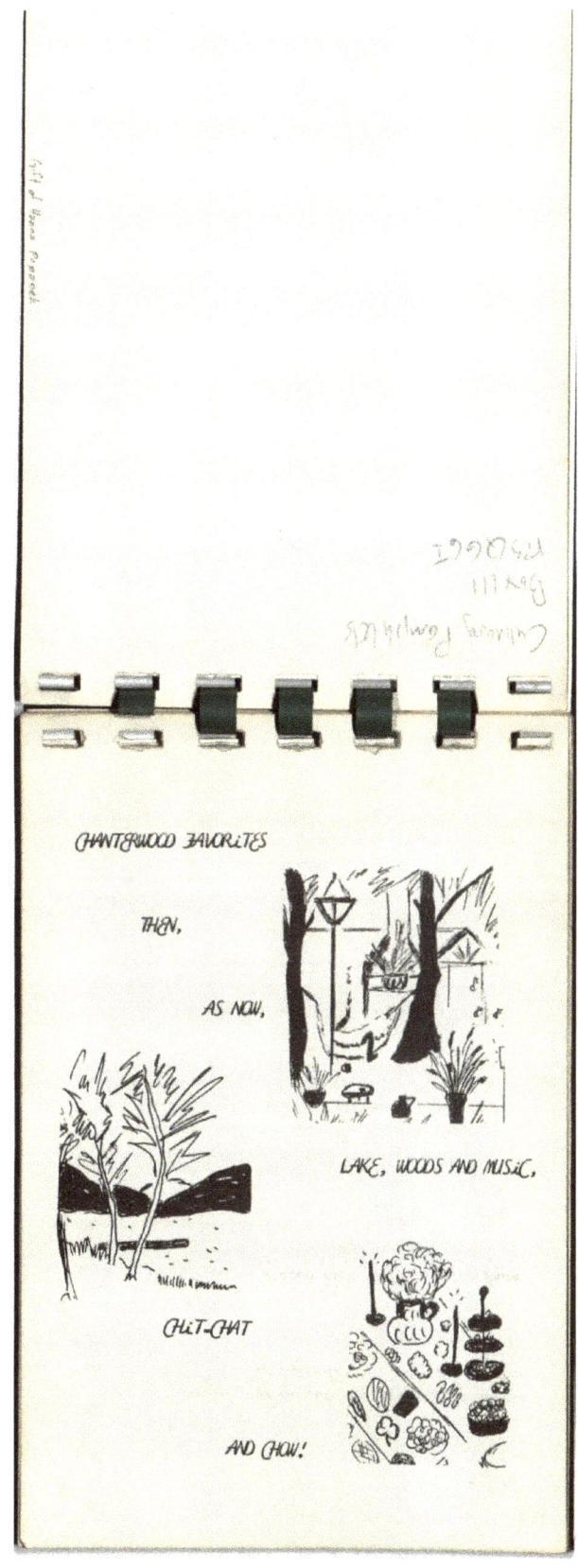

When people ask how we get our recipes, I always tell them that all our friends are good cooks. And it's TRUE!

Many things in this book have been adapted from suggestions of kind Chanterwoodians, and to all of them go our grateful thanks.

Thanks also must go to all the boys and girls who have worked with us over these many summers, whose good-natured comments, and prodigious appetites, were a continuing challenge.

And finally to Joe, our long-suffering boss, appreciation for patience (and good digestion!) as he bore with our experimentations and improvisations.

If there are other recipes you would like, please tell us - perhaps next year, Volume 2.

INDEX

CRESCENT COOKIES	1
CHOCOLATE ChipMunk COOKIES	2-3
LEMON MERINGUE PIE	4-5
BROWNIES	6
MISS MAY'S SPONGE CAKE	7
CHOCOLATE LAYER CAKE	8
GREAT AUNT MARGIE'S COFFEE CAKE	9
DUTCH APPLE CAKE	10-11
CRULLERS	12-13
MISS SYBIL'S BANANA BREAD	14
SWEDISH MEAT BALLS	15
CHEESE SOU-FONDUE	16-17
SEA-FONDUE	17
CHICKEN NOODLE CASSEROLE	18-19
RED CABBAGE	19
SEAFOOD CASSEROLE	20
GOLDENGLOW SALAD	21
ROQUEFORT CHEESE DIP	22
CORN FRITTERS	23
CHICKEN MARYLAND	24-25
MEAT LOAF	26
BROILED SWORDFISH	27
BAR-B-QUE SHORT RIBS OF BEEF	28-29

CRESCENT COOKIES

Butter	1 Cup
Almond Extract (or Vanilla or Orange)	1/2 tsp.
Confectioner's Sugar	1/2 Cup
Cornstarch	1/2 Cup
Flour	1-1/2 Cups
Salt	Pinch
Chopped Almonds (or Filberts or Walnuts)	1/2 Cup

CREAM butter, add extract. Sift together sugar, cornstarch, flour and salt and add. Stir in nuts and mix well. Shape into rolls about as long and round as your pinkie, bend into crescents and place 1-1/2" apart on ungreased cookie sheet.

BAKE 25-30 mins. in slow (325°) oven, or until delicately browned. Cool on racks, sprinkle with additional sifted conf. sugar.   Yield: about 36

::

HINT NO. 1.

All recipes specify "butter". However, in this day of cholesterol worries, many prefer margarine, and I find no significant difference in flavor or consistency, especially if the product is to be consumed immediately.

I do think butter has slightly better keeping qualities, if cookies are to be stored.

1

Chocolate "Chipmunk" Cookies

One lovely day a woods-roaming guest returned with an armload of fragrant pine branches, and stacked them on the flower table behind the kitchen.

Suddenly Leo, the Chipmunk, appeared on a branch, ecstatically sniffing the aroma of cooling cookies.

I pulled the window down in front of him - and have you ever seen a frustrated chipmunk? He could _see_ them, probably still _smell_ them, and he pawed the glass frantically in the hope of sampling something new and exotic.

Of course he got one - who could resist such flattery!

Butter	1 Cup
Granulated Sugar	3/4 Cup
Light Brown Sugar, firmly packed	3/4 Cup
Eggs, lightly beaten	2
Baking Soda	1 tsp.
Flour	2-1/4 Cups
Salt	1 tsp.
Hot water	Few Drops
Chopped nuts	1 Cup
Vanilla	1 tsp.
Chocolate Chips	12 ozs.

CREAM butter, add sugars and mix well. Add eggs, then sifted dry ingredients and few drops hot water. Blend in nuts and vanilla, then chocolate chips.

Drop by teaspoonful onto lightly greased cookie sheets, about 2" apart, and bake in 375° oven 10 to 12 mins., or until light brown.

Cool on racks.   Yield: Approx. 8 doz.

::

AND the only thing more wistful than Leo, the Chipmunk's, expression was that of Charlie Rowell, as, hand-in-hand with Harriet, he peered silently over the kitchen window sill; and the only thing more satisfied was his beatific smile when it was finally LEMON PIE DAY!

LEMON MERINGUE PIE

Cornstarch	7 TBsps.
Water	2 Cups
Sugar	1 Cup
Salt	1/4 tsp.
Egg yolks, well beaten	3
Butter	3 TBsps.
Lemon Juice, strained	1/2 Cup
Lemon Rind, grated	2 TBsps.

::::::::::::::::::::::::::::

Egg Whites	3
Sugar	6 TBsps.

PLACE 1 cup cold water in top of double boiler, dissolve cornstarch in this, then add 1 cup HOT water. Stir in sugar & salt and cook over medium heat, stirring constantly, until it comes to a boil.

Cover, place over boiling water and cook 10 mins. Remove from heat, stir a little of the hot mixture into yolks, then combine yolks with the remaining hot mixture. Reserve 1/2 tsp. each rind and juice for meringue. Gradually add remaining rind and juice until desired tartness is obtained. Add butter, stir well, and set aside to cool.

Now ready your pie shell. If you are willing to start from scratch -

In large, shallow bowl combine 1-1/2 Cups All-Purpose Flour, 1/2 Cup Cold Shortening, and 3/4 tsp. Salt.

BLEND with pastry blender, or rub quickly between your palms until about pea size. DON'T SQUEEZE!

With fork, quickly stir in 3-4 TBsps. ice water, just enough to have dough hold together. Roll out on floured board with light, quick strokes to diameter 1" larger than your pie pan. Fold in half, lift into pan and center. Turn edges under, pressing between thumb and forefinger to make fluted ridge. Prick all over with heavy-tined fork. Bake in 425° oven for 15-18 mins., or until light brown all over. If air bubbles form in first five mins., collapse with fork.

Cool on rack. When cold, fill with thoroughly cooled filling.

Beat 3 egg whites at medium (NOT high) speed together with a pinch of salt and the 1/2 tsp. reserved juice. When foamy, begin adding sugar gradually, and beat until meringue is satiny and will hold its shape when bowl is inverted. Stir in the reserved lemon rind.

Spread meringue over filling, making sure to cover completely and touch pastry rim all around.

Bake in 450° for 5-8 mins., or until delicately browned. When cool, cut with buttered knife.

This filling quantity is for 9" pie. You should have some pastry dough left over.

SUGGESTION: Fill little circle with a tsp. of jam, fold over, seal edges with fork and bake.

BROWNiES

Sugar	1 Cup
Eggs, well beaten	2
Bitter Chocolate, Baker's	2 Sqs.
Butter	1/2 Cup
Flour	1 Cup
Salt	Pinch
Chopped nuts - any kind	1/2 Cup
Vanilla	1/2 tsp.

GRADUALLY add sugar to beaten eggs. Melt chocolate and butter together over hot water. Cool slightly, then add to first mixture. Stir in flour, salt, vanilla and nuts.

Pour into greased pan, approximately 11" x 7" x 2", and bake 25-30 mins. in slow (325°) oven. Cool in pan, then cut into squares.

::

HINT NO. 2

To make all cake baking simpler, grease pan lightly, then cover with wax paper, folding corners snugly and letting paper come up almost to top of pan.

Then grease again, especially over the mitered corner folds.

Let finished cake rest in pan for 5 mins., then invert and cake will slip out beautifully.

Peel off paper at once.

MISS MAY'S SPONGE CAKE

Egg Yolks	4
Sugar, granulated	1 Cup
Cold Water	3 TBsps.
Cornstarch	2 TBsps.
Flour	1cup - 2tbsp
Salt	1/4 tsp.
Baking Powder	1-1/4 tsp.
Almond Extract	1 tsp.
Egg whites	4

ANOTHER recipe from Camp Morse days is Miss May's Sponge Cake, a Sunday specialty.

Beat egg yolks and water until thick and lemon colored. Add extract, then sugar very gradually, beating well after each addition so that sugar is thoroughly absorbed.

Put cornstarch in cup, fill cup with flour. Then sift together with baking powder and salt. Fold gently into first mixture. When thoroughly blended, fold in egg whites which have been beaten into stiff, but not dry, peaks.

Pour batter into greased and lined cake pan, approximately 11" x 7" x 2" and bake in 350° oven about 30-35 mins., or until top springs back when lightly pressed. Turn out on rack immediately and peel off paper. When cool, sprinkle with sifted conf. sugar.

CHOCOLATE LAYER CAKE

ANY standard cookbook will give you a recipe for a basic chocolate cake, and you can choose the one that suits you best - cocoa type, bitter chocolate, or devil's food. But, if you're the lazy type (as I am!) use one of the excellent mixes now on the market.

But NOW------ glamorize it with this icing!!

Sugar, granulated	1 Cup
Coffee	1/2 Cup
Hot water	1/2 Cup
Butter	1 TBsp.
Bitter Chocolate (Baker's)	2 Squares
Salt	Pinch
Vanilla	1/2 tsp.

Mix everything (except vanilla) and heat over medium flame until chocolate is melted, stirring constantly. Thicken with 3 Tablespoons of cornstarch dissolved in a little cold water, and cook until mixture is thick and smooth. Remove from fire, add vanilla and beat well. Icing will remain soft. It is best to put this on cake while cake is still warm. Enough for two 9" layers.

GREAT AUNT MARGIE'S COFFEE CAKE

A family joke, too long to explain, but everyone seems to like the results.

Flour	4-1/2 Cups
Sugar	3 Cups
Butter	3/4 Cup
Baking Powder	1 TBsp.
Salt	3/4 tsp.
Cinnamon	1 TBsp.
Chopped Nuts (walnuts, filberts)	1 Cup

PUT all the above into a large bowl and blend well with pastry blender, or with a quick, rubbing motion of your own two hands. JUST DON'T SQUEEZE! It should be about the consistency of coarse corn-meal. Take out 1-1/2 cups and reserve for topping.

Eggs	3
Milk	3/4 Cup
Vanilla	1-1/2 tsp.

Beat eggs, add milk and vanilla. Stir in all of the dry mix (except reserved topping). If desired, add 1/2 cup raisins or chopped dates. Pour into a greased, unlined, cake pan approximately 11" x 17" x 2". Sprinkle topping evenly over batter and bake 30-35 mins. in 375° oven. Cool in pan.

Keeps well - some think it better the next day.

DUTCH APPLE CAKE

THO why it's Dutch I really can't say, since friend Tom Cunningham contributed this one. Tom, a man of many talents, is the one who single-handedly moved Cabin #4 from the top of the hill to it's present position midway. Wife Helen, one of the best cooks I know, says she can't make this turn out as good as Tom's. Do you suppose he's holding out on us?

Apples, peeled and thinly sliced (Greenings are best)	6-8
Butter	1/2 Cup
Flour	1-1/4 Cup
Baking Powder	1 tsp.
Salt	1/2 tsp.
Sugar	1 TBsp.
Egg - yolk only	1
Milk	2 TBsps.

CREAM butter, and blend in all other ingredients (except apples). Spread dough thinly in shallow 10" pie pan. Starting from outer edge and working to center, place apple slices close together, turning edges down into the dough.

When dough is fully covered with apples, sprinkle on the following topping:

Topping

Sugar	3/4 Cup
Flour	1-1/2 TBsp.
Cinnamon	1/4 tsp.
Butter	3 TBsp.

Mix all together and sprinkle evenly over the apples. Bake 50 mins. in 350° oven. Serves 8.

If you have to use canned apple slices, trim them to uniform size, and sprinkle with a little lemon juice and a dash of salt. Also, reduce topping to 2/3 rds of above recipe.

::

HINT NO. 3

When you have surplus bread of any kind, try this:
Melt butter, season with Worcestershire sauce, Tabasco, powdered garlic (or onion) paprika & salt.
Spread generously on bread cut into strips and triangles, and sprinkle with any one of the following: Celery seed, caraway seed, Parmesan cheese, poppy seed or sesame seed. Toast in very slow oven until thoroughly crisp. Delicious with soup.

CRULLERS

So many people have asked for this recipe that I've decided to include it, but the only way I know to make a proper cruller is to get the "feel" of it.

Butter	1/4 Cup
Sugar, granulated	1 Cup
Eggs, well beaten	2
Baking Powder	3-1/2 tsps.
Nutmeg	1/4 tsp.
Salt	1/2 tsp.
Vanilla	1/2 tsp.
Milk	1 Cup
Flour	4 Cups

CREAM butter, add sugar and eggs, mixing well. Sift 1 cup of the flour with baking powder, salt & nutmeg, and add to first mixture alternately with the combined milk and vanilla. Stir in remaining flour gradually, all but 1/2 cup. The trick is to use as little flour as possible.

Flour a board well, and dump dough onto it. Sprinkle with a little of the reserved flour & pat gently with light quick strokes of a floured rolling pin to a thickness of about 1/3".

If it sticks too badly, add a little more flour, knead gently, and re-roll. Run a spatula knife under dough to be sure it is not stuck to board.

Cut with well-floured doughnut cutter, and fry in about 2" of fat heated to approx. 365° in a heavy iron skillet. Test by dropping one of the "holes" in -

It should rise to the top immediately, and begin to brown around the edges. Never allow fat to smoke.

Turn crullers only once, allow to brown evenly on both sides, then lift from pan by slipping fork thru center hole. Let drip a minute, then drain on heavy brown paper.

When cool, sprinkle with sifted confectioner's sugar.   Yield: about 36

::

WHAT'S the difference between a cruller and a doughnut? Well, I call anything made of cake type batter, such as this, a cruller, regardless of shape, and anything made of yeast dough a doughnut. I really never looked it up in WEBSTER, tho.

::

MISS SYBIL'S BANANA BREAD

Our dear Miss Sybil Morse, now retired to Tryon, North Carolina, gave us this favorite from Camp Morse days.

Bananas, very ripe	3
Water	1 Tbsp.
Sugar	1 Cup
Shortening	1/2 Cup
Eggs, well beaten	2
Flour	2 Cups
Baking Soda	1 tsp.
Baking Powder	1 tsp.
Salt	1 tsp.

Mash bananas, add sugar and water and let stand 15 mins. Cream shortening well, add banana mixture and blend thoroughly. Add eggs, then sifted dry ingredients and blend all well.

Optional: At this point you may add 1/2 Cup chopped nuts, or 1/3 Cup All-Bran.

Bake, in greased or lined tins 50-60 mins. in 350° oven, or until straw inserted in center comes out clean.

Makes 1 large or 2 small loaves.

SWEDISH MEAT BALLS

Soft Bread Crumbs (cut crusts from day old white bread and cube)	1-1/2 Cups
Milk	3/4 Cup
Nutmeg	1/4 tsp.
Parsley, finely chopped	3 Tbsps.
Onion, finely chopped	3 Tbsps.
Salt	1-1/2 tsp.
Pepper	1/8 tsp.
Butter	4 Tbsps.
Egg, slightly beaten	1
Ground beef (round preferably)	1 Lb.
Consomme, Campbell's Condensed	1 Can
Cornstarch	2 Tbsps.

COOK onion in 2 Tbsps. of butter until just limp, but not brown.

Soften bread in milk, and add all other ingredients (except consomme & cornstarch). Chill mixture in refrigerator a few hours to facilitate handling.

Form into small balls, brown on all sides in remaining butter. Place in casserole. Heat consomme to boiling, thicken with cornstarch dissolved in a little cold water. Pour over meat balls, cover and finish cooking in 350° oven for about 20 mins. May be prepared ahead of time and reheated.

CHEESE SOU-FONDUE

HE says it's a fondue, because no souffle has bread in it.

I say it's a souffle, because no fondue was ever as high, handsome and dependable as this luscious thing.

Bread, one day old	8 Slices
American Cheese	6 ozs.
(or use half Amer., half Cheddar)	
Eggs, beaten	3
Milk (or half Evaporated, half water)	2 Cups
Salt	1/2 tsp.
Pepper	1/8 tsp.
Paprika	1/2 tsp.
Mustard, dry	1/2 tsp.

SLICE bread diagonally, fit a layer into the bottom of an ungreased 1 quart casserole. Cover with a layer of sliced or diced cheese, then more bread until all is used.

Mix together all remaining ingredients and pour over the bread and cheese layers.

Cover casserole and let stand at least 1 hour.

Bake in preheated 350° oven 1 hour, or until puffed and brown.

Good friend and good cook Eleanor Smith came up with the following interesting variation of the above. (Husband Tommy is the one responsible for our wonderful stereo set-up. How much talent can one family have?)

We call this a

SEA-FONDUE

To the recipe given above, add

1 Small Can Shrimp (deveined)
1 Small Can Crabmeat

Dice the bread instead of leaving it in slices. Reserve one piece for topping.

Using 1 quart casserole, put in layer of bread, layer of cheese (use a sharp cheese here) and layer of seafood, then repeat. Mix eggs, milk and seasonings and pour over. Top with the reserved bread cubes, which have been buttered. Cover and refrigerate overnight.

Bake 1 hour in preheated 350° oven.

A friend, after reading the rough draft, suggested gently that I state at the beginning that I am not an artist. I felt this unnecessary, for, by the time you have gotten this far, you will have guessed it.

CHICKEN NOODLE CASSEROLE

Butter	1/3 Cup
Onion, minced	1 Tbsp.
Flour	6 Tbsps.
Chicken Stock	1 Pint
Cream, Light (_or_ Evaporated milk)	1 Pint
Dry Mustard	1/8 tsp.
Salt	1 tsp.
Pepper	1/8 tsp.
Accent	1 tsp.
Noodles, medium wide	4 ozs.
Chicken, fryer or broiler, about 2-1/2 to 3 lbs.	1
Mushrooms, canned sliced	1/2 Cup
Almonds, blanched and sliced	1/4 Cup

MELT butter, add onion and cook gently two mins. Do not allow to brown. Blend in flour, then add chicken stock, cream, mustard, salt and pepper. Cook until smooth and thickened, stirring constantly. (It will be similar to a light cream sauce.)

Cook noodles in boiled salted water as directed, drain well, and add to sauce together with chicken and mushrooms.

Place in large casserole and cover lightly with dry bread crumbs, dash of paprika, and almonds, which have been lightly buttered and toasted.

(continued)

If you're ambitious, buy your chicken, wash it well, removing all "innards", and poach gently in just enough water to cover, to which you have added 1 tsp. salt, 1 chopped onion, handful celery top.

When fork-tender, remove chicken from broth and take meat from bones in as large pieces as possible.

Return all skin and bones to broth and cook an additional 1/2 hour.

Strain and use for stock.

And if you're too busy, you can get by quite well with canned chicken broth, and canned chicken meat.

Serves four to six.

::

RED CABBAGE

We had many requests for this recipe, and I could give you a nice, long, complicated one learned from Grandma.

But today they do such a marvelous job commercially, that I really recommend trying one of the glass-jarred variety, and saving your strength for something the experts haven't yet been able to do satisfactorily (at least, as far as I've seen) such as Lemon Meringue Pie.

SEAFOOD CASSEROLE

Butter	1/4 Lb.
Flour	1/2 Cup
Milk	3-1/2 Cups
Tomato soup, condensed	1/2 Cup
Salt	2 tsps.
Red Pepper	1/4 tsp.
Paprika	1 tsp.
Garlic - finely minced	1 Clove
Accent	1 Tbsp.
Gruyere Cheese - diced	3 ozs.
American Cheese	2 ozs.

MELT butter, blend in flour and cook 1 min., stirring constantly. Add all other ingredients and continue cooking and stirring until mixture is thick and smooth.

This will make enough sauce for 3 to 4 pounds of cooked and cleaned seafood, and you can make up your own combinations. I like shrimp, lobster & crab, but any variation can be used. Scallops, for instance, Langousta (baby lobster tails) etc.

Place in deep casserole, sprinkle top lightly with fine dry breadcrumbs, dash of paprika, and a little grated Parmesan cheese. Heat slowly in 350° oven until piping hot - about 45 mins.

Good served with fluffy parsley rice.

GOLDENGLOW SALAD

Even MEN like this one - and you know that's saying a lot for a molded salad.

Lemon Jello (9 ozs.)	3 Pkgs.
Hot Water	2 Cups
Vinegar, Cider	1/2 Cup
Cold Water	1-1/3 Cups
Fruit Juice	2 Cups
Carrots, peeled and shredded	1 Lb.
Crushed Pineapple, well drained	1 #2 Can

POUR hot water over jello. When dissolved, add cold water, vinegar and fruit juices. (Use the juice drained from the pineapple, plus any other light colored juice such as grapefruit, orange, etc., to make up the necessary 2 cups.)

Mix carrots and pineapple, stir into liquid and pour into 1-1/2 quart mold, which has been previously rinsed in cold water.

Refrigerate until set. Dip mold briefly into hot water and invert on chilled plate. Surround with greens and garnish with extra fruit if desired.

ROQUEFORT CHEESE DIP

PROBABLY our most requested dressing - excellent with raw vegetables, tantalizing over a lettuce wedge, and a happy surprise on baked potato.

Scallions - chopped, all but root end	3 TBsps.
Mayonnaise	1 Cup
Garlic - grated	1 Clove
Parsley - finely chopped	1/3 Cup
Anchovy Filets - mashed with fork	4
Thick Sour Cream	1/2 Cup
Tarragon Vinegar	1/4 Cup
Lemon Juice	1 TBsp.
Roquefort or Bleu Cheese	1/4 Lb.

Mash anchovy filets, crumble cheese and beat together with all other ingredients. Chill for two hours to blend.

Base without scallions can be made a day ahead.

Yield: 2 Cups

Any remainder, if promptly covered and chilled, will keep well in refrigerator for a few days.

CORN FRITTERS

Eggs	2
Milk	3 Tbsps.
Flour	1/2 Cup
Baking Powder	1 tsp.
Salt	1-1/4 tsp.
Pepper	1/4 tsp.
Mashed Potato	1 Cup
Kernel Corn, drained	1 Cup
Parsley, finely cut	2 TBsps.
Pimento, drained & chopped	1 TBsp.

BEAT together eggs and milk, then add sifted dry ingredients. Add mashed potato and mix very well. If using a mixer, turn off now, and fold in corn, parsley and pimento by hand.

Heat shortening in small iron frying pan to 365° and keep level about 1-1/2" deep. Drop batter by tablespoon into hot fat, and turn as soon as edges are brown.

Lift from fat with slotted spoon, drain on brown paper. Keep warm in oven until all are cooked. They go very fast, so a small pan will let you keep up with them.

Yield: about 12 large

Good with crisp bacon, applesauce or spiced apple rings.

CHICKEN MARYLAND

Chicken - Fryer or broiler, 2-1/2 to 3# - cut into quarters	1
Flour	1/3 Cup
Evaporated Milk	3/4 Cup
Bread Crumbs, dry coarse	2 Cups
Salt	1-1/2 tsp.
Marjoram, dried & crumbled	1/4 tsp.
Dry Mustard	1/4 tsp.
Pepper	Dash
Accent	1 tsp.
Poultry Seasoning	1/4 tsp.

WASH chicken thoroughly, then cut off wing tip at first joint. SKIN pieces completely - it's really not hard. If the wings give you a little trouble, peel back as much as you can with a pair of scissors and snip off all excess.

Put skin, wing tips, neck and giblets in stew pot, cover with water, add handful celery leaves, 1 chopped onion, and 1 small bay leaf. Do not add salt. Simmer gently until giblets are tender.

In one shallow soup dish combine flour, mustard, marjoram and 1/2 tsp. salt.

In second shallow dish put evap. milk, 1 tsp. salt, Accent and dash of pepper.

Place bread crumbs in third deeper dish, add poultry seasonings and now you are ready to go.

Dry chicken pieces on paper towel. Dip first into flour, patting in well, then into milk, then breadcrumbs, making sure all surface is well covered.

Lay chicken pieces in well-greased shallow baking pan (and if you line pan with alum. foil before greasing, you'll save a lot of clean-up time). Sprinkle with a little paprika.

Bake in hot (475°) oven for 10 mins. Remove, baste each piece with 1 TBsp. melted butter, and return to oven. Reduce heat to 350° and continue cooking until fork-tender, about 45 mins.

For gravy, make a roux of 2 TBsps. melted butter and 2 TBsps. flour (use what is left from chicken). Strain evap. milk used for dipping, and add sufficient extra milk to make 1 Cup. Strain chicken broth, measure 1 Cup and add both milk and broth to the roux. Heat, stirring constantly, until thick & smooth.

A few dashes of curry powder lend an interesting note - but be cautious here - you don't want to overwhelm the delicate herb flavor of the chicken.

PLEASE don't ask me what to do with the cooked giblets - I don't like them! Do you have a cat?

MEAT LOAF

Chopped Beef	1-1/2 Lbs.
(**or** mixture of beef, veal & pork)	
Rye Bread - Large slices	6
Salt	2 tsp.
Poultry Seasoning	1/2 tsp.
Accent	1 tsp.
Pepper	1/4 tsp.
Onion, grated	1 Large
Carrot, grated	1 Large
Parsley, minced fresh	1 TBsp.
Egg	1 Large

SOAK bread in warm water until thoroughly soft. Drain in colander and press out all excess water.

Break egg in large bowl, add bread and all seasonings. Break up meat into bowl and knead all firmly until thoroughly mixed.

Spank into firm, even loaf shape and place in a shallow baking pan. Spread a little chili sauce over top and sides of loaf. Surround loaf with water to depth of 1/2 inch, and bake in 350° oven 1 to 1-1/4 hrs. (Allow a little longer if you are using part pork.)

For extra flavor, cut 2 Bacon Strips in half & place across top of loaf.

 BROILED SWORDFISH

USE fresh or frozen filets of Swordfish, allow 6 to 8 oz. per portion. Trim all dark skin from edges.

Lay in shallow baking pan just large enough to accommodate pieces.

Sprinkle with salt, pepper and dash of paprika. Brush with lemon butter mix and broil about 6 inches from flame for 10 mins., or until nicely browned.

Pour remainder of lemon butter over the fish and finish in medium (350°) oven for about 20 mins., or until fork tender. If necessary to hold longer, cover and add additional liquid as needed. Never allow to dry out.

(And if you don't feel like squeezing more lemons, try a little dry white wine for the extra liquid.)

For 2 lbs. of fish you would need approximately:
   6 TBsps. Butter
   2 Lemons - juice of - squeesed & strained.

::

HINT NO. 4

Run, don't walk, to the nearest housewares department and purchase a wire whisk, if you haven't already discovered these marvelous things. Never again, a lumpy sauce, curdled soup, or so-so gravy.

BAR-B-QUE SHORT RIBS OF BEEF

THE most important ingredient in this recipe is a good butcher! Tell him you want meaty, lean ribs, not the bony, fatty things seen so often in markets. Allow about 3/4 lb. per person.

Dip ribs lightly in flour, then brown in melted shortening. If you have a pressure cooker, use it. When ribs are thoroughly browned, add 1 sliced carrot, 2 chopped onions, handful of celery top, 1 bay leaf, 1 tsp. salt and dash of pepper. Add 1 cup of water, cover, bring to 15 lbs. pressure and cook 25 mins.

If you don't have a pressure cooker, cover stew pot tightly and simmer slowly until very tender, but you don't want the meat to fall from the bones.

Now drain, and lay ribs in shallow baking pan. Coat lightly with following sauce, and bake in moderate oven until well browned (about 30 mins.), basting often with sauce.

Vinegar, cider	1 Cup
Garlic	1 Clove
Worcestershire Sauce	2 TBsps.
Tabasco	1/2 tsp.
Sugar	1 TBsp.
Catsup	1/2 Cup
Salt	1 tsp.
Dry Mustard	1 tsp.

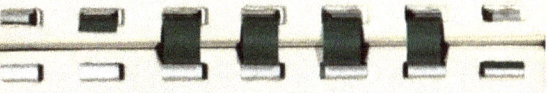

Combine all ingredients and simmer for 10 mins.

You probably won't use all this sauce at once, but it keeps very well in the refrigerator.

It is excellent also for spare ribs, or barbequed chicken.

Our ever-popular Helen Waitkevicz, hostess and housekeeper for many summers, donated this one.

AND I hope you didn't discard the liquid left in the stew pot or pressure cooker. Strain and refrigerate. The next day you can remove all that fat in one piece, and you will have a rich, beefy broth which can be used for gravy, soup or what-you-will.

CLOSED GENTIAN

Reflections on Upper Goose Pond

CHAPTER 17

A DUGOUT CANOE

*M*YSTERIES, BOTH REAL AND FICTIONAL, often go unsolved for long periods, going cold as it were, only to be solved many years later after long-buried truths, previously unknown, emerge. Goose Pond's dugout canoe story is just such a mystery, going unsolved for years, but only because of some good-natured mischief worthy of a good laugh.

It was July 1959, and a local Boy Scout troupe was exploring the wilderness surrounding Upper Goose Pond. Wolcott Hamblin, a founding member of the Mohhekennuck Club, was quite likely the scoutmaster. As the boys entered the swampy area at the far end of Upper Goose they came upon the remains of a wooden dugout canoe, ten feet long and sixteen inches wide. One can only imagine the boys' excitement when their scoutmaster became immediately convinced that this canoe had been carved by the Mohican Indians many years before. The scoutmaster promptly made inquiries with Mr. Frank Korkosz, the Director of the Springfield Museum of Natural History.

Archeologist's 'Indian' Boat Attributed to Civil War Vet

Figure 17.1 Headline about the Upper Goose Pond dugout canoe discovery. From The Berkshire Evening Eagle, *July 14, 1959.*

Korkosz launched an exploratory expedition later that month, finding the canoe in "a boggy section of Upper Goose Pond," and described it "in a pretty good state of preservation," with one side broken off the log canoe. He reported, "Upon close examination, there are indications that the dugout may have been made with steel implements" and that there were possible axe marks on the canoe. Korkosz said, "It looks to me as if it's about twenty years old."[111]

Figure 17.2 Dugout canoe was discovered on Upper Goose Pond in 1959. Courtesy of David Stilwell.

Nevertheless, Korkosz, a humble man, acknowledged his lack of expertise in archeology, and planned a second expedition with more experts: Dr. John Brainerd, biology professor at Springfield College; Dr. Menzies Whitelaw, retired head of the American International College history department; and William R. Young, head of the Connecticut Valley Archeology Association. It is not known if such an expedition occurred or what its findings may have been.

Figure 17.3 Korkosz expedition to dugout canoe find on Upper Goose Pond 1959. Courtesy of the Tyringham Historical Commission.

Unsurprisingly, at least two other theories about this canoe surfaced. The writer of the 1959 *Berkshire Evening Eagle* article, postulated, without attribution, that the canoe "may have been used on Goose Pond sixty-five years ago by a Civil War veteran." From this statement, it would be concluded that the canoe was being paddled around as early as 1894.

Joseph "Hooker" Moore, who grew up at the MacDarby farmhouse on Goose Pond, and was then the operator of the Moore Boat Livery, weighed in with an alternative story, claiming that he recalled seeing the dugout canoe when he was a small boy living on Goose Pond and that the canoe was built by George Pichenor, who was half Indian and half Dutch. It is not clear if Pichenor was a Civil War veteran or not. Hooker was born in 1890, so any childhood sightings of this canoe would likely have occurred before 1905.

During his initial 1959 expedition, Korkosz interviewed Marguerite Murphy (Duncan and Ted's sister) who was then staying at the Murphy cabin on Upper Goose. She professed absolutely no knowledge of the canoe's origins -- only to have a good laugh after the interview.[112] It appears that good-natured, but mischievous tendencies were widespread among these Murphy kids.

Here's the back story. It was in 1936 when young Duncan Murphy, Marguerite's brother, had discovered a recently fallen elm tree on the shore of Lower Goose. After first cutting off its branches, Duncan and his younger brother Ted floated the heavy tree trunk through Sucker Brook to their camp, somehow managing to lift it onto a pair of sawhorses. Duncan, Ted, Bob Stilwell, and any visitors that could get roped into helping spent the next two summers chopping, carving, hacking, gouging, hollowing, and burning their tree trunk into the shape of a dugout canoe.

Figure 17.4 From left to right is Bob Stilwell, Marguerite Murphy, and Ted Murphy, c1938.
Doesn't Marguerite look a bit mischievous to you?
Courtesy of Ted Murphy.

When it was finished, they launched it on Upper Goose, they climbed in, and it promptly rolled over. Back to the drawing board, they fixed this problem by adding an outrigger, which solved the rolling-over problem but created a new challenge with the paddling part. Not to be discouraged, they added a mast and a sail (well, a blanket), which apparently worked fairly well.[113]

By this time, Hooker would have been forty-eight years old and not really any longer considered a child. So, unless there were two dugout canoes on Upper Goose, it appears that Hooker either had a vivid imagination or a foggy memory.

Storing the canoe over the long winters was a challenge, the boat being far too heavy to bring firmly onto dry land. Each winter, Duncan and Ted would drag it as high as they were able and secure it however they could. One spring, upon returning to camp, the canoe had floated off and disappeared – until it was re-discovered in 1959 by the Boy Scouts. So much for the Civil War veteran, a half-Indian and half-Dutch Pichenor, and Hooker's memory.

The fate of the rediscovered canoe remains a mystery. Rumors long circulated that it landed in either a Springfield Museum or the Peabody Museum at Harvard University. Recent inquiries to these museums have come up empty so I'm guessing the boat just rotted away.[114]

Appalachian Trail in Tyringham

CHAPTER 18

THE APPALACHIAN TRAIL

*I*F YOU WERE TO BE GENEROUS ENOUGH to overlook the fifty-plus years I have been on, in, and around Goose Pond, you might forgive me for having generally considered the Appalachian Trail as just an extraordinarily long dirt path through the woods. While there is, to be sure, a long dirt path out there in the woods surrounding Goose Pond, I have since realized that the soul of the trail is not in this narrow dirt path, but in the *people* who hike along it and the *people* who lovingly care for it. By way of having joined the volunteers of the Western Massachusetts Chapter of the Appalachian Mountain Club, and by serving as a caretaker at the Upper Goose Pond hiker cabin, I have been fortunate to connect with these *people* of the Trail — including thru-hikers with trail names like Type Two, Squirrely, Hiking Viking (and his so-sweet limping dog Catori), Captain Calves, JJ, Top Shelf, Full Moon, and Mothman to name a few. It was eye-opening for me -- transformative in fact — to so belatedly discover that such a vibrant community had been quietly thriving all around me on Goose Pond -- the living soul of the Appalachian Trail.

There are, to be sure, myriad motivations for people to lace up a pair of hiking boots, grab a walking stick, pack some supplies, and take to trekking on trails deep in the woods. Some seek solitude, others seek companionship. There are those who simply love nature and fresh air or seek the joys of vigorous exercise. Some are looking for life "resets," or entering life transitions, or perhaps following in a parent's footsteps, while others aim to set, and meet, a challenging personal goal. Many hike alone, some with companions, others with a dog. Often, new friends are made on the way. While many of us have enjoyed day hikes on short sections, there is something about the Appalachian Trail, winding its way from the mountains of Maine to the forests of Georgia, that lures thousands of hikers each year to longer excursions.

Approximately 3,000 so-called "thru-hikers", representing only a small fraction of the trail's three million annual visitors, set out each year to trek the entire trail, from start to finish during a single season. Some plan to do this continuously in one direction, while others, known as "flip-floppers," intend to cover one section northbound and the other section southbound, often starting each leg in Harpers Ferry, West Virginia, or another midpoint. There are also countless "section hikers" whose goal is typically to hike all or most of the A.T. but in a series of shorter sections, often over a period of years. Many, like myself, are the so-called "day-hikers," who are lucky enough to live near the trail, pack a snack, explore a few miles, and still get home for dinner. What all us hikers have in common is that we each put one foot in front of the other as we follow the ubiquitous vertical 2" x 6" white "blazes" painted on the trail's bordering trees marking the route.

In 1905, a twenty-six-year-old man named Benton MacKaye, from Shirley, Massachusetts, graduated with a degree in geology from a reasonably well-known local school, 100 miles east of Goose Pond known as Harvard University. In the years that followed, he joined the Harvard faculty and worked in various roles in the US Forest Service, the Tennessee Valley Authority, and the US Department of Labor. Benton's primary interest was balancing the needs of humans with those of the natural environment. In 1921 he published an article entitled *An Appalachian Trail: A Project in Regional Planning*, proposing the creation of a continuous trail along the length of the Appalachian Mountains. This groundbreaking article motivated sixteen years of work by private citizens and volunteers up and down the East Coast to construct such a trail, making the Appalachian Trail a reality by 1937. It is difficult to imagine how a project like this (or anything else for that matter) could have been accomplished without email, cell phones, GPS, and social media. The trail traverses fourteen states and stretches unbroken for 2197.4 miles from the summit of Georgia's 3,782-foot peak of Springer Mountain to Maine's 5,260-foot peak of Mount Katahdin. Its path through Massachusetts lies entirely in the Berkshire Mountains and wraps its thin, sinewy arms intimately around Goose Pond.

Figure 18.1 *A typical "white blaze" which mark the entire Appalachian Trail. This particular blaze is on the trail in Tyringham, south of Tyringham Road.*

During the first forty years of its existence, the immensely popular Appalachian Trail, enthusiastically created and maintained by a small army of barely organized volunteers, lacked any official status or regulatory oversight, and existed substantially on private land. In the absence of such oversight, the 1970s saw some chaos on Upper Goose, a consequence of uncontrolled camping, partying, campfires, and littering; with Goose Ponders typically blaming the "hippies". Concerned Goose Pond residents formed the "Goose Pond Voters Association," expending much energy to bring this disorder under control, an effort complicated by limited law enforcement resources and a lack of any clear jurisdiction. The problem ultimately improved after the Appalachian Mountain Club —— without bothering to wait for any official jurisdiction — posted a seasonal ranger in an Upper Goose cabin in the late 1970s.

The trail's unstructured existence improved dramatically in 1978, with the passage of "HR 8803", a Congressional bill officially entitled "An Act to Amend the National Trails System Act" but most commonly known simply as the "Appalachian Trail Bill." The bill called for the federal government to purchase a 1000-foot-wide corridor along the entire length of the Trail, and provided $90 million, over three years, to complete the acquisitions. The bill was passed in the House of Representatives by a vote count of 409 yea to twelve nay, a wide margin the likes of which we don't generally see any longer. After easily passing in the Senate, the bill was signed into law by President Jimmy Carter. I vaguely remember when the Government used to work like this.

Figure 18.2 President Jimmy Carter signing into law the Appalachian Trail Act, 1978.
Courtesy of the Appalachian Trail Conservancy.

The numerous federal land acquisitions mandated by HR 8803 were to be allocated either to the US Forest Service (in the Department of Agriculture) or to the National Park Service (in the Department of the Interior). The acquisition around Upper Goose Pond fell to the National Park Service (NPS). The Stilwell family, who owned the preponderance of Upper Goose shoreline, were deeply committed to the preservation of the natural state of Upper Goose and insisted that the National Park Service's land purchase around Upper Goose include, not just the 1000-foot-wide corridor around the trail, but Upper Goose's entire shoreline. A prolonged period of negotiations followed between the NPS and the various landowners around Upper Goose Pond: the Stilwells, the Smiths, the Murphy's, and the Mohhekennuck Club. When the deed transfers were executed in 1981, they encompassed 684 acres and included the entire shoreline of Upper Goose, along with several existing cabins. This purchase represented one of the largest single acquisitions under HR 8803, and ensured the forested land surrounding Upper Goose would forever remain in its natural state.

Figure 18.3 National Park Service purchases trail corridor around Upper Goose Pond. *From* The Berkshire Eagle, *May 21, 1981.*

Prior to the passage of the Appalachian Trail Bill, northbound hikers following the white blazes out of the Tyringham valley would hike up George Canon Road, head east for a short distance on Goose Pond Road, walk a short stretch on Cooper Creek Road, and then follow the trail to the right up the hill south of Lower Goose Pond. The trail then followed the south shore of Upper Goose Pond, wrapped around its far eastern tip, crossed Higley Brook, and hugged the northern shoreline of Upper Goose, before turning northward towards the great state of Maine.

HR 8803, however, prohibited the A.T. from using public roads. In order to comply with this requirement, the trail needed to be rerouted off George Canon, Goose Pond, and Cooper Creek Roads. This task was accomplished in 1982 by rerouting the trail into the woods east of George Canon, across Goose Pond Road near the far eastern end of Lower Goose, to rejoin the pre-existing trail above the south shore of Upper Goose. Additionally, a short side trail, marked with blue blazes, was created, connecting the trail on Upper Goose's northeastern shore to the newly designated hiker cabin on the west end of Upper Goose.

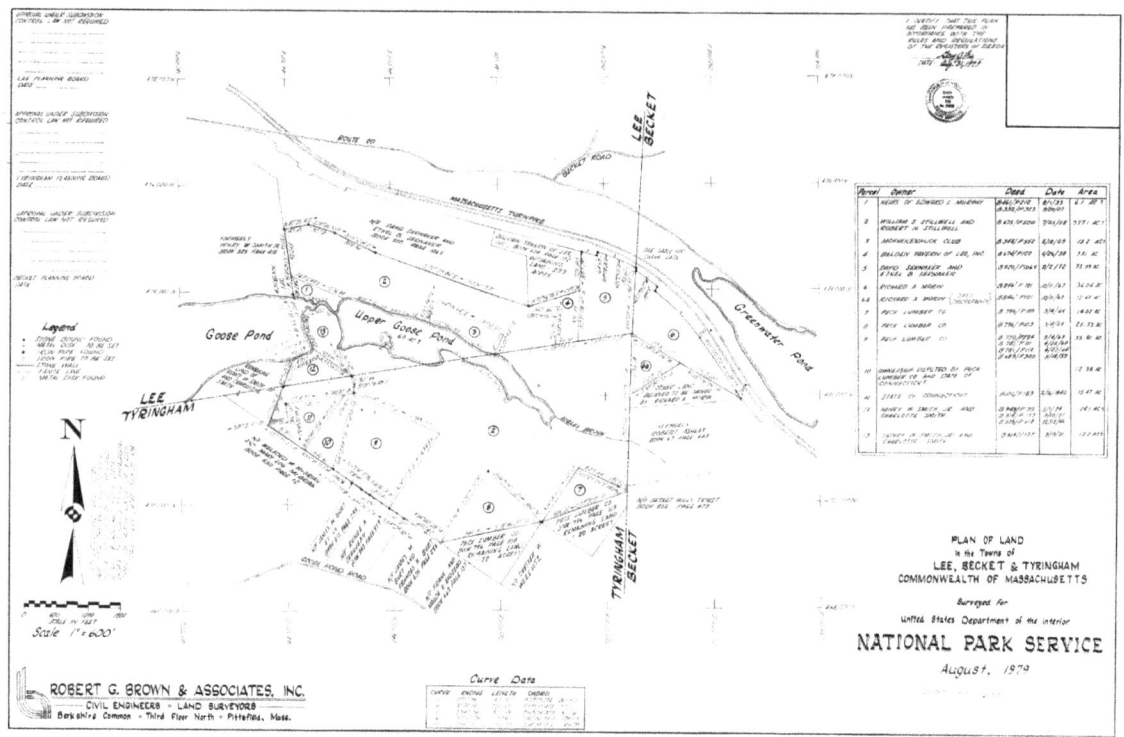

Figure 18.4 Survey map (1979) identifying the lots related to the National Parks Service purchase of Upper Goose Pond trail corridor. Courtesy of the National Parks Service.

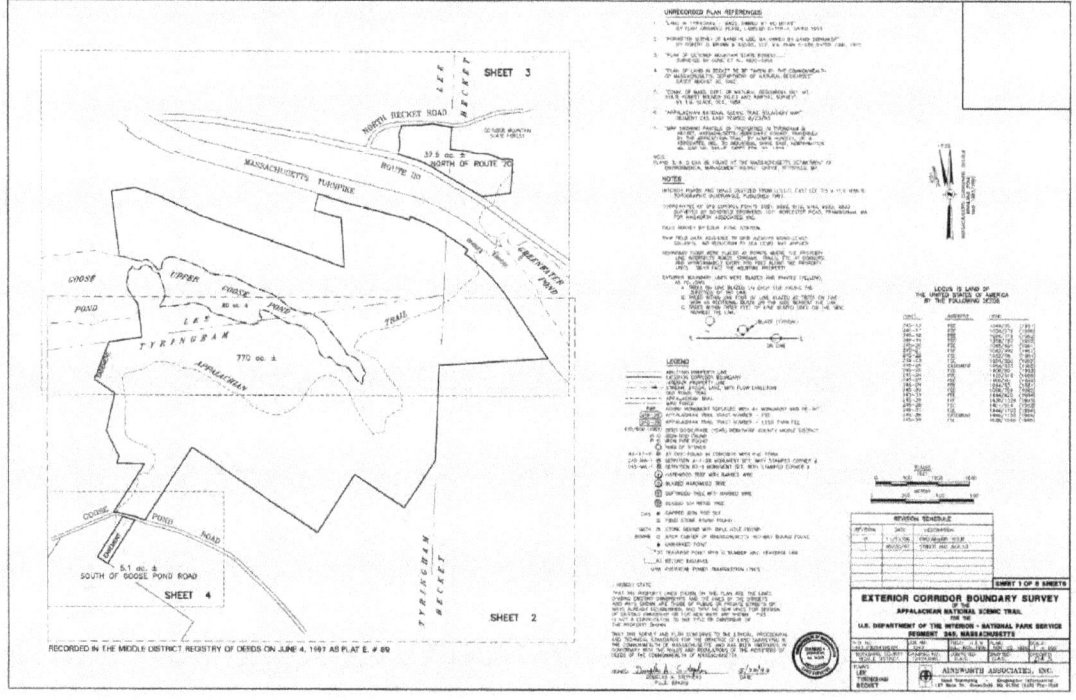

Figure 18.5 Survey map of Appalachian Trail Corridor in 1997 indicating the boundaries of the 684-acre corridor around Upper Goose Pond. From Middle Registry of Deeds, Berkshire County.

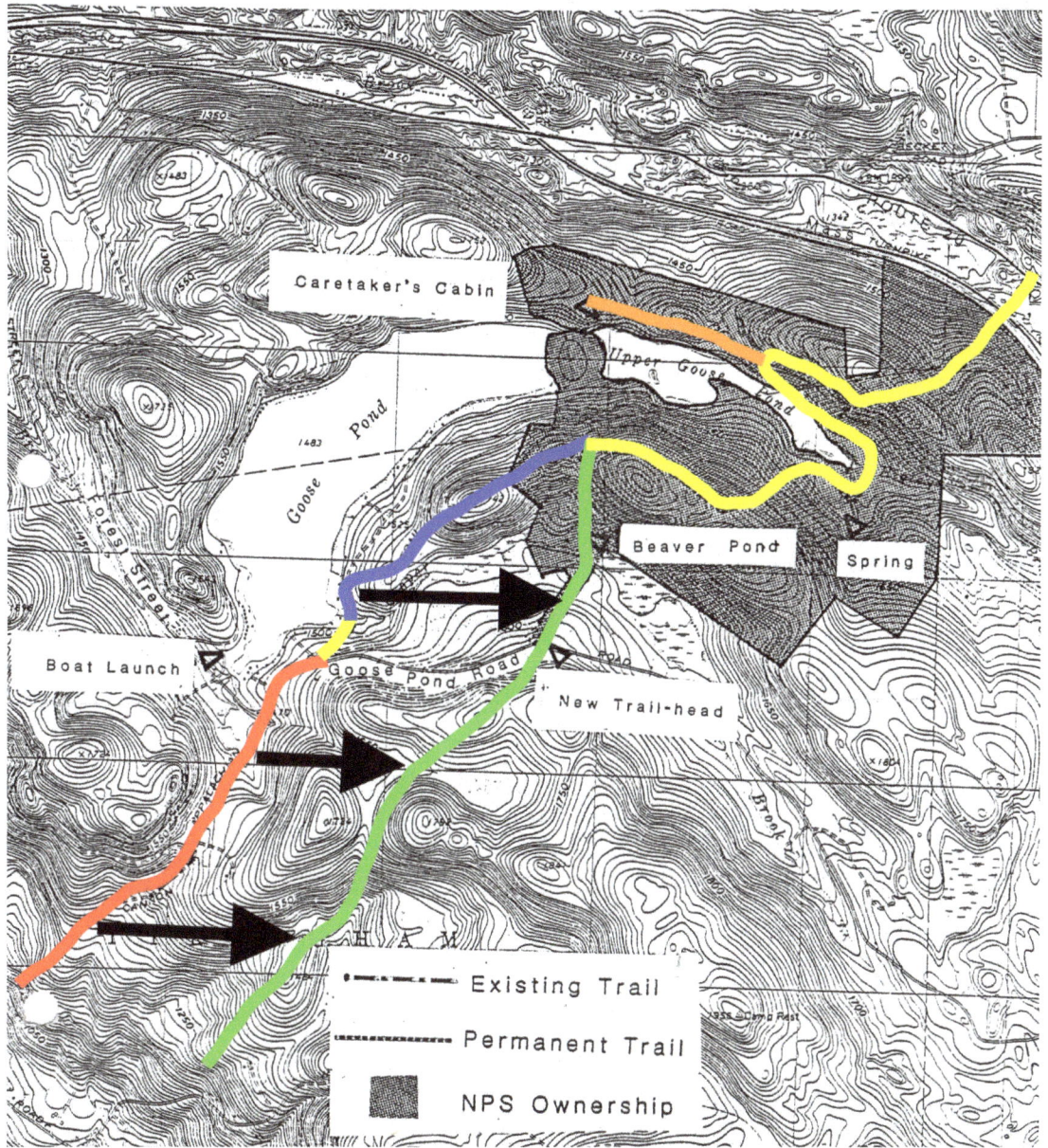

Figure 18.6 Map of the 1982 re-location (black arrows) of the Appalachian Trail around Upper Goose Pond. Note the original trail locations on George Canon Road (red), Cooper Creek Road (yellow), and on the mountain south of Lower Goose (blue). The trail was relocated to the new trail (approximated in green). The new trail meets the original trail (yellow) just south of the junction of Lower and Upper Goose Ponds. Note the new side trail (orange) linking the trail to the hiker cabin ("caretaker cabin"). The dark-gray-colored section indicates the extent of the federally-owned corridor around the trail and Upper Goose. The 1982 ceremony took place at the junction of the dotted and solid green lines, indicated by "New Trailhead." Courtesy of the National Parks Service.

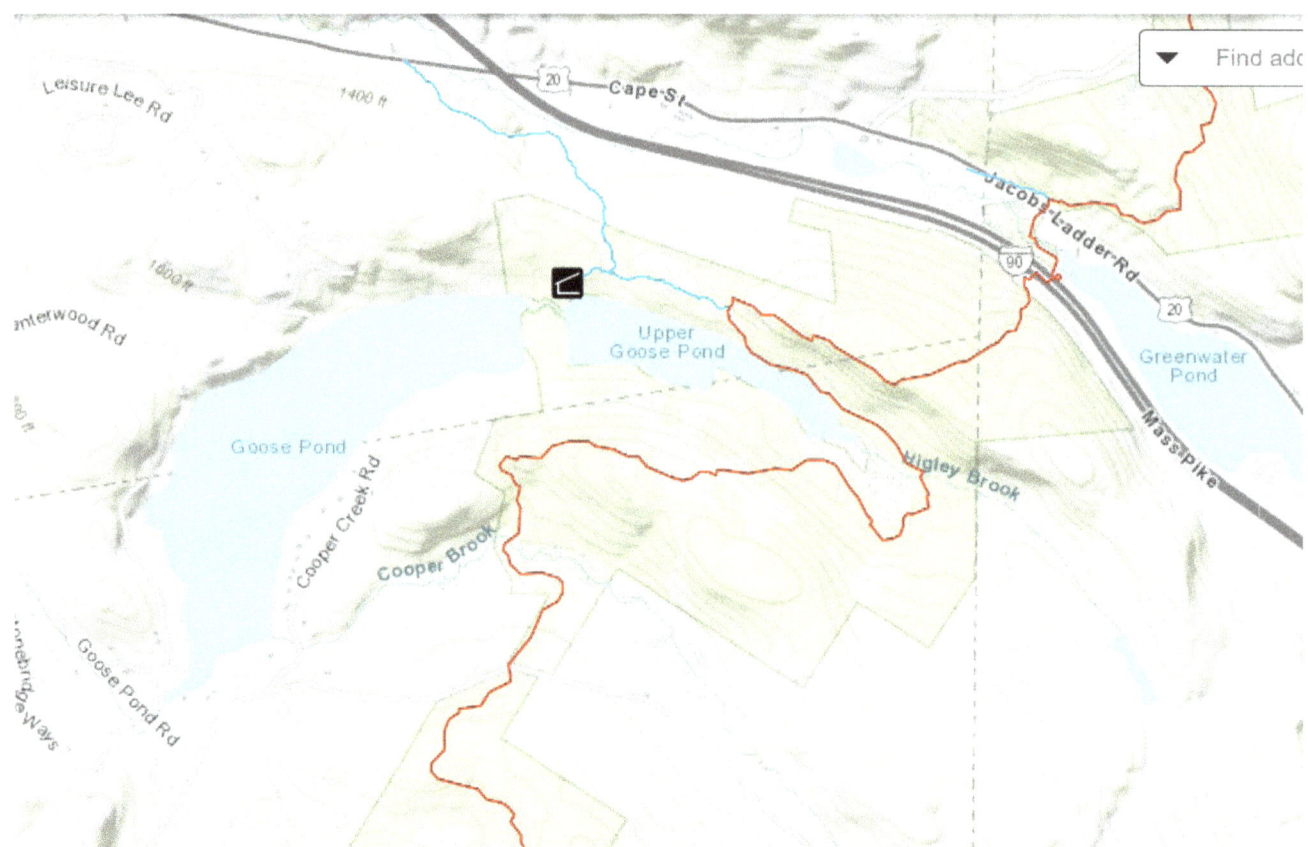

Figure 18.7 *Current route of Appalachian Trail around Goose Pond (red). Note the blue line which indicates the side trail to the hiker cabin (black icon). The darker green section represents the current land corridor owned by the National Parks Service. From the Appalachian Trail Conservancy.*

An official ceremony to celebrate the recently completed rerouting of the trail around Goose Pond took place at 1 p.m. on July 24, 1982, attended by U.S. Representative Sylvio O. Conte along with numerous officials from the Appalachian Mountain Club (AMC), the Berkshire Natural Resources Defense Council, and the Mohhekennuck Club. U.S. Senators Edward Kennedy and Paul Tsongas were both invited but did not attend. Attendees gathered at the boat ramp and were taken by a shuttle bus to the new Appalachian Trail trailhead on Goose Pond Road where a ribbon-cutting ceremony took place, with Rep. Conte cutting the ribbon, and AMC's George Osgood acting as the Master of Ceremonies. After the ribbon-cutting, attendees either hiked along the newly rerouted trail from Goose Pond Road to Upper Goose or paddled to Upper Goose from the boat ramp. A barbeque on Upper Goose followed, paid for by the Berkshire National Resource Council, with some guests sleeping overnight at the newly opened hiker cabin.

Notably, three important attendees arrived at the barbeque in their canoe a little late, laughing and soaking wet. On the morning of this event, Dr. Wolcott "Bud" Hamblin, who was then secretary-treasurer of the Mohhekennuck Club (and also the grandson of one of the club's founding members) along with his wife Dagne, met another club member, James McVey, at the boat ramp,

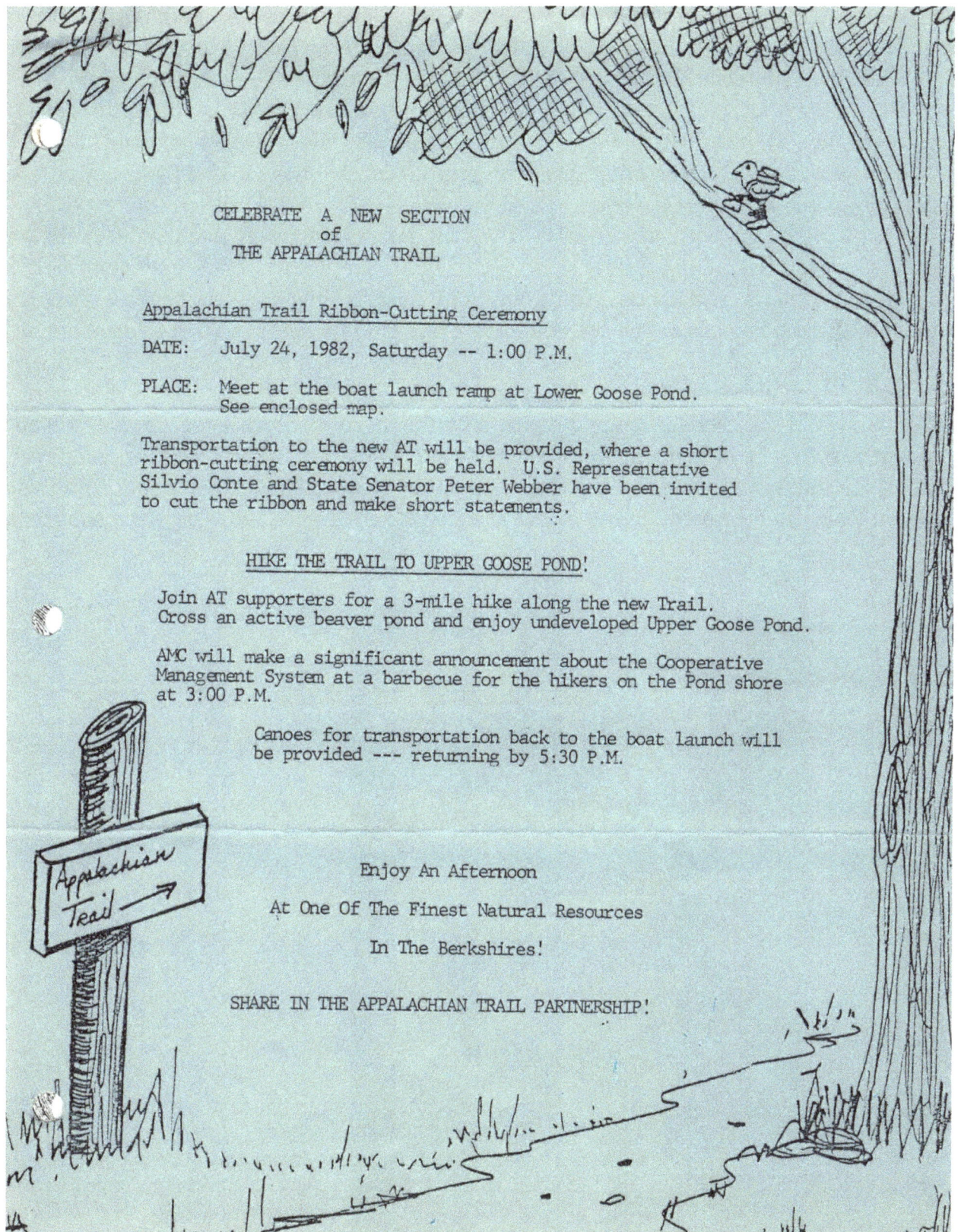

Figure 18.8 *Invitation to the ribbon-cutting ceremony for the newly re-routed Appalachian Trail.*

with the plan to take a canoe to the 1 p.m. ceremony on Upper Goose. Although the Mohhekennuck Club cabin had burned down in 1971, its members still owned its thirteen acres on Upper Goose's northern shoreline. Out of the $36,000 that the government paid for this property, Club members had previously voted to donate $12,000 to the Appalachian Mountain Club to cover the expenses of the new hiker cabin. Before climbing into their canoe, McVey handed Hamblin the $12,000 check, made out to the Appalachian Mountain Club. Hamblin folded the check and, a bit too casually, put it in his shirt pocket.

Those of us familiar with canoes have likely had the experience of paddling over the wake of a nearby motorboat pulling a water skier. With a skier in tow, motorboats cannot always alter their course or speed, and canoes, being the tippy vessels they are, can become alarmingly unstable in these boat wakes. Bud Hamblin and his able crew had just such an experience on their way to Upper Goose and, after encountering just such a motorboat and skier, proceeded to capsize in Lower Goose. The motorboat's operator, thankfully well aware of his maritime responsibilities, rescued the swamped canoers by towing the upturned canoe, along with its three wet passengers, to shore, after which the trio bailed the boat and made it, belatedly, to the barbecue. But in this water-soaked chaos, the $12,000 check had slipped out of Bud's shirt pocket and sank to the lake's bottom. McVey's camera, valued at $200, suffered a similar fate.

Figure 18.9 U.S. Representative Sylvio O. Conte (left) and Appalachian Mountain Club's George Osgood (right) at the ceremony marking the relocation of the Appalachian Trail. From The Berkshire Eagle *July 26, 1982.*

Bud stopped payment on the drowned check (an action that was hardly necessary) and issued a new one a few days later. The funds from this re-issued check, responsibly invested by the AMC, continue to completely fund the ongoing expenses needed to maintain and operate the hiker cabin on Upper Goose Pond.[115]

Once the old Jacot/Stevenson cabin became the property of the National Parks Service in 1982, AMC volunteers converted it to a hiker cabin by adding a fire escape and bunk beds on the second floor. The cabin, which continues to be staffed with full-time volunteer caretakers from May to October, is unique on the entire 2190 miles of the Appalachian Trail, providing interior sleeping quarters for fifteen hikers on a first-come first-serve basis, and free of charge. The cabin has a cozy living room with a stone fireplace, a small collection of books, a reading couch, a dining table, a kitchen equipped with propane lighting and a propane stove, a spacious covered porch, a large upstairs bunk room and a separate bedroom for a caretaker. There is no electricity or running water. During the summer months, the cabin and surrounding tent sites often host over thirty hikers each night. The cabin is actively maintained, staffed, and operated by energetic volunteers of the Western Massachusetts Appalachian Trail Management Committee.

Figure 18.10 Hiker cabin on Upper Goose Pond.

Typical for the entire Appalachian Trail, the land surrounding Upper Goose Pond today has a nearly undecipherable structure of ownership, oversight, and management. The land is owned by the National Park Service, which manages the trail through its "Appalachian National Scenic Trail Office", whose acronym is simply "APPA". Then there is the Appalachian Trail Conservancy (ATC), a non-profit, non-governmental entity that contracts with APPA to support and manage volunteers, assist with resource protection, and provide advocacy for the trail. The ATC, which receives millions of dollars in federal funds to support the trail, provides vital assistance to thirty-one local "trail clubs" such as our local Western Massachusetts Chapter of the Appalachian Mountain Club (AMC). The AMC, a large, private conservation organization located in northeast and mid-Atlantic states, is divided into local chapters such as our Western Massachusetts Chapter.[116] The Western Massachusetts Appalachian Trail Management Committee is an arm of the Western Massachusetts Chapter that directly oversees the trail and cabin around Goose Pond. Volunteers provide direct hands-on trail management and maintenance. As complicated as these arrangements certainly sound, they have continued to successfully nurture the traditions of the Trail all these years and to protect Upper Goose Pond, and its hiker community, in perpetuity.

Early autumn on Goose Pond

CHAPTER 19

WILDLIFE

I CRAWLED OUT OF BED well before sunrise one day in early September 2010. In the dark, I found my kayak, loaded it with some granola, a thermos of black coffee, and a good camera, and set off to paddle across Lower Goose and then through the channel into Upper Goose. I arrived at the marsh at the far end just before sunrise.

I knew there was an inhabited beaver lodge here but I had never encountered any beaver before now. But on that morning, as the sun rose, several beaver, either oblivious to my presence or, more likely, not minding it, spent the better part of an hour swimming, diving, and flapping their tails all around me.

Figure 19.1 *Beaver in the Upper Goose Pond swamp (2010).*

Figure 19.2 *Beaver near Goose Pond (2011). Courtesy of Richard Greene.*

It turns out that 2010 was an active year for beaver on Goose Pond. I saw a large beaver dam on Sucker Brook that year, and I caught some sightings of beaver in Lower Goose. I even found evidence of their work on a large tree in front of my house.

Figure 19.3 The work of beaver on a Pinepoint tree (2010).

Figure 19.4 A small beaver dam in Sucker Brook (fall of 2013).

Figure 19.5 *Remnants of beaver dam (red arrows) in Upper Goose Pond swamp in 2023. This dam and the nearby lodge were functional until the beaver disappeared a few years ago and since then has gradually broken down.*

Figure 19.6 *Remmants of beaver lodge (red arrow). This lodge was larger, well-maintained, and fully active until a few years ago.*

On Memorial Day in 2020, while paddling my kayak, I spotted a North American River Otter swimming in the eastern end of Lower Goose. These sleek animals are endemic but not commonly seen on Goose Pond. (See Figure 19.23)

Bald Eagles are soaring over Goose Pond all year round, diving for fish and perched high on shoreline trees. While these magnificent birds used to be abundant in Massachusetts in the past, the pesticide DDT resulted in their rapid decline in the 1950s and 1960s. With the federal government having banned the use of DDT in 1972, the Massachusetts Division of Fisheries & Wildlife later teamed up with Mass Audubon and spearheaded an initiative to re-introduce Bald Eagle nestlings in the state. In all, forty-one Bald Eagle chicks from Manitoba, Nova Scotia, and Michigan were released at the Quabbin Reservoir in central Massachusetts in 1982. This re-introduction was wildly successful, and Bald Eagles are now breeding and thriving across the entire state of Massachusetts and beyond, including on Goose Pond.

The wildlife photographs that follow were all taken in the vicinity of Goose Pond over the years.

Figure 19.7 Bald eagle at the Lakeside Drive beach (2023).

Figure 19.8 Bald eagle flying over a frozen Goose Pond (2022).

Figure 19.9 A young Bald eagle over Goose Pond (2024).
Bald eagles do not get their signature white heads and tails until they are a few years old.

Figure 19.10 Black bear. Courtesy of Richard Greene.

Figure 19.11 Coyote (2011). Courtesy of Richard Greene.

Figure 19.12 Coyote on Goose Pond ice (Christmas Day 2019).

Figure 19.13 Bobcat. Courtesy of Richard Greene.

Figure 19.14 Bobcat leaping to catch a squirrel (2023). Courtesy of Jim Pelletier.

Figure 19.15 Red fox (2006). Courtesy of Richard Greene.

Figure 19.16 Red fox in winter. Taken from my bedroom window. (2023).

Figure 19.17 *Red fox pups on Stonebridge Ways. Courtesy of Andy Potler.*

Figure 19.18 *Gray fox on Pinepoint, taken from my bedroom window (2021).*

Figure 19.19 Porcupine. Courtesy of Andy Potler.

Figure 19.20 *Porcupine climbing a tree on Upper Goose (2023).*

Figure 19.21 *Fisher. Although commonly called Fisher "Cats" these are not cats. Courtesy of Richard Greene.*

Figure 19.22 Raccoons (2011). Courtesy of Richard Greene.

Figure 19.23 River otter. Courtesy of Richard Greene.

Figure 19.24 Deer (2011). Courtesy of Richard Greene.

Figure 19.25 *Young moose in Sucker Brook (2017). This was captured on a trail cam. A few minutes after this moose swam across Sucker Brook a boat motored by. Courtesy of Jim Pelletier.*

Figure 19.26 Moose. Courtesy of Richard Greene.

Figure 19.27 Snapping turtle on Pinepoint (2010) and on Forest Street (2023). Top photo courtesy of Sandy Cohen.

Figure 19.28 Snapping turtle baby. Courtesy of Richard Greene.

Figure 19.29 *Green turtle in the swamp in Upper Goose (2022). This fella was a regular on this log until the log finally became submerged a few years ago and the turtle hasn't been sighted since.*

Figure 19.30 *Largemouth bass caught by Nate Laprade (2024), ice-fishing during the winter of 2024. The Division of Fisheries and Wildlife (DFW) stocks the Pond twice a year with Rainbow Trout. Additionally, DFW surveys of Goose Pond have recently also found Bluegill, Pumpkinseed, Redbreast Sunfish, Yellow Perch, Brown Bullhead, Golden Shiner, Chain Pickerel, Smallmouth Bass, and White Sucker. Goose Pond is also a habitat for the bridle shiner, a species listed as a "special concern" by the Massachusetts National Heritage and Endangered Species Program and therefore protected under the Wetlands Protection Act. Courtesy of Joe Janis.*

Figure 19.31 Turkey vulture (2010). Courtesy of Richard Greene.

Figure 19.32 Wild turkey (2024).

Figure 19.33 *Hummingbird (2024).*

Figure 19.34 *Owl on George Canon Road (2022).*

Figure 19.35 Loon. Courtesy of Andy Potler.

Figure 19.36 Loon. Courtesy of Roger Brown.

Figure 19.37 Great Blue heron. Courtesy of Andy Potler.

Figure 19.38 *Great Blue heron taking off from the hiker cabin dock on Upper Goose (2021).*

Figure 19.39 *Great Blue heron rookery. Courtesy of Richard Greene.*

Figure 19.40 Dark Fishing spider on Pinepoint (2023).

Figure 19.41 Eurasian Mergansers, male (black and white) and female (gray). Courtesy of Roger Brown.

This book would be woefully incomplete without a word about Canadian Geese (*Branta canadensis*) which, after all, are the animals after which Goose Pond was named so long ago. Today, there are two distinct populations of Canadian Geese in Western Massachusetts.[117] The first population is the migrating birds that for centuries have been using Massachusetts lakes for resting but not for nesting. These birds winter in the United States and summer in Canada, and can be seen flying overhead in large "V" formations. The second population, which is now much larger than the first, is descended from captive birds that had been used by waterfowl hunters as live decoys in eastern Massachusetts. When the use of live decoys was outlawed in the 1930s, these captive birds were released into the wild. Having developed no migratory habits, these released birds began nesting in Eastern Massachusetts. In the 1960s, MassWildlife began relocating these birds to central and western Massachusetts. This non-migrating population, which continues to nest in western Massachusetts, has grown dramatically since the 1960s.[118]

Figure 19.42 *A Giant Gaggle of Geese Gather on Goose Pond. Courtesy of Roger Brown.*

Upper Boynes Cove in autumn

EPILOGUE

THE SUN HAS JUST slipped down below the trees behind me, and the humid August air is already a little cooler. I am sitting on our dock, in one of the nice wooden Adirondack chairs my brother had made for us, still wet from my brief plunge just a few minutes ago, and contemplating the vista of Goose Pond before me. The view is so familiar, yet somehow always a little different every time I look at it. On this side of the lake, the "golden hour" is passing and soon evening will descend. Yet the opposite shore is still basking in the late afternoon sunshine which is now horizontal and reflecting brightly off the windows of the houses on Cooper Creek. A rocks glass holding an amber finger of Basil Hayden and a few ice cubes rests on the arm of my chair.

I hear a young girl whooping it up on the far end of Lower Goose as she slaloms behind a motorboat, pulling hard in a tight turn outside the wake, the sun's last rays catching her impressive fan tail. In the old days, evening was our favorite time to ski Goose Pond too.

My eyes drift in the direction of the Chanterwood section, where I spy a lone fisherman standing in the bow of his small rowboat. His gossamer fishing line, reflecting a lingering ray of sunlight, is visible floating weightlessly above the water as he casts his lure. I wonder if this cast will get him a nice bass or not. Odds are not, but that's okay because I know what the fisherman also knows, that the joys of fishing are not only to be found in the catching part.

There are feathery puffs of breeze, heavy and thick on my slowly drying skin, coming from ever-shifting directions and creating evanescent dark patches that dance across the water's glassy surface and then disappear as quickly as they appear. I hear the annoying whine of a single mosquito near my left ear, and I wave it away with my baseball cap. I hope she's not going to come back for more. A swallow of the bourbon goes down cool at first, and then warm.

The young girl on the ski has fallen with another whoop and a pretty dramatic splash. I recall, like it was yesterday, how soothing it would feel, in my much younger days of course, sliding down into the pond's warm water after a hard slalom circuit, breathing hard and every muscle taut and screaming for, and then receiving, relief. The boat has picked our tired girl up and returned home, leaving the Pond now blissfully silent. The haunting call of a loon drifts over to me, lonely and sad, and reminds me of that classic Katherine Hepburn movie. I hear a child's brief squeal of delight from somewhere on the other side. A dog barks, just once.

Yet another dreamy summer day on Goose Pond is slowly winding down for us. In the late summer heat, we had been swimming most of the day of course, but also napping in the shade, enjoying leftovers for lunch, paddling our kayaks, reading novels, choosing to temporarily ignore the utter craziness of the world out there, and reminiscing about our early years on the lake with mom and dad — so many years ago.

Goose Pond's marvelous stories, played out over countless years, for centuries, millions of years even, resonate in my mind. My good fortune to be here, right here, right now, overwhelms me. Goose Pond makes me feel whole. Just imagine if she could do that for everyone in the world.

ACKNOWLEDGEMENTS

So many people, from so many walks of life, enthusiastically responded to my outreach, each making their unique contribution to this project. Without the help of all these people, this book would certainly not exist.

My first stop on this project was to call on Joe Janis, my friend and neighbor. Joe has been on Goose Pond even longer than I have, and I knew he shared my love of the lake. Joe showered me with stories, sent me old maps, connected me with countless people, and took me on long, off-trail woodland treks to show me all the historical artifacts hiding silently among the trees.

The Stilwell family, especially David and Caroline, opened their voluminous archives to me and shared with me the stories of some of the founding families on Goose Pond. They spent hours with me pouring over stacks of photographs, maps, guest books, deeds, and documents. Richard and Verna helped decipher some mysteries too, and in the process, hospitably treated us to some delicious culinary treats at their Upper Goose camp. The Stilwells' love for Upper Goose, and its stories, was contagious.

While I always did have a general affinity for rocks, I possessed no meaningful understanding of geology or glaciers. For the geology and Ice Age chapters, I am profoundly indebted to Nick Ratcliff, a retired geologist from the US Geological Survey, and to Steve Mabee, the Massachusetts State Geologist and a Senior Lecturer in Geology at the University of Massachusetts/Amherst. They spent endless hours trying to help me, like a struggling college freshman, to wrap my head around the complicated geological and glacial processes that gave rise to Goose Pond. And then, on a crisp, sunny day in November 2021, they took me on a day-long geology tour of the Goose Pond environs. Nick, who arguably knows more about Goose Pond's underlying bedrock than anyone on the planet, continued to respond to my countless, hopelessly confused emails and then generously, and meticulously edited the geology chapter. I am nevertheless certain I still got a lot wrong and that's all on me. Surely, I have not been their best student. Just maybe I have not been their worst. Other geologists at U Mass who weighed in are Mike Williams and Julie Brigham-Grette. And thanks also to Lee's marble quarry for permitting our visit there.

The Lee Library's Historical Collection is a well-organized and robust online archive busting with images and information, created and managed by another Goose Ponder, Mary Philpot. Many of the old paper mill photographs you see in this book and most of the references to the *The Berkshire Gleaner* are here only because of Mary's love of local history and the resources of the Lee Library. She went out of her way to provide me with the very best historical images available. Mary also thought to send me an ingenious clue, a recent obituary of all things, which, once pursued (with the help of Mike Kelly) led to the discovery of the heretofore unknown photographs of the Mohhekennuck Club.

The Western Massachusetts Chapter of the Appalachian Mountain Club, and more specifically the Western Massachusetts Appalachian Trail Management Committee, connected me with the extraordinary culture of the Appalachian Trail. Cosmo Catalano, the volunteer coordinator and manager of the Upper Goose Pond Cabin, shared his deep knowledge of the Appalachian Trail and provided detailed editing of that chapter. Jim Pelletier, the committee's guru on flora and fauna, shared his spectacular trail cam images of local wildlife and guided me on an exploratory hike around Upper Goose which was full of discoveries. Pete Rentz took me on my very first tour of the hiker cabin and told me his first-hand account of the lost, and found, Mohhekennuck Club plaque.

I am so grateful to Chuck Mecklum for his extraordinary effort to locate the original copy of Madge Cavarly's story about Pinepoint in his aunt Adrienne's attic, and for providing me with a high-resolution scan of this marvelous memoir. I also thank Chuck's aunt, Adrienne Cavarly, for preserving this document, and for providing her Pinepoint memories along with the choice photograph of the stump island arrowhead.

Warren Rapelye White shared his extraordinary collection of never-before-seen photographs of the Mohhekennuck Club, as well as his memories of the vivid childhood summers he spent there. Much of that marvelous story would have gone forever untold without his enthusiastic contribution.

I am grateful to Pamela Haskell and Tracie Schneyer for taking the time to share with me their collections of photographs of the old MacDarby family and the Moore Boat Livery. It was Pamela's collection that gave us those images of the mysterious U.S. Navy operation on Goose Pond. Maybe someday someone will figure that one out.

My thanks go out to another Goose Ponder, Edward Habermehl, who provided me with over a hundred emails with all sorts of artifacts and valuable tidbits of Goose Pond lore and history. His enthusiasm for this project was wonderful and his information was fascinating, some of it sending me off in unanticipated directions; like the Higley story and the pre-Revolution maps.

The chapter on Grover Cleveland would not have been possible without the generous resources provided to me by Reese and Linda Gilder Palmer at the Four Brooks Farm in Tyringham. The photographs they provided for this book are precious, especially to me, because it shows Mr. and Mrs. Cleveland, Richard Watson Gilder, and Cecelia Beaux all on my property in the early 1900s. They share my passion for local history, and I wish them well with their preservation efforts. Also, thanks to Nini Gilder and the Hop Brook Community Club for putting me in touch with them in the first place!

Well, we didn't find Hooker's sunken car, but it wasn't for lack of trying. Thank you to my good friend and fellow Goose Ponder, Roger Brown, who was the fearless captain of our great sonar exploration vessel with which we explored the targeted sections of lakebed, and also to

Acknowledgements

Zack Maxfield, master scuba diver, who drove all the way here from Boston, braved frigid waters and utter darkness, all for the cause, even if coming up only with a cool souvenir shell.

Sophie Sterling shared her childhood memories of Chanterwood as well as of her aunt, Eva Bender, the proprietor for so many years. I am so grateful to Sophie and to Gary Bender for finally bringing to the surface a rare photograph of Eva. And sincere thanks to Mike Kelly, of Kelly Funeral Home, who always responded to my periodic outreach, and whose local connections ultimately led to my discovery of most of the Mohhekennuck Club photographs.

Special thanks are due to the Massachusetts Historical Society, for getting me a copy of the 1886 treatise on the Mud Pond dam disaster, and to Ilse Allen at the Brandeis University Library for providing me with the 1895 Weston book on Berkshire papermaking. Also, thank you to the Boston Public Library and its marvelous Norman B. Leventhal Map & Education Center. I also was helped by two reference librarians at the Boston Public Library; Diane Parks and John Devine. It was Rosemarie Corbo at the North Haledon Free Public Library (in New Jersey) who first directed me to the Massachusetts Historical Society in the first place. The library at Harvard University provided me with Eva Bender's cookbook. Also, thanks are due to Danielle Kovacs, the Curator of Collections at the UMass/Amherst Libraries for rummaging through endless dusty cardboard boxes trying to fulfill my ask about Congressman Sylvio O. Conte's archives.

Others to thank include those at the Lee Historical Society, especially Caroline Young, Linda Buttery, Gary Wallen, Karen Norton, Linda Cysz, and Mal Eckert. Thanks also to Ann Gallo and Carol Hardy-Fanta of the Tyringham Historical Commission who guided me through their archives in the old schoolhouse during an afternoon that provided me with some terrific material. Larry Bravo, also of the Tyringham Historical Commission, shared with me a veritable storehouse of information and resources on the history of Tyringham. And of course, thank you to the late Clint Elliott, the great organizer of the Tyringham historical archives, and one of my very first interviews for this project.

Donald Warfield, in the Local History department of the Berkshire Athenaeum, assembled a nice collection of relevant materials for my perusal. Other thanks go to the Becket Historical Commission, the National Parks Service, Tracy Lind at the Appalachian Trail Conservancy, and Doug Winiarski, Professor of Religious Studies at the University of Richmond. I even tracked down Steve Golden, who had worked for the National Parks Service and organized the 1982 ceremony on Upper Goose.

I am grateful for the enthusiastic responses from Elizabeth Massa, of the Western Massachusetts Hilltown Hikers, Judith Monachina, Director of the Housatonic Heritage Oral History Center at Berkshire Community College, Dan Bolognani, the Executive Director of the Upper Housatonic Valley National Heritage Area, Jenna Ware, the director at the Crane Museum of Papermaking, and Jeremy Davis, Founder of the New England Lost Ski Areas Project. Also, thanks are due to Denis Boudreau of DCR Ridgerunners, for his excellent old maps of the A.T. I would also like to thank the Environmental Business Council of New England for its resources on the Mud Pond dam disasters.

Ancestry.com became a surprisingly valuable resource, particularly when I needed help establishing relationships or identifying and contacting some important sources. TopoMaps was a great app for recording my treks in the woods and my sonar survey of the lake bed.

Although the mystery of the US Navy operation on Goose Pond has not been solved, my research efforts were nonetheless supported by Nathan Patch of the Naval Archives II Reference Branch in Maryland and by Joanie Gearin, Archivist at the National Naval Archives at Boston.

By quite a large margin, my most senior assistant was almost certainly Ted Murphy, who shared many vivid and snarky stories about his childhood summers spent on Upper Goose. On the day of our interview, he was just a few weeks shy of his 100th birthday. Happy Birthday, Ted!

Much of my material on the Mohican Indians was derived from a recent exhibit at the Mission House in Stockbridge, courtesy of the Trustees for Reservations. Thank you, Trustees, for this exhibit and for everything else you do for us on Goose Pond.

Tim Puntin was an early contributor to this project, and his recent book, *Goose Tails*, filled in a lot of gaps, and surely represents a nice companion book to this one. I am also grateful to both Flint Henry Smiths (Jr. and Sr.) and Holly Coon, for their interest and their permission to include those wonderful illustrations from RW Smith's *Three Thumbnails*.

While writing this book, I attended an online writing course given by Lou-Ellen Barkan, sponsored by Berkshire OLLI. Not only did I learn much about writing in general, but some passages in this book are derived directly from exercises in this class. I will leave it to the reader to try to figure out which ones. Her direction and challenging classes hopefully made me at least a little better as a writer. I hope she likes the work product.

My neighbor, Stephen A. Cohen (no relation) applied his mathematical and engineering skills to some complicated calculations about the dam, as well as providing some image enhancement projects, and some excellent leads on the Indian grave topic. Another Lakeside neighbor, Bruce Walton, provided me with a viewing of his father's fantastic collection of Goose Pond arrowheads. My son Zach helped me with the highly successful FOIA inquiry we filed with the National Parks Service. Wallace Prysock, drone pilot extraordinaire, created some truly amazing aerial photographs of Upper Goose Pond.

Special thanks to Gregory Crewdson, who provided me with information on Upper Upper Goose Pond and so generously provided a beautiful photograph of this lake. I am honored to include one of his photographs in this volume.

There were so many others who did their part for this book, including (and in no particular order): Ginger Elvin, Jay McBrian, Sarah Gapinski, Stephen Novak, Gail Bleifer, Sarah Schultz, Pat Martin, Ellen and Bill Apfel, Jeff Coons, Gerry LePrevost, William Matthew, Karen Firebaugh, Dorothy Naventi, Dr. Ingrid H.H. Zabel, Barbara and Michael Borys, Mary Wolf, Bonnie and Rob Cramp, Dennis Welch, Kathleen Bort, Paul Giarolo, Glen and Doug Wilcox, Lee Wooten, David Carrington, James McVey, and the people at Studley Press. If I left anyone out, you know who you are. I apologize and extend my thanks here.

My local Pond buddies, Richard Greene, Andy Potler, Stephen Hodgin, and Roger Brown always provided me with ideas and consistent encouragement. They also provided me with many of the best wildlife photographs in this book. Lastly, they consistently gave me great confidence

Acknowledgements

that I would sell at least four copies of this book when it finally came out. And a special thanks to Andy for introducing me to the Grover Cleveland photograph in *Views of the Valley*, which opened the door to that chapter.

And then there is my editor, Gary Smailes, of Bubblecow, who provided me with inspiration and encouragement all the way from Liverpool, UK, provided wonderful creative ideas, improved the manuscript dramatically, and meticulously restructured, reworded, and repunctuated the mess I had sent him. My sincere thanks also go to my book designer, Amit Dey, who, all the way from India, put it all together, and created the visually beautiful volume you are holding in your hands.

It would be rather self-serving for me to express gratitude to all the people at Berkshire Mountain Books for their tireless support of this project, but I know they would like to thank Mel and Nick Cohen for creating the company's most excellent logo.

David Carriere, my publicist, provided me with his bottomless enthusiasm for this story along with some great editorial suggestions, and applied his deep understanding of book publicity to this project, and was instrumental in getting this volume into so many hands.

Dan Lewis was immeasurably helpful and encouraging, readily sharing with me his extensive experience in creating books of photography and history and spending many long hours improving the many faded, historical images in this book.

Susan, Lesle, Stephen, and Ron have always been there for me, all of them writers themselves, and generously offering me various combinations of endless encouragement, plenty of critique, shared memories, and meaningful editorial comments. Susan also offered me excellent publicity ideas as well as her legal expertise to help me navigate some copyright questions. Ron was invaluable with his memories of Chanterwood.

Zach, Mel, Nick, and Rachel provided terrific feedback on several sections of the manuscript and helped me navigate some thorny questions about political correctness.

I cannot imagine my life without Goose Pond in it. What would my life be like today if it wasn't for my mom and dad's inspiration on that Saturday morning back in 1971? Certainly, if not for their decision that day you would be reading something else right now.

And to Sandy, thank you for quietly tolerating the endless hours I spent hunched over at my desk these five years, researching, interviewing, reading, and writing. And for watching me leave to meet this person or that person, or hike here or there. And for listening to me retelling the same stories over and over again. She was also a critical reader of many passages, a cheerleader, and my soulmate. She celebrated with me when cool discoveries were made and calmed me down when the going got tough. Of course, I suspect she would sometimes roll her eyes when I wasn't looking. Thank you, Sandy, from the bottom of my heart for your encouragement, patience, and love.

AUTHOR BIO

This photograph of the author was taken while caretaker at the Upper Goose Pond hiker cabin.

David E. Cohen has written a children's book about water, which sold forty-six copies, and a four-volume genealogy study of his ancestors in the travelling circus, which sold even fewer than that, and thus does not consider himself an overly accomplished author. David's long career as an interventional cardiologist in New Jersey, and later as a physician practicing in the Berkshires, may have helped a lot of people, but did not really provide him with any additional skills even remotely useful to the creation of this book. In the end, however, these challenges turned out to be easily surmounted obstacles when pitched against the rich tapestry of Goose Pond's stories — stories that fascinated the author for over fifty years of visiting his family's lakehouse. It has been said that everyone has at least one good book in them. For David, *Reflections on Goose Pond* is that book. He now lives full time on the pond with his wife, his dog and a veritable armada of small boats.

RECOMMENDED READING

See All the People, 1978, by Florence Consolati

Most Wonderful Machine, Mechanization and Social Change in Berkshire Paper Making, 1801-1885, 1987, by Judith A. McGaw

Three Thumbnails, 1978, by R.W. Smith,

Rag Paper Manufacture in the United States, 1801-1900, by AJ Valente, 2010.

Lee. The Centennial Celebration and Centennial History of Lee, Mass, 1878, by Charles M. Hyde, Alexander Hyde,

Goose Tails, by Tim Puntin, 2024

Roadside Geology of Massachusetts, by James W. Skehan, 2001

Exploring the Berkshire Hills, by Ed Kirby, 1995

Grover Cleveland: A Record of Friendship, by Richard Watson Gilder, 1910

History of the Town of Lee, Mass, A Lecture, Delivered Before the Young Men's Association of Lee, March 22, 1854, 1854, By Amory Gale

Views of the Valley, Tyringham 1739-1989, by Cornelia Brook Gilder

A Hinterland Settlement, by Eloise Myers, 1989

ENDNOTES

1. For those readers interested in teaching stories of water to their young children, at the risk of some shameless self-promotion, the author can highly recommend his own book, *The Amazing Life of Squirt the Water Drop*, by Dr. David E. Cohen, affordably available on Amazon
2. *Three Thumbnails*, 1978, by R.W. Smith, p45
3. *The Berkshire Gleaner*, May 1, 1931
4. *The Berkshire Eagle*, April 13, 1965
5. William Matthew, Lee Water Department Superintendent, personal communication to Joe Janis
6. All photographs in this book not otherwise attributed were created by the author.
7. *Lee. The Centennial Celebration and Centennial History of Lee, Mass*, 1878, by Charles M. Hyde, Alexander Hyde, p57
8. *The Berkshire Eagle*, June 24, 1958
9. *Goose Tails*, by Tim Puntin, 2024, p56
10. *Three Thumbnails*, 1978, by R.W. Smith, p65
11. *1777-1977 Two Hundred Years, The History of the town of Washington Massachusetts*, Compiled by Mrs. Louise Elliot
12. *A Hinterland Settlement*, by Eloise Myers, 1989
13. https://founders.archives.gov/documents/Adams/06-02-02-0007-0007
14. *Three Thumbnails*, 1978, by RW Smith, p59
15. *History of the Town of Lee, Mass, A Lecture, Delivered Before the Young Men's Association of Lee, March 22, 1854*, 1854, By Amory Gale, p5
16. *Lee. The Centennial Celebration and Centennial History of Lee, Mass*, 1878, by Charles M. Hyde, Alexander Hyde, p299
17. *Lost Ski Areas of the Berkshires*, 2018, by Jeremy K. Davis, p201
18. *The Berkshire Eagle*, June 1, 2019
19. *Three Thumbnails*, 1978, by R.W. Smith, p67
20. *A Complete Account of the Terrible Disaster at East Lee, on Tuesday Apr 20th, 1886*, 1886, by Edward S. Rogers, p31
21. David Stilwell, personal communication
22. *The Higleys and Their Ancestry: An Old Colonial Family*, by Mary Coffin Johnson, 1898, p300
23. *Three Thumbnails*, 1978, by R.W. Smith, Figure p56
24. *Goose Tails*, by Tim Puntin, 2024, p133
25. *Geophysical Research Letters*, May 7, 2024, Quan Yuan et al.
26. *The New York Times*, June 12, 2024
27. *Tectonic Sythesis of the Taconian Orogeny in Western New England*, Bulletin Geological Society of America: Vol. 96.10, pp1227-1250, by Stanley, RS and Ratcliffe, NM, 1985

28 https://earthathome.org/hoe/ne/geologic-history/)
29 This stylish wig is available for online purchase for $47.99 at Lightinthebox.com, Item #7965805
30 The author has redacted any content referring to the precise location of this "Indian grave" in the interest of protecting this sacred site from any further risk of desecration. The author can attest that the grave's markers still stand.
31 Three Thumbnails, 1978, by R.W. Smith, p57
32 Berkshire Athenaeum, historical section files
33 "Credit is due where credit is due" for the remarkable discovery of this 1822 article which was found in 1970 by Lanesboro researcher Edward Knurrow
34 Wikipedia, article on Berkshire County Massachusetts
35 In the 1960s, a Danish-born carpenter named Ejner Handberg operated a furniture workshop in Lee producing fine furniture in the Shaker style. He became interested in Shaker furniture after repairing multiple Shaker pieces brought to him by local customers. He published four books on Shaker furniture.
36 *See All the People*, 1978, by Florence Consolati, p287.
37 *See All the People*, 1978, by Florence Consolati, p288.
38 History of Paper Making in Berkshire County, Berkshire Historical Scientific Society, 1895, by Byron Weston
39 The Housatonic Railroad, incorporated in 1836, connected western Massachusetts to points south in Connecticut. After a series of mergers, this railroad became the New York, New Haven and Hartford Railroad. This rail system provided Lee paper mills a robust transportation system linking to the New York City markets.
40 *Rag Paper Manufacture in the United States, 1801-1900*, by AJ Valente, 2010
41 Most Wonderful Machine, Mechanization and Social Change in Berkshire Paper Making, 1801-1885, by Judith A. McGaw, p192
42 Mario, a barber at Steve's Barber Shop in Lee, personal communication
43 Most Wonderful Machine, Mechanization and Social Change in Berkshire Paper Making, 1801-1885, by Judith A. McGaw, p42
44 History of Paper Making in Berkshire County, Berkshire Historical Scientific Society, 1895, by Byron Weston, p.3.
45 *Three Thumbnails*, 1978, by R.W. Smith, p9.
46 *Most Wonderful Machine, Mechanization and Social Change in Berkshire Paper Making, 1801-1885*, by Judith A. McGaw, p65
47 *Lee. The Centennial Celebration and Centennial History of Lee, Mass*, 1878, by Charles M. Hyde, Alexander Hyde, p298
48 Kathleen Bort, personal communication
49 *Lee. The Centennial Celebration and Centennial History of Lee, Mass*, 1878, by Charles M. Hyde, Alexander Hyde, p299
50 There were also two gunpowder mills constructed in downtown Lee in the early 1800s supplying a strong market for explosives needed to build the Erie Canal. Multiple explosions of these mills killed several people in Lee between 1823-1825. There were no gunpowder mills along the Goose Pond stream.
51 *A Complete Account of the Terrible Disaster at East Lee, on Tuesday Apr 20th, 1886*, 1886, by Edward S. Rogers, p31
52 *Rag Paper Manufacture in the United States, 1801-1900*, by AJ Valente, 2010.
53 *History of Paper Making in Berkshire County*, Berkshire Historical Scientific Society, 1895, by Byron Weston, p4
54 *Lee. The Centennial Celebration and Centennial History of Lee, Mass*, 1878, by Charles M. Hyde, Alexander Hyde, p70
55 *History of Paper Making in Berkshire County*, Berkshire Historical Scientific Society, 1895, by Byron Weston, p7

56 *History of Paper Making in Berkshire County*, Berkshire Historical Scientific Society, 1895, by Byron Weston, p9. Also: *The Berkshire Eagle*, January 5, 2013

57 *Most Wonderful Machine, Mechanization and Social Change in Berkshire Paper Making, 1801-1885*, by Judith A. McGaw, p215

58 *Lee. The Centennial Celebration and Centennial History of Lee, Mass*, 1878, by Charles M. Hyde, Alexander Hyde, p297

59 *Most Wonderful Machine, Mechanization and Social Change in Berkshire Paper Making, 1801-1885*, by Judith A. McGaw, p230

60 *History of Paper Making in Berkshire County*, Berkshire Historical Scientific Society, 1895, by Byron Weston, p9

61 *See All the People*, 1978, by Florence Consolati, p232

62 *See All the People*, 1978, by Florence Consolati, p232

63 *Three Thumbnails*, 1978, by R.W. Smith, p31

64 *See All the People*, 1978, by Florence Consolati, p232

65 Paperheritage.org

66 *A Complete Account of the Terrible Disaster at East Lee, on Tuesday Apr 20th, 1886*, 1886, by Edward S. Rogers

67 *A Complete Account of the Terrible Disaster at East Lee, on Tuesday Apr 20th, 1886*, 1886, by Edward S. Rogers, p31

68 *Lee. The Centennial Celebration and Centennial History of Lee, Mass*, 1878, by Charles M. Hyde, Alexander Hyde, p298.

69 *Most Wonderful Machine, Mechanization and Social Change in Berkshire Paper Making, 1801-1885*, by Judith A. McGaw, p218

70 *Rag Paper Manufacture in the United States, 1801-1900*, by AJ Valente, 2010

71 *The Valley Gleaner*, May 4, 1887

72 *The Berkshire Eagle*, September 22, 1938

73 "*The Grande Old Dam of Foster's Pond Turns 162, An Engineer's Take*" A presentation by Lee Wooten, P.E. of GEI Consultants, Inc.

74 "*Part 1: Historical Dam Failures in New England*" A presentation by the Environmental Business Council of New England's Dam Management Webinar Series.

75 For the story of how the Goose Pond Maintenance District came to be, there is no better reference than *Goose Tails*, by Tim Puntin.

76 Tim Puntin, personal communication.

77 Stephen A. Cohen, personal communication

78 United States Department of Energy

79 *The Electrical Engineer*, September 11, 1895, p263

80 *Electrical World*, Vol. 79, No. 12, March 25, 1922, pp573-576

81 Directory of Electric Utilties in the United States, 1941.

82 *Hydroelectric Power Resources of the United States*, January 1, 1968, Table 2

83 Information and images of this salvage can be seen at *Frenchriverland.com/lake_may_pelton_wheel_removal.htm*

84 "*Huckleberry Trolley Line, Lee-Huntington Trolley Line*" Becket Historical Commission

85 "*Huckleberry Trolley Line, Lee-Huntington Trolley Line*" Becket Historical Commission

86 *See All The People*, by Florence Consolati, p232

87 *Goose Tails*, by Tim Puntin, 2024, p45

88 Pamela Margaret Haskell, personal communication

89 *The Berkshire Eagle*, February 23, 1932

90 *The Berkshire County Eagle*, February 29, 1932

91 *Goose Tails*, by Tim Puntin, 2024, p48

92 *Goose Tails*, by Tim Puntin, 2024, p44

93 *Goose Tails*, by Tim Puntin, 2024, p52

94 Interested readers are encouraged to visit www.fourbrooksfarm.org

95 Wikipedia, Grover Cleveland

96 *Grover Cleveland: A Record of Friendship*, by Richard Watson Gilder, 1910

97 *Grover Cleveland: A Record of Friendship*, by Richard Watson Gilder, 1910

98 Linda Gilder Palmer, personal communication.

99 *The Berkshire Gleaner*, September 14, 1910.

100 Warren Rapelye White, personal communication

101 *The Berkshire Eagle*, August 6, 1982

102 *Goose Tails*, by Tim Puntin, 2024, p5

103 Dr. Peter Rentz, personal communication

104 *Berkshire Appalachian Trail newsletter*, February 2, 2019

105 Legend has it (Hyde, p140) that Jonathan Foote's grandfather, Nathaniel Foote, had put King Charles of England into the trunk of an oak tree to shield the King from his pursuers. The story goes that the King rewarded Nathaniel with a tract of land in Connecticut and that this story is emblazoned in the Foote Coat of Arms. Some Foote descendants contest the veracity of this story.

106 Ted Murphy, personal communication, just weeks before his 100th birthday.

107 *Pittsfield Berkshire Evening Eagle*, April 27, 1928

108 Ron Cohen, personal communication

109 Ron Cohen, personal communication

110 *Family Sketches: The Albert F. Bender Family*, by Edward J. Bender. This volume is self published book by Eva's brother. The book included a chapter about Eva and also a chapter about each of Eva's nine siblings. Unfortunately I was unable to obtain a copy of this book.

111 *Berkshire Evening Eagle*, July 14, 1959

112 Ted Murphy, at age 99.9, personal communication

113 Ted Murphy, at age 99.9, personal communication

114 Caroline Stilwell, personal communication

115 *The Berkshire Eagle*, August 6, 1982

116 Cosmo Catalano, Western Massachusetts Chapter, Appalachian Mountain Club, personal communication

117 Massachusetts Division of Fisheries and Wildlife, https://www.mass.gov/doc/living-with-geese-fact-sheet/download

118 In *Three Thumbnails*, R.W. Smith wrote (p54) that he had never seen geese on Goose Pond, and he wondered why the lake would have ever been given this name. Since Smith was born in 1905, his childhood would have been prior to the 1930s release. It appears that the extensive presence of geese on Goose Pond did not develop until after the 1930s release of captive geese, or perhaps not before their deliberate 1960s relocation to western Massachusetts. This of course begs the unanswered question, why the lake was named "Goose", back in the 1700s, when only the rare migratory populations were present.

www.ingramcontent.com/pod-product-compliance
Lightning Source LLC
Chambersburg PA
CBHW051328110526
44582CB00003B/86

*9 7 8 9 9 9 2 8 4 8 3 0 4 *